THE COMPLETE GREEK TRAGEDIES

VOLUME II

SOPHOCLES

1891-1991

A CENTENNIAL PUBLICATION OF

The University of Chicago Press

THE COMPLETE GREEK TRAGEDIES

CENTENNIAL EDITION

Edited by David Grene and Richmond Lattimore

VOLUME II

SOPHOCLES

THE UNIVERSITY OF CHICAGO PRESS

Chicago & London

PUBLISHER'S NOTE: In this edition of *Sophocles,* new translations by David
Grene replace Robert Fitzgerald's translation of *Oedipus at Colonus* (1941 and
1954) and Elizabeth Wyckoff's translation of *Antigone* (1954).

The University of Chicago Press, Chicago 60637
The University of Chicago Press, Ltd., London
© 1942, 1954, 1957, 1991 by The University of Chicago
All rights reserved
Volume 2 published 1992
Printed in the United States of America

00 99 98 97 96 95 94 93 92   5 4 3 2 1

ISBN (4-vol. set) 0-226-30763-8
ISBN (vol. 2) 0-226-30765-4

Library of Congress Cataloging-in-Publication Data

The complete Greek tragedies / edited by David Grene and Richmond
    Lattimore.—Centennial ed.
        p.   cm.
        Contents: v. 1 Aeschylus—v. 2. Sophocles—v. 3–4. Euripides.
        1. Greek drama (Tragedy)—Translations into English.   I. Grene,
    David.   II. Lattimore, Richmond Alexander, 1906–   .
PA3626.A2G67   1992
882'.0108—dc20
                                                                        91-45936
                                                                        CIP

⊗ The paper used in this publication meets
the minimum requirements of the American
National Standard for Information Sciences—
Permanence of Paper for Printed Library Materials,
ANSI Z39.48-1984.

CONTENTS

INTRODUCTION

"*The Theban Plays*" *by Sophocles*

THIS series of plays, *Oedipus the King*, *Oedipus at Colonus*, and *Antigone*, was written over a wide interval of years. The dating is only approximate, for reliable evidence is lacking; but the *Antigone* was produced in 441 B.C. when Sophocles was probably fifty-four, and *Oedipus the King* some fourteen or fifteen years later. *Oedipus at Colonus* was apparently produced the year after its author's death at the age of ninety in 405 B.C. Thus, although the three plays are concerned with the same legend, they were not conceived and executed at the same time and with a single purpose, as is the case with Aeschylus' *Oresteia*. We can here see how a story teased the imagination of Sophocles until it found its final expression. We can see the degrees of variation in treatment he gave the myth each time he handled it. And perhaps we can come to some notion of what the myths meant to Sophocles as raw material for the theater.

The internal dramatic dates of the three plays do not agree with the order of their composition. As far as the legend is concerned, the story runs in sequence: *Oedipus the King, Oedipus at Colonus, Antigone*. But Sophocles wrote them in the order: *Antigone, Oedipus the King, Oedipus at Colonus*. In view of this and the long interval between the composition of the individual plays, we would expect some inconsistencies between the three versions. And there are fairly serious inconsistencies—in facts, for instance. At the conclusion of *Oedipus the King*, Creon is in undisputed authority after the removal of Oedipus. Though he appeals to him to look after his daughters, Oedipus refrains from asking Creon to do anything for his sons, who, he says, will be all right on their own (*OK* 1460). It is Creon who will succeed Oedipus in Thebes, and there is no question of any

« 1 »

legitimate claim of Oedipus' descendants (*OK* 1418). But in *Antigone,* Creon tells the chorus that he has favorably observed their loyalty first to Oedipus and then to his sons, and so has hope of their devotion to himself. In *Oedipus at Colonus*—the last of the three plays he wrote—Sophocles makes one of his very few clumsy efforts to patch the discrepancies together. In *Oedipus at Colonus* (ll. 367 ff.), Ismene says that *at first* the two sons were willing to leave the throne to Creon in view of their fatal family heritage, but after a while they decided to take over the monarchy and the quarrel was only between themselves as to who should succeed. At this point Creon has vanished out of the picture altogether! Again, the responsibility for the decision to expel Oedipus from Thebes and keep him out rests, in *Oedipus the King,* entirely with Creon, who announces that he will consult Apollo in the matter. In *Oedipus at Colonus* his sons' guilt in condemning their father to exile is one of the bitterest counts in Oedipus' indictment of them (*OC* 1360 ff.). These are important differences. We do not know anything really certain about the manner of publication of the plays after their production. We know even less about Sophocles' treatment of his own scripts. Maybe he simply did not bother to keep them after he saw them as far as the stage, though that seems unlikely. Or it is possible and likelier that Sophocles, as he wrote the last play in extreme old age and in what seems to be the characteristic self-absorption of the last years of his life, cared little about whether *Oedipus at Colonus* exactly tallied, in its presentation, with the stories he had written thirty-seven and twenty-two years earlier.

Let us for the moment disregard the details of the story and concentrate on what would seem to be the central theme of the first two plays in order of composition. And here we find something very curious. Most critics have felt the significance of the *Antigone* to lie in the opposition of Creon and Antigone and all that this opposition represents. It is thus a play about something quite different from *Oedipus the King.* And yet what a remarkable similarity there is in the dilemma of Creon in *Antigone* and Oedipus himself in the first Oedipus play. In both of them a king has taken a decision which is disobeyed or questioned by his subjects. In both, the ruler misconstrues the role of the rebel and his own as a sovereign. In both, he has a crucial encounter with the priest Teiresias, who warns him that the forces of religion are against him. In both, he charges that the priest has been suborned. There the resemblance ends; for, after abusing the old prophet, Creon is overcome with fear of his authority and, too late, tries to undo his mistake. In *Oedipus the King* the king defies all assaults upon his decision until the deadly self-knowledge which starts to work in him has accomplished its course and he is convicted out of his own mouth.

Usually, as we know, the *Antigone* is interpreted entirely as the conflict between Creon and Antigone. It has often been regarded as the classical statement of the struggle between the law of the individual conscience and the central power of the state. Unquestionably, these issues are inherent in the play. Unquestionably, even, Sophocles would understand the modern way of seeing his play, for the issue of the opposition of the individual and the state was sufficiently present to his mind to make this significant for him. But can the parallelism between the position of Oedipus in the one play and Creon in the other be quite irrelevant to the interpretation of the two? And is it not very striking that such a large share of the *Antigone* should be devoted to the conclusion of the conflict, as far as Creon is concerned, and to the destruction of his human happiness?

What I would suggest is this: that Sophocles had at the time of writing the first play (in 442 B.C.) a theme in mind which centered in the Theban trilogy. One might express it by saying that it is the story of a ruler who makes a mistaken decision, though in good faith, and who then finds himself opposed in a fashion which he misunderstands and which induces him to persist in his mistake. This story is later on going to be that of a man who breaks divine law without realizing that he is doing so, and whose destruction is then brought about by the voice of the divine law in society. Between the *Antigone* and *Oedipus the King*, the theme has developed further, for in the latter play Sophocles is showing how the ruler who breaks the divine law may, for all he can see and understand, be entirely innocent, but nonetheless his guilt is an objective fact. In the third play, *Oedipus at Colonus*, this issue reaches its final statement. The old Oedipus is admittedly a kind of monster. Wherever he comes, people shrink from him. Yet his guilt carries with it some sort of innocence on which God will set his seal. For the old man is both cursed and blessed. The god gives him an extraordinary end, and the last place of his mortal habitation is blessed forever.

What this interpretation would mean, if correct, is that Sophocles started to write about the Theban legend, the story of Oedipus and his children, without having fully understood what he wanted to say about it. He may have been, and probably was, drawn, unknown to himself, to the dramatization of this particular legend because in it lay the material of the greatest theme of his later artistic life. But first he tried his hand at it in the opposition of Creon and Antigone. However, even while he did this, the character of Creon and his role in the play were shaping what was to be the decisive turn in the story he was going to write—the Oedipus saga.

Thus there is a certain elasticity in the entire treatment of myth. The author will accent a certain character at one time to suit a play and change the accent to suit another. Or he may even discover the same theme in a different myth. This is suggested by a short comparison of the *Philoctetes* and *Oedipus at Colonus,* both written in the last few years of Sophocles' life. The figure of Philoctetes, though occurring in a totally different legend from Oedipus, is a twin child with Oedipus in Sophocles' dramatic imagination. In both these plays, the *Philoctetes* and *Oedipus at Colonus,* the hero is a man whose value is inextricably coupled with his offensive quality. Philoctetes is the archer whose bow will overcome Troy. He is also the creature whose stinking infested wound moves everyone to disgust who has to do with him. Oedipus is accursed in the sight of all men; he had committed the two crimes, parricide and incest, which rendered him an outcast in any human society. But he is also the one to whom, at his end, God will give the marks of his favor, and the place where he is last seen on earth will be lucky and blessed. This combination of the evil and the good is too marked, in these two plays, to be accidental. It is surely the idea which inspired the old Sophocles for his two last plays. There is, however, an important further development of the theme in the *Oedipus at Colonus.* For there in Oedipus' mind the rational innocence—the fact that he had committed the offenses unknowingly—is, for him at least, important in God's final justification of him. Sophocles is declaring that the sin of Oedipus is real; that the consequences in the form of the loneliness, neglect, and suffering of the years of wandering are inevitable; but that the will and the consciousness are also some measure of man's sin—and when the sinner sinned necessarily and unwittingly, his suffering can be compensation enough for his guilt. He may at the end be blessed and a blessing. This is not the same doctrine as that of Aeschylus, when he asserts that through suffering comes wisdom. Nor is it the Christian doctrine of a man purified by suffering as by fire. Oedipus in his contact with Creon, in his interview with Polyneices shows himself as bitter, sudden in anger, and implacable as ever. He is indeed a monstrous old man. But at the last, he is, in a measure, *vindicated*. Yet in *Philoctetes* the theme of the union of the offensive and the beneficial, which in *Oedipus at Colonus* becomes the curse and the blessing, is seen without the addition of conscious innocence and unconscious guilt. Can we say that Sophocles finally felt that the consciousness of innocence in Oedipus is the balancing factor in the story? That in this sense *Oedipus at Colonus* is the further step beyond *Philoctetes* in the clarification of the dramatic subject which occupied the very old author? Or that the consciousness of innocence when linked with objective guilt is only the human shield against the cruelty of the irrational—that Oedipus is meaningful in his combination of guilt and innocence as a manifestation of God and of destiny and that his explanation of his conscious innocence is only the poor human inadequate explanation? Everyone will answer this according to his own choice. But, clearly, the theme of Philoctetes and the theme of the old Oedipus are connected.

If an analysis such as this has importance, it is to show the relation of Sophocles to the raw material of his plays—the myth. It is to show the maturing of a theme in Sophocles' mind and his successive treatments of it in the same and different legends. In the Oedipus story it is a certain fundamental situation which becomes significant for Sophocles, and the characters are altered to suit the story. Creon in the first, Oedipus in the second, are examples of the same sort of dilemma, even though the dilemma of Creon in the *Antigone* is incidental to the main emphasis of the play, which is on Antigone. But the dilemma was to be much more fruitful for Sophocles as a writer and thinker than the plain issue between Antigone and Creon. The dilemma resolves itself in the last play at the end of Sophocles' life into the dramatic statement of a principle, of the union of the blessed and the cursed, of the just and the unjust, and sometimes (not always) of the consciously innocent and the unconsciously guilty. The fact that Sophocles could in two successive treatments of the play fifteen years apart switch the parts of Creon and Oedipus indicates that neither the moral color of the characters nor even their identity was absolutely fixed in his mind. The same conclusion is borne out by the great similarity between the *Philoctetes* and the *Oedipus at Colonus*. Sophocles in his last days was incessantly thinking of the man who is blessed and cursed. For the theater he became once the lame castaway Philoctetes, who yet, in virtue of his archery, is to be the conqueror of Troy; in the next play he is Oedipus, who sinned against the order of human society but is still to be the blessing of Athens and the patron saint of Colonus. It is the theme and not the man that matters. Consequently, it is the kernel of the legend, as he saw it for the moment, that is sacred for Sophocles, not the identification of all the characters in a certain relation to one another. True, he has treated the Oedipus story three times in his life, which means that the Oedipus story had a certain fascination for him—that somehow hidden in it he knew there was what he wanted to say. But he did not have to think of the whole story and the interdependence of its characters when he made his changes each time. One stage of the theme borne by the hero is given to a character in a totally different myth. The sequence is Creon, Oedipus, Philoctetes, Oedipus. It may seem absurd to link Creon, the obvious form of tyrant (as conceived by the Athenians), and Philoctetes. But it is the progression we should notice. The tyrant who with true and good intentions orders what is wrong, morally and religiously, is crudely represented in Creon; he is much more subtly represented in Oedipus himself in the next play. But the similarity of the situation and the nature of the opposition to him proves how generically the character is conceived. You can switch the labels, and Creon becomes Oedipus. But if the character is generic, the situation is deepening. We are beginning to understand *why* a certain sort of tyrant may be a tyrant and in a shadowy way how conscious and unconscious guilt are related. In the *Philoctetes* and *Oedipus at Colonus* the situation is being seen in its last stages. We are no longer concerned with how Philoctetes came to sin or how Oedipus is the author of his own ruin. But only how does it feel to be an object both of disgust and of fear to your fellows, while you yourself are simultaneously aware of the injustice of your treatment and at last, in *Oedipus at Colonus,* of the objective proofs of God's favor.

For Sophocles the myth was the treatment of the generic aspect of human dilemmas. What he made of the myth in his plays was neither history nor the kind of dramatic creation represented by *Hamlet* or *Macbeth*. Not history, for in no sense is the uniqueness of the event or the uniqueness of the character important; not drama in the Shakespearean sense, because Sophocles' figures do not have, as Shakespeare's do, the timeless and complete reality in themselves. Behind the figure of Oedipus or Creon stands the tyrant of the legend; and behind the tyrant of the legend, the meaning of all despotic authority. Behind the old Oedipus is the beggar and wanderer of the legend, and behind him the mysterious human combination of opposites—opposites in meaning and in fact. And so the character may fluctuate or the names may vary. It is the theme, the generic side of tragedy, which is important; it is there that the emphasis of the play rests.

FURTHER INTRODUCTORY NOTE, 1991

My version of *Oedipus the King* was written fifty years ago. Of the two other translations which also formerly appeared in this volume, Robert Fitzgerald's *Oedipus at Colonus* is of almost the same vintage and Elizabeth Wyckoff's *Antigone* is more than thirty years old. As the remaining editor of *The Complete Greek*

Tragedies I have been looking through the series, at the suggestion of the Press, and have been making some alterations. Perhaps some of my criticisms may have been misplaced, but certain features of these translations by Wyckoff and Fitzgerald seemed unsatisfactory. Besides, despite the small inconsistencies in the story of the three plays, which I mentioned earlier, there is certainly a unity of tone and style in these Theban plays that greatly favors the same translator for all of them. So I have translated the *Antigone* and the *Oedipus at Colonus* and have substituted them for the previous renderings of Wyckoff and Fitzgerald.

Though the numbered lines of my *Oedipus the King* appear to match fairly thoroughly those of the Greek text, I have not been so successful with the combination of the Greek and the English in these last two plays. Often I have needed more space than the limitation of a line would allow. I decided that my numbering should correspond with the lines of the English translation rather than with those of the Greek, since if anyone wanted to cite a passage it would be unlikely that he or she would refer to the Greek. I hope this will not lead to too much confusion.

Some years ago the Court Theatre asked Wendy Doniger and me to do a new prose version of the *Antigone* for their repertory company. We worked in very close collaboration with the actors. Because the Court Theatre rendering was in prose, and all the other plays in the series of *The Complete Greek Tragedies* were overwhelmingly in verse, I decided to write the *Antigone* in my new translation in verse. But I owe a great deal to the earlier prose version, which I gladly acknowledge, and to Wendy Doniger's participation in it.

UNIVERSITY OF CHICAGO   DAVID GRENE

OEDIPUS THE KING

Translated by David Grene

CHARACTERS

Oedipus, King of Thebes

Jocasta, His Wife

Creon, His Brother-in-Law

Teiresias, an Old Blind Prophet

A Priest

First Messenger

Second Messenger

A Herdsman

A Chorus of Old Men of Thebes

OEDIPUS THE KING

SCENE: *In front of the palace of Oedipus at Thebes. To the right of the stage near the altar stands the Priest with a crowd of children. Oedipus emerges from the central door.*

Oedipus

    Children, young sons and daughters of old Cadmus,
    why do you sit here with your suppliant crowns?
    The town is heavy with a mingled burden
    of sounds and smells, of groans and hymns and incense;   5
    I did not think it fit that I should hear
    of this from messengers but came myself,—
    I Oedipus whom all men call the Great.

                               (He turns to the Priest.)

    You're old and they are young; come, speak for them.
    What do you fear or want, that you sit here   10
    suppliant? Indeed I'm willing to give all
    that you may need; I would be very hard
    should I not pity suppliants like these.

Priest

    O ruler of my country, Oedipus,
    you see our company around the altar;   15
    you see our ages; some of us, like these,
    who cannot yet fly far, and some of us
    heavy with age; these children are the chosen
    among the young, and I the priest of Zeus.
    Within the market place sit others crowned   20
    with suppliant garlands, at the double shrine
    of Pallas and the temple where Ismenus
    gives oracles by fire. King, you yourself
    have seen our city reeling like a wreck
    already; it can scarcely lift its prow
    out of the depths, out of the bloody surf.

A blight is on the fruitful plants of the earth, 25
A blight is on the cattle in the fields,
a blight is on our women that no children
are born to them; a God that carries fire,
a deadly pestilence, is on our town,
strikes us and spares not, and the house of Cadmus
is emptied of its people while black Death
grows rich in groaning and in lamentation. 30
We have not come as suppliants to this altar
because we thought of you as of a God,
but rather judging you the first of men
in all the chances of this life and when
we mortals have to do with more than man.
You came and by your coming saved our city, 35
freed us from tribute which we paid of old
to the Sphinx, cruel singer. This you did
in virtue of no knowledge we could give you,
in virtue of no teaching; it was God
that aided you, men say, and you are held
with God's assistance to have saved our lives.
Now Oedipus, Greatest in all men's eyes, 40
here falling at your feet we all entreat you,
find us some strength for rescue.
Perhaps you'll hear a wise word from some God,
perhaps you will learn something from a man
(for I have seen that for the skilled of practice
the outcome of their counsels live the most). 45
Noblest of men, go, and raise up our city,
go,—and give heed. For now this land of ours
calls you its savior since you saved it once.
So, let us never speak about your reign
as of a time when first our feet were set
secure on high, but later fell to ruin. 50
Raise up our city, save it and raise it up.
Once you have brought us luck with happy omen;
be no less now in fortune.

If you will rule this land, as now you rule it,
better to rule it full of men than empty. 55
For neither tower nor ship is anything
when empty, and none live in it together.

Oedipus

I pity you, children. You have come full of longing,
but I have known the story before you told it
only too well. I know you are all sick, 60
yet there is not one of you, sick though you are,
that is as sick as I myself.
Your several sorrows each have single scope
and touch but one of you. My spirit groans
for city and myself and you at once. 65
You have not roused me like a man from sleep;
know that I have given many tears to this,
gone many ways wandering in thought,
but as I thought I found only one remedy
and that I took. I sent Menoeceus' son
Creon, Jocasta's brother, to Apollo, 70
to his Pythian temple,
that he might learn there by what act or word
I could save this city. As I count the days,
it vexes me what ails him; he is gone
far longer than he needed for the journey. 75
But when he comes, then, may I prove a villain,
if I shall not do all the God commands.

Priest

Thanks for your gracious words. Your servants here
signal that Creon is this moment coming.

Oedipus

His face is bright. O holy Lord Apollo, 80
grant that his news too may be bright for us
and bring us safety.

Priest

It is happy news,
I think, for else his head would not be crowned
with sprigs of fruitful laurel.

Oedipus

     We will know soon,
he's within hail. Lord Creon, my good brother,   85
what is the word you bring us from the God?

               (Creon enters.)

Creon

A good word,—for things hard to bear themselves
if in the final issue all is well
I count complete good fortune.

Oedipus

     What do you mean?
What you have said so far
leaves me uncertain whether to trust or fear.   90

Creon

If you will hear my news before these others
I am ready to speak, or else to go within.

Oedipus

Speak it to all;
the grief I bear, I bear it more for these
than for my own heart.

Creon

     I will tell you, then,   95
what I heard from the God.
King Phoebus in plain words commanded us
to drive out a pollution from our land,
pollution grown ingrained within the land;
drive it out, said the God, not cherish it,
till it's past cure.

Oedipus

     What is the rite
of purification? How shall it be done?

Creon

> By banishing a man, or expiation   100
> of blood by blood, since it is murder guilt
> which holds our city in this destroying storm.

Oedipus

> Who is this man whose fate the God pronounces?

Creon

> My Lord, before you piloted the state
> we had a king called Laius.

Oedipus

> I know of him by hearsay. I have not seen him.   105

Creon

> The God commanded clearly: let some one
> punish with force this dead man's murderers.

Oedipus

> Where are they in the world? Where would a trace
> of this old crime be found? It would be hard
> to guess where.

Creon

> The clue is in this land;   110
> that which is sought is found;
> the unheeded thing escapes:
> so said the God.

Oedipus

> Was it at home,
> or in the country that death came upon him,
> or in another country travelling?

Creon

> He went, he said himself, upon an embassy,
> but never returned when he set out from home.   115

Oedipus

> Was there no messenger, no fellow traveller
> who knew what happened? Such a one might tell
> something of use.

Creon

    They were all killed save one. He fled in terror
    and he could tell us nothing in clear terms
    of what he knew, nothing, but one thing only.

Oedipus

    What was it?   120
    If we could even find a slim beginning
    in which to hope, we might discover much.

Creon

    This man said that the robbers they encountered
    were many and the hands that did the murder
    were many; it was no man's single power.

Oedipus

    How could a robber dare a deed like this
    were he not helped with money from the city,
    money and treachery?   125

Creon

                        That indeed was thought.
    But Laius was dead and in our trouble
    there was none to help.

Oedipus

    What trouble was so great to hinder you
    inquiring out the murder of your king?

Creon

    The riddling Sphinx induced us to neglect   130
    mysterious crimes and rather seek solution
    of troubles at our feet.

Oedipus

    I will bring this to light again. King Phoebus
    fittingly took this care about the dead,
    and you too fittingly.
    And justly you will see in me an ally,   135
    a champion of my country and the God.
    For when I drive pollution from the land

I will not serve a distant friend's advantage,
but act in my own interest. Whoever
he was that killed the king may readily
wish to dispatch me with his murderous hand;　　　140
so helping the dead king I help myself.

Come, children, take your suppliant boughs and go;
up from the altars now. Call the assembly
and let it meet upon the understanding
that I'll do everything. God will decide　　　145
whether we prosper or remain in sorrow.

Priest
　　Rise, children—it was this we came to seek,
　　which of himself the king now offers us.
　　May Phoebus who gave us the oracle
　　come to our rescue and stay the plague.　　　150

　　　　　　　　　　　(*Exeunt all but the Chorus.*)

Chorus
　　Strophe
　　What is the sweet spoken word of God from the shrine of Pytho
　　　　rich in gold
　　that has come to glorious Thebes?
　　I am stretched on the rack of doubt, and terror and trembling
　　　　hold
　　my heart, O Delian Healer, and I worship full of fears
　　for what doom you will bring to pass, new or renewed in the　　　155
　　　　revolving years.
　　Speak to me, immortal voice,
　　child of golden Hope.

　　Antistrophe
　　First I call on you, Athene, deathless daughter of Zeus,
　　and Artemis, Earth Upholder,　　　160
　　who sits in the midst of the market place in the throne which
　　　　men call Fame,
　　and Phoebus, the Far Shooter, three averters of Fate,

come to us now, if ever before, when ruin rushed upon the state,   165
you drove destruction's flame away
out of our land.

Strophe
Our sorrows defy number;
all the ship's timbers are rotten;
taking of thought is no spear for the driving away of the plague.   170
There are no growing children in this famous land;
there are no women bearing the pangs of childbirth.
You may see them one with another, like birds swift on the
     wing,   175
quicker than fire unmastered,
speeding away to the coast of the Western God.

Antistrophe
In the unnumbered deaths
of its people the city dies;
those children that are born lie dead on the naked earth
unpitied, spreading contagion of death; and grey haired mothers
     and wives
everywhere stand at the altar's edge, suppliant, moaning;   182–85
the hymn to the healing God rings out but with it the wailing
     voices are blended.
From these our sufferings grant us, O golden Daughter of Zeus,
glad-faced deliverance.

Strophe
There is no clash of brazen shields but our fight is with the War
     God,
a War God ringed with the cries of men, a savage God who burns   191
us;
grant that he turn in racing course backwards out of our coun-
     try's bounds
to the great palace of Amphitrite or where the waves of the   195
     Thracian sea
deny the stranger safe anchorage.
Whatsoever escapes the night

at last the light of day revisits;
so smite the War God, Father Zeus,
beneath your thunderbolt,
for you are the Lord of the lightning, the lightning that
  carries fire.   200

Antistrophe
And your unconquered arrow shafts, winged by the golden
  corded bow,
Lycean King, I beg to be at our side for help;   205
and the gleaming torches of Artemis with which she scours the
  Lycean hills,
and I call on the God with the turban of gold, who gave his name
  to this country of ours,   210
the Bacchic God with the wind flushed face,
Evian One, who travel
with the Maenad company,
combat the God that burns us
with your torch of pine;
for the God that is our enemy is a God unhonoured among the   215
  Gods.
                                        (*Oedipus returns.*)

Oedipus
For what you ask me—if you will hear my words,
and hearing welcome them and fight the plague,
you will find strength and lightening of your load.

Hark to me; what I say to you, I say
as one that is a stranger to the story
as stranger to the deed. For I would not   220
be far upon the track if I alone
were tracing it without a clue. But now,
since after all was finished, I became
a citizen among you, citizens—
now I proclaim to all the men of Thebes:
who so among you knows the murderer   225
by whose hand Laius, son of Labdacus,

died—I command him to tell everything
to me,—yes, though he fears himself to take the blame
on his own head; for bitter punishment
he shall have none, but leave this land unharmed.
Or if he knows the murderer, another, 230
a foreigner, still let him speak the truth.
For I will pay him and be grateful, too.
But if you shall keep silence, if perhaps
some one of you, to shield a guilty friend,
or for his own sake shall reject my words— 235
hear what I shall do then:
I forbid that man, whoever he be, my land,
my land where I hold sovereignty and throne;
and I forbid any to welcome him
or cry him greeting or make him a sharer 240
in sacrifice or offering to the Gods,
or give him water for his hands to wash.
I command all to drive him from their homes,
since he is our pollution, as the oracle
of Pytho's God proclaimed him now to me.
So I stand forth a champion of the God
and of the man who died. 245
Upon the murderer I invoke this curse—
whether he is one man and all unknown,
or one of many—may he wear out his life
in misery to miserable doom!
If with my knowledge he lives at my hearth 250
I pray that I myself may feel my curse.
On you I lay my charge to fulfill all this
for me, for the God, and for this land of ours
destroyed and blighted, by the God forsaken.

Even were this no matter of God's ordinance 255
it would not fit you so to leave it lie,
unpurified, since a good man is dead
and one that was a king. Search it out.

Since I am now the holder of his office,
and have his bed and wife that once was his,   260
and had his line not been unfortunate
we would have common children—(fortune leaped
upon his head)—because of all these things,
I fight in his defence as for my father,
and I shall try all means to take the murderer   265
of Laius the son of Labdacus
the son of Polydorus and before him
of Cadmus and before him of Agenor.
Those who do not obey me, may the Gods
grant no crops springing from the ground they plough   270
nor children to their women! May a fate
like this, or one still worse than this consume them!
For you whom these words please, the other Thebans,
may Justice as your ally and all the Gods
live with you, blessing you now and for ever!   275

Chorus

As you have held me to my oath, I speak:
I neither killed the king nor can declare
the killer; but since Phoebus set the quest
it is his part to tell who the man is.

Oedipus

Right; but to put compulsion on the Gods   280
against their will—no man can do that.

Chorus

May I then say what I think second best?

Oedipus

If there's a third best, too, spare not to tell it.

Chorus

I know that what the Lord Teiresias
sees, is most often what the Lord Apollo   285
sees. If you should inquire of this from him
you might find out most clearly.

Oedipus

    Even in this my actions have not been sluggard.
    On Creon's word I have sent two messengers
    and why the prophet is not here already
    I have been wondering.

Chorus

                    His skill apart   290
    there is besides only an old faint story.

Oedipus

    What is it?
    I look at every story.

Chorus

                    It was said
    that he was killed by certain wayfarers.

Oedipus

    I heard that, too, but no one saw the killer.

Chorus

    Yet if he has a share of fear at all,
    his courage will not stand firm, hearing your curse.   295

Oedipus

    The man who in the doing did not shrink
    will fear no word.

Chorus

              Here comes his prosecutor:
    led by your men the godly prophet comes
    in whom alone of mankind truth is native.

                  (Enter Teiresias, led by a little boy.)

Oedipus

    Teiresias, you are versed in everything,   300
    things teachable and things not to be spoken,
    things of the heaven and earth-creeping things.
    You have no eyes but in your mind you know
    with what a plague our city is afflicted.
    My lord, in you alone we find a champion,

in you alone one that can rescue us.
Perhaps you have not heard the messengers,   305
but Phoebus sent in answer to our sending
an oracle declaring that our freedom
from this disease would only come when we
should learn the names of those who killed King Laius,
and kill them or expel from our country.
Do not begrudge us oracles from birds,   310
or any other way of prophecy
within your skill; save yourself and the city,
save me; redeem the debt of our pollution
that lies on us because of this dead man.
We are in your hands; pains are most nobly taken
to help another when you have means and power.   315

Teiresias
Alas, how terrible is wisdom when
it brings no profit to the man that's wise!
This I knew well, but had forgotten it,
else I would not have come here.

Oedipus
                    What is this?
How sad you are now you have come!

Teiresias
                    Let me
go home. It will be easiest for us both   320
to bear our several destinies to the end
if you will follow my advice.

Oedipus
                    You'd rob us
of this your gift of prophecy? You talk
as one who had no care for law nor love
for Thebes who reared you.

Teiresias
Yes, but I see that even your own words
miss the mark; therefore I must fear for mine.   325

Oedipus

    For God's sake if you know of anything,
    do not turn from us; all of us kneel to you,
    all of us here, your suppliants.

Teiresias

    All of you here know nothing. I will not
    bring to the light of day my troubles, mine—
    rather than call them yours.

Oedipus

                 What do you mean?
    You know of something but refuse to speak.   330
    Would you betray us and destroy the city?

Teiresias

    I will not bring this pain upon us both,
    neither on you nor on myself. Why is it
    you question me and waste your labour? I
    will tell you nothing.

Oedipus

    You would provoke a stone! Tell us, you villain,   335
    tell us, and do not stand there quietly
    unmoved and balking at the issue.

Teiresias

    You blame my temper but you do not see
    your own that lives within you; it is me
    you chide.

Oedipus

    Who would not feel his temper rise
    at words like these with which you shame our city?   340

Teiresias

    Of themselves things will come, although I hide them
    and breathe no word of them.

Oedipus

                Since they will come
    tell them to me.

Teiresias

I will say nothing further.
Against this answer let your temper rage
as wildly as you will.

Oedipus

Indeed I am   345
so angry I shall not hold back a jot
of what I think. For I would have you know
I think you were complotter of the deed
and doer of the deed save in so far
as for the actual killing. Had you had eyes
I would have said alone you murdered him.

Teiresias

Yes? Then I warn you faithfully to keep   350
the letter of your proclamation and
from this day forth to speak no word of greeting
to these nor me; you are the land's pollution.

Oedipus

How shamelessly you started up this taunt!
How do you think you will escape?   355

Teiresias

I have.
I have escaped; the truth is what I cherish
and that's my strength.

Oedipus

And who has taught you truth?
Not your profession surely!

Teiresias

You have taught me,
for you have made me speak against my will.

Oedipus

Speak what? Tell me again that I may learn it better.

Teiresias

Did you not understand before or would you
provoke me into speaking?   360

Oedipus

                    I did not grasp it,
not so to call it known. Say it again.

Teiresias

I say you are the murderer of the king
whose murderer you seek.

Oedipus

                    Not twice you shall
say calumnies like this and stay unpunished.

Teiresias

Shall I say more to tempt your anger more?

Oedipus

As much as you desire; it will be said   365
in vain.

Teiresias

             I say that with those you love best
you live in foulest shame unconsciously
and do not see where you are in calamity.

Oedipus

Do you imagine you can always talk
like this, and live to laugh at it hereafter?

Teiresias

Yes, if the truth has anything of strength.

Oedipus

It has, but not for you; it has no strength   370
for you because you are blind in mind and ears
as well as in your eyes.

Teiresias

              You are a poor wretch
to taunt me with the very insults which
every one soon will heap upon yourself.

Oedipus

Your life is one long night so that you cannot
hurt me or any other who sees the light.   375

Teiresias
> It is not fate that I should be your ruin,
> Apollo is enough; it is his care
> to work this out.

Oedipus
>   Was this your own design
> or Creon's?

Teiresias
>   Creon is no hurt to you,
> but you are to yourself.

Oedipus
> Wealth, sovereignty and skill outmatching skill   380
> for the contrivance of an envied life!
> Great store of jealousy fill your treasury chests,
> if my friend Creon, friend from the first and loyal,   385
> thus secretly attacks me, secretly
> desires to drive me out and secretly
> suborns this juggling, trick devising quack,
> this wily beggar who has only eyes
> for his own gains, but blindness in his skill.
> For, tell me, where have you seen clear, Teiresias,   390
> with your prophetic eyes? When the dark singer,
> the sphinx, was in your country, did you speak
> word of deliverance to its citizens?
> And yet the riddle's answer was not the province
> of a chance comer. It was a prophet's task
> and plainly you had no such gift of prophecy   395
> from birds nor otherwise from any God
> to glean a word of knowledge. But I came,
> Oedipus, who knew nothing, and I stopped her.
> I solved the riddle by my wit alone.
> Mine was no knowledge got from birds. And now
> you would expel me,
> because you think that you will find a place   400
> by Creon's throne. I think you will be sorry,

both you and your accomplice, for your plot
to drive me out. And did I not regard you
as an old man, some suffering would have taught you
that what was in your heart was treason.

Chorus

We look at this man's words and yours, my king,
and we find both have spoken them in anger.   405
We need no angry words but only thought
how we may best hit the God's meaning for us.

Teiresias

If you are king, at least I have the right
no less to speak in my defence against you.
Of that much I am master. I am no slave   410
of yours, but Loxias', and so I shall not
enroll myself with Creon for my patron.
Since you have taunted me with being blind,
here is my word for you.
You have your eyes but see not where you are
in sin, nor where you live, nor whom you live with.
Do you know who your parents are? Unknowing   415
you are an enemy to kith and kin
in death, beneath the earth, and in this life.
A deadly footed, double striking curse,
from father and mother both, shall drive you forth
out of this land, with darkness on your eyes,
that now have such straight vision. Shall there be
a place will not be harbour to your cries,   420
a corner of Cithaeron will not ring
in echo to your cries, soon, soon,—
when you shall learn the secret of your marriage,
which steered you to a haven in this house,—
haven no haven, after lucky voyage?
And of the multitude of other evils
establishing a grim equality
between you and your children, you know nothing.   425

So, muddy with contempt my words and Creon's!
Misery shall grind no man as it will you.

Oedipus
Is it endurable that I should hear
such words from him? Go and a curse go with you!   430
Quick, home with you! Out of my house at once!

Teiresias
I would not have come either had you not called me.

Oedipus
I did not know then you would talk like a fool—
or it would have been long before I called you.

Teiresias
I am a fool then, as it seems to you—   435
but to the parents who have bred you, wise.

Oedipus
What parents? Stop! Who are they of all the world?

Teiresias
This day will show your birth and will destroy you.

Oedipus
How needlessly your riddles darken everything.

Teiresias
But it's in riddle answering you are strongest.   440

Oedipus
Yes. Taunt me where you will find me great.

Teiresias
It is this very luck that has destroyed you.

Oedipus
I do not care, if it has saved this city.

Teiresias
Well, I will go. Come, boy, lead me away.

Oedipus
Yes, lead him off. So long as you are here,   445

you'll be a stumbling block and a vexation;
once gone, you will not trouble me again.

Teiresias

                    I have said
what I came here to say not fearing your
countenance: there is no way you can hurt me.
I tell you, king, this man, this murderer
(whom you have long declared you are in search of,
indicting him in threatening proclamation   450
as murderer of Laius)—he is here.
In name he is a stranger among citizens
but soon he will be shown to be a citizen
true native Theban, and he'll have no joy
of the discovery: blindness for sight
and beggary for riches his exchange,   455
he shall go journeying to a foreign country
tapping his way before him with a stick.
He shall be proved father and brother both
to his own children in his house; to her
that gave him birth, a son and husband both;
a fellow sower in his father's bed
with that same father that he murdered.
Go within, reckon that out, and if you find me   460
mistaken, say I have no skill in prophecy.

                    (*Exeunt separately Teiresias and Oedipus.*)

Chorus

    Strophe
Who is the man proclaimed
by Delphi's prophetic rock
as the bloody handed murderer,   465
the doer of deeds that none dare name?
Now is the time for him to run
with a stronger foot
than Pegasus
for the child of Zeus leaps in arms upon him   470
with fire and the lightning bolt,

and terribly close on his heels
are the Fates that never miss.

Antistrophe
Lately from snowy Parnassus
clearly the voice flashed forth,
bidding each Theban track him down,   475
the unknown murderer.
In the savage forests he lurks and in
the caverns like
the mountain bull.
He is sad and lonely, and lonely his feet
that carry him far from the navel of earth;   480
but its prophecies, ever living,
flutter around his head.

Strophe
The augur has spread confusion,
terrible confusion;
I do not approve what was said   485
nor can I deny it.
I do not know what to say;
I am in a flutter of foreboding;
I never heard in the present
nor past of a quarrel between   490
the sons of Labdacus and Polybus,
that I might bring as proof
in attacking the popular fame
of Oedipus, seeking
to take vengeance for undiscovered
death in the line of Labdacus.   495

Antistrophe
Truly Zeus and Apollo are wise
and in human things all knowing;
but amongst men there is no   500
distinct judgment, between the prophet
and me—which of us is right.

One man may pass another in wisdom
but I would never agree
with those that find fault with the king
till I should see the word
proved right beyond doubt. For once
in visible form the Sphinx
came on him and all of us
saw his wisdom and in that test
he saved the city. So he will not be condemned by my mind.   512

(*Enter Creon.*)

Creon

Citizens, I have come because I heard
deadly words spread about me, that the king
accuses me. I cannot take that from him.
If he believes that in these present troubles   515
he has been wronged by me in word or deed
I do not want to live on with the burden
of such a scandal on me. The report   520
injures me doubly and most vitally—
for I'll be called a traitor to my city
and traitor also to my friends and you.

Chorus

Perhaps it was a sudden gust of anger
that forced that insult from him, and no judgment.

Creon

But did he say that it was in compliance   525
with schemes of mine that the seer told him lies?

Chorus

Yes, he said that, but why, I do not know.

Creon

Were his eyes straight in his head? Was his mind right
when he accused me in this fashion?

Chorus

I do not know; I have no eyes to see   530
what princes do. Here comes the king himself.

(*Enter Oedipus.*)

Oedipus

You, sir, how is it you come here? Have you so much
brazen-faced daring that you venture in
my house although you are proved manifestly
the murderer of that man, and though you tried,
openly, highway robbery of my crown?   535
For God's sake, tell me what you saw in me,
what cowardice or what stupidity,
that made you lay a plot like this against me?
Did you imagine I should not observe
the crafty scheme that stole upon me or
seeing it, take no means to counter it?   540
Was it not stupid of you to make the attempt,
to try to hunt down royal power without
the people at your back or friends? For only
with the people at your back or money can
the hunt end in the capture of a crown.

Creon

Do you know what you're doing? Will you listen
to words to answer yours, and then pass judgment?

Oedipus

You're quick to speak, but I am slow to grasp you,   545
for I have found you dangerous,—and my foe.

Creon

First of all hear what I shall say to that.

Oedipus

At least don't tell me that you are not guilty.

Creon

If you think obstinacy without wisdom
a valuable possession, you are wrong.   550

Oedipus

And you are wrong if you believe that one,
a criminal, will not be punished only
because he is my kinsman.

« 33 »

Creon
>   This is but just—
> but tell me, then, of what offense I'm guilty?

Oedipus
> Did you or did you not urge me to send   555
> to this prophetic mumbler?

Creon
>   I did indeed,
> and I shall stand by what I told you.

Oedipus
> How long ago is it since Laius. . . .

Creon
> What about Laius? I don't understand.

Oedipus
> Vanished—died—was murdered?   560

Creon
>   It is long,
> a long, long time to reckon.

Oedipus
>   Was this prophet
> in the profession then?

Creon
>   He was, and honoured
> as highly as he is today.

Oedipus
> At that time did he say a word about me?

Creon
> Never, at least when I was near him.   565

Oedipus
> You never made a search for the dead man?

Creon
> We searched, indeed, but never learned of anything.

Oedipus
> Why did our wise old friend not say this then?

Creon
    I don't know; and when I know nothing, I
    usually hold my tongue.

Oedipus
                 You know this much,   570
    and can declare this much if you are loyal.

Creon
    What is it? If I know, I'll not deny it.

Oedipus
    That he would not have said that I killed Laius
    had he not met you first.

Creon
                 You know yourself
    whether he said this, but I demand that I   575
    should hear as much from you as you from me.

Oedipus
    Then hear,—I'll not be proved a murderer.

Creon
    Well, then. You're married to my sister.

Oedipus
                 Yes,
    that I am not disposed to deny.

Creon
                 You rule
    this country giving her an equal share
    in the government?

Oedipus
                 Yes, everything she wants   580
    she has from me.

Creon
                 And I, as thirdsman to you,
    am rated as the equal of you two?

Oedipus
    Yes, and it's there you've proved yourself false friend.

Creon

Not if you will reflect on it as I do.
Consider, first, if you think any one
would choose to rule and fear rather than rule   585
and sleep untroubled by a fear if power
were equal in both cases. I, at least,
I was not born with such a frantic yearning
to be a king—but to do what kings do.
And so it is with every one who has learned
wisdom and self-control. As it stands now,
the prizes are all mine—and without fear.   590
But if I were the king myself, I must
do much that went against the grain.
How should despotic rule seem sweeter to me
than painless power and an assured authority?
I am not so besotted yet that I
want other honours than those that come with profit.   595
Now every man's my pleasure; every man greets me;
now those who are your suitors fawn on me,—
success for them depends upon my favour.
Why should I let all this go to win that?
My mind would not be traitor if it's wise;   600
I am no treason lover, of my nature,
nor would I ever dare to join a plot.
Prove what I say. Go to the oracle
at Pytho and inquire about the answers,
if they are as I told you. For the rest,   605
if you discover I laid any plot
together with the seer, kill me, I say,
not only by your vote but by my own.
But do not charge me on obscure opinion
without some proof to back it. It's not just
lightly to count your knaves as honest men,   610
nor honest men as knaves. To throw away
an honest friend is, as it were, to throw
your life away, which a man loves the best.

In time you will know all with certainty;
time is the only test of honest men,
one day is space enough to know a rogue.   615

Chorus
   His words are wise, king, if one fears to fall.
   Those who are quick of temper are not safe.

Oedipus
   When he that plots against me secretly
   moves quickly, I must quickly counterplot.
   If I wait taking no decisive measure   620
   his business will be done, and mine be spoiled.

Creon
   What do you want to do then? Banish me?

Oedipus
   No, certainly; kill you, not banish you.[1]

Creon
   I do not think that you've your wits about you.   626

Oedipus
   For my own interests, yes.

Creon
                              But for mine, too,
   you should think equally.

Oedipus
                              You are a rogue.

Creon
   Suppose you do not understand?

Oedipus
                              But yet
   I must be ruler.

   1. Two lines omitted here owing to the confusion in the dialogue consequent on
the loss of a third line. The lines as they stand in Jebb's edition (1902) are:
Oed.: That you may show what manner of thing is envy.
Creon: You speak as one that will not yield or trust.
[Oed. lost line.]

Creon

                        Not if you rule badly.

Oedipus

  O, city, city!

Creon

                     I too have some share   630
  in the city; it is not yours alone.

Chorus

  Stop, my lords! Here—and in the nick of time
  I see Jocasta coming from the house;
  with her help lay the quarrel that now stirs you.

                            (*Enter Jocasta.*)

Jocasta

  For shame! Why have you raised this foolish squabbling
  brawl? Are you not ashamed to air your private   635
  griefs when the country's sick? Go in, you, Oedipus,
  and you, too, Creon, into the house. Don't magnify
  your nothing troubles.

Creon

                 Sister, Oedipus,
  your husband, thinks he has the right to do
  terrible wrongs—he has but to choose between   640
  two terrors: banishing or killing me.

Oedipus

  He's right, Jocasta; for I find him plotting
  with knavish tricks against my person.

Creon

  That God may never bless me! May I die
  accursed, if I have been guilty of   645
  one tittle of the charge you bring against me!

Jocasta

  I beg you, Oedipus, trust him in this,
  spare him for the sake of this his oath to God,
  for my sake, and the sake of those who stand here.

Chorus

Be gracious, be merciful,   649
we beg of you.

Oedipus

In what would you have me yield?

Chorus

He has been no silly child in the past.
He is strong in his oath now.
Spare him.

Oedipus

Do you know what you ask?

Chorus

Yes.

Oedipus

Tell me then.

Chorus

He has been your friend before all men's eyes; do not cast him   656
away dishonoured on an obscure conjecture.

Oedipus

I would have you know that this request of yours
really requests my death or banishment.

Chorus

May the Sun God, king of Gods, forbid! May I die without God's   660
blessing, without friends' help, if I had any such thought. But my
spirit is broken by my unhappiness for my wasting country; and   665
this would but add troubles amongst ourselves to the other
troubles.

Oedipus

Well, let him go then—if I must die ten times for it,   669
or be sent out dishonoured into exile.
It is your lips that prayed for him I pitied,
not his; wherever he is, I shall hate him.

Creon

> I see you sulk in yielding and you're dangerous
> when you are out of temper; natures like yours
> are justly heaviest for themselves to bear. 675

Oedipus

> Leave me alone! Take yourself off, I tell you.

Creon

> I'll go, you have not known me, but they have,
> and they have known my innocence.

> (*Exit.*)

Chorus

> Won't you take him inside, lady?

Jocasta

> Yes, when I've found out what was the matter. 680

Chorus

> There was some misconceived suspicion of a story, and on the
> other side the sting of injustice.

Jocasta

> So, on both sides?

Chorus

> Yes.

Jocasta

> What was the story?

Chorus

> I think it best, in the interests of the country, to leave it where 685
> it ended.

Oedipus

> You see where you have ended, straight of judgment
> although you are, by softening my anger.

Chorus

> Sir, I have said before and I say again—be sure that I would have 689
> been proved a madman, bankrupt in sane council, if I should put
> you away, you who steered the country I love safely when she

was crazed with troubles. God grant that now, too, you may   695
prove a fortunate guide for us.

Jocasta

Tell me, my lord, I beg of you, what was it
that roused your anger so?

Oedipus

                  Yes, I will tell you.   700
I honour you more than I honour them.
It was Creon and the plots he laid against me.

Jocasta

Tell me—if you can clearly tell the quarrel—

Oedipus

                  Creon says
that I'm the murderer of Laius.

Jocasta

Of his own knowledge or on information?

Oedipus

He sent this rascal prophet to me, since   705
he keeps his own mouth clean of any guilt.

Jocasta

Do not concern yourself about this matter;
listen to me and learn that human beings
have no part in the craft of prophecy.
Of that I'll show you a short proof.   710
There was an oracle once that came to Laius,—
I will not say that it was Phoebus' own,
but it was from his servants—and it told him
that it was fate that he should die a victim
at the hands of his own son, a son to be born
of Laius and me. But, see now, he,
the king, was killed by foreign highway robbers   715
at a place where three roads meet—so goes the story;
and for the son—before three days were out
after his birth King Laius pierced his ankles

and by the hands of others cast him forth
upon a pathless hillside. So Apollo   720
failed to fulfill his oracle to the son,
that he should kill his father, and to Laius
also proved false in that the thing he feared,
death at his son's hands, never came to pass.
So clear in this case were the oracles,
so clear and false. Give them no heed, I say;
what God discovers need of, easily
he shows to us himself.   725

Oedipus

              O dear Jocasta,
as I hear this from you, there comes upon me
a wandering of the soul—I could run mad.

Jocasta

    What trouble is it, that you turn again
and speak like this?

Oedipus

              I thought I heard you say
that Laius was killed at a crossroads.   730

Jocasta

    Yes, that was how the story went and still
that word goes round.

Oedipus

            Where is this place, Jocasta,
where he was murdered?

Jocasta

           Phocis is the country
and the road splits there, one of two roads from Delphi,
another comes from Daulia.

Oedipus

           How long ago is this?   735

Jocasta

    The news came to the city just before

you became king and all men's eyes looked to you.
What is it, Oedipus, that's in your mind?

Oedipus

What have you designed, O Zeus, to do with me?

Jocasta

What is the thought that troubles your heart?

Oedipus

Don't ask me yet—tell me of Laius—   740
How did he look? How old or young was he?

Jocasta

He was a tall man and his hair was grizzled
already—nearly white—and in his form
not unlike you.

Oedipus

             O God, I think I have
called curses on myself in ignorance.   745

Jocasta

What do you mean? I am terrified
when I look at you.

Oedipus

             I have a deadly fear
that the old seer had eyes. You'll show me more
if you can tell me one more thing.

Jocasta

                   I will.
I'm frightened,—but if I can understand,
I'll tell you all you ask.

Oedipus

             How was his company?   750
Had he few with him when he went this journey,
or many servants, as would suit a prince?

Jocasta

In all there were but five, and among them
a herald; and one carriage for the king.

Oedipus
It's plain—its plain—who was it told you this?   755

Jocasta
The only servant that escaped safe home.

Oedipus
Is he at home now?

Jocasta
                    No, when he came home again
and saw you king and Laius was dead,
he came to me and touched my hand and begged   760
that I should send him to the fields to be
my shepherd and so he might see the city
as far off as he might. So I
sent him away. He was an honest man,
as slaves go, and was worthy of far more
than what he asked of me.

Oedipus
O, how I wish that he could come back quickly!   765

Jocasta
He can. Why is your heart so set on this?

Oedipus
O dear Jocasta, I am full of fears
that I have spoken far too much; and therefore
I wish to see this shepherd.

Jocasta
                  He will come;
but, Oedipus, I think I'm worthy too
to know what it is that disquiets you.   770

Oedipus
It shall not be kept from you, since my mind
has gone so far with its forebodings. Whom
should I confide in rather than you, who is there
of more importance to me who have passed
through such a fortune?

Polybus was my father, king of Corinth,
and Merope, the Dorian, my mother.   775
I was held greatest of the citizens
in Corinth till a curious chance befell me
as I shall tell you—curious, indeed,
but hardly worth the store I set upon it.
There was a dinner and at it a man,
a drunken man, accused me in his drink   780
of being bastard. I was furious
but held my temper under for that day.
Next day I went and taxed my parents with it;
they took the insult very ill from him,
the drunken fellow who had uttered it.
So I was comforted for their part, but   785
still this thing rankled always, for the story
crept about widely. And I went at last
to Pytho, though my parents did not know.
But Phoebus sent me home again unhonoured
in what I came to learn, but he foretold   790
other and desperate horrors to befall me,
that I was fated to lie with my mother,
and show to daylight an accursed breed
which men would not endure, and I was doomed
to be murderer of the father that begot me.
When I heard this I fled, and in the days
that followed I would measure from the stars   795
the whereabouts of Corinth—yes, I fled
to somewhere where I should not see fulfilled
the infamies told in that dreadful oracle.
And as I journeyed I came to the place
where, as you say, this king met with his death.
Jocasta, I will tell you the whole truth.   800
When I was near the branching of the crossroads,
going on foot, I was encountered by
a herald and a carriage with a man in it,
just as you tell me. He that led the way

and the old man himself wanted to thrust me   805
out of the road by force. I became angry
and struck the coachman who was pushing me.
When the old man saw this he watched his moment,
and as I passed he struck me from his carriage,
full on the head with his two pointed goad.
But he was paid in full and presently   810
my stick had struck him backwards from the car
and he rolled out of it. And then I killed them
all. If it happened there was any tie
of kinship twixt this man and Laius,
who is then now more miserable than I,   815
what man on earth so hated by the Gods,
since neither citizen nor foreigner
may welcome me at home or even greet me,
but drive me out of doors? And it is I,
I and no other have so cursed myself.   820
And I pollute the bed of him I killed
by the hands that killed him. Was I not born evil?
Am I not utterly unclean? I had to fly
and in my banishment not even see
my kindred nor set foot in my own country,
or otherwise my fate was to be yoked   825
in marriage with my mother and kill my father,
Polybus who begot me and had reared me.
Would not one rightly judge and say that on me
these things were sent by some malignant God?
O no, no, no—O holy majesty   830
of God on high, may I not see that day!
May I be gone out of men's sight before
I see the deadly taint of this disaster
come upon me.

Chorus

Sir, we too fear these things. But until you see this man face to
face and hear his story, hope.   835

Oedipus

Yes, I have just this much of hope—to wait until the herdsman comes.

Jocasta

And when he comes, what do you want with him?

Oedipus

I'll tell you; if I find that his story is the same as yours, I at least will be clear of this guilt.   840

Jocasta

Why what so particularly did you learn from my story?

Oedipus

You said that he spoke of highway *robbers* who killed Laius. Now if he uses the same number, it was not I who killed him. One man cannot be the same as many. But if he speaks of a man travelling   845 alone, then clearly the burden of the guilt inclines towards me.

Jocasta

Be sure, at least, that this was how he told the story. He cannot unsay it now, for every one in the city heard it—not I alone. But,   850 Oedipus, even if he diverges from what he said then, he shall never prove that the murder of Laius squares rightly with the prophecy—for Loxias declared that the king should be killed by his own son. And that poor creature did not kill him surely,—   855 for he died himself first. So as far as prophecy goes, henceforward I shall not look to the right hand or the left.

Oedipus

Right. But yet, send some one for the peasant to bring him here;   860 do not neglect it.

Jocasta

I will send quickly. Now let me go indoors. I will do nothing except what pleases you.

(*Exeunt.*)

Chorus

Strophe

May destiny ever find me

pious in word and deed   865
prescribed by the laws that live on high:
laws begotten in the clear air of heaven,
whose only father is Olympus;
no mortal nature brought them to birth,
no forgetfulness shall lull them to sleep;   870
for God is great in them and grows not old.

   Antistrophe
Insolence breeds the tyrant, insolence
if it is glutted with a surfeit, unseasonable, unprofitable,   875
climbs to the roof-top and plunges
sheer down to the ruin that must be,
and there its feet are no service.
But I pray that the God may never   880
abolish the eager ambition that profits the state.
For I shall never cease to hold the God as our protector.

   Strophe
If a man walks with haughtiness
of hand or word and gives no heed   885
to Justice and the shrines of Gods
despises—may an evil doom
smite him for his ill-starred pride of heart!—
if he reaps gains without justice
and will not hold from impiety   890
and his fingers itch for untouchable things.
When such things are done, what man shall contrive
to shield his soul from the shafts of the God?
When such deeds are held in honour,   895
why should I honour the Gods in the dance?

   Antistrophe
No longer to the holy place,
to the navel of earth I'll go
to worship, nor to Abae
nor to Olympia,   900
unless the oracles are proved to fit,
for all men's hands to point at.

O Zeus, if you are rightly called
the sovereign lord, all-mastering,
let this not escape you nor your ever-living power!   905
The oracles concerning Laius
are old and dim and men regard them not.
Apollo is nowhere clear in honour; God's service perishes.   910

(Enter Jocasta, carrying garlands.)

Jocasta

Princes of the land, I have had the thought to go
to the Gods' temples, bringing in my hand
garlands and gifts of incense, as you see.
For Oedipus excites himself too much
at every sort of trouble, not conjecturing,   915
like a man of sense, what will be from what was,
but he is always at the speaker's mercy,
when he speaks terrors. I can do no good
by my advice, and so I came as suppliant
to you, Lycaean Apollo, who are nearest.
These are the symbols of my prayer and this   920
my prayer: grant us escape free of the curse.
Now when we look to him we are all afraid;
he's pilot of our ship and he is frightened.

(Enter Messenger.)

Messenger

Might I learn from you, sirs, where is the house of Oedipus? Or   925
best of all, if you know, where is the king himself?

Chorus

This is his house and he is within doors. This lady is his wife and
mother of his children.

Messenger

God bless you, lady, and God bless your household! God bless   930
Oedipus' noble wife!

Jocasta

God bless you, sir, for your kind greeting! What do you want
of us that you have come here? What have you to tell us?

Messenger

Good news, lady. Good for your house and for your husband.

Jocasta

What is your news? Who sent you to us? 935

Messenger

I come from Corinth and the news I bring will give you pleasure.
Perhaps a little pain too.

Jocasta

What is this news of double meaning?

Messenger

The people of the Isthmus will choose Oedipus to be their king. 940
That is the rumour there.

Jocasta

But isn't their king still old Polybus?

Messenger

No. He is in his grave. Death has got him.

Jocasta

Is that the truth? Is Oedipus' father dead?

Messenger

May I die myself if it be otherwise!

Jocasta (to a servant)

Be quick and run to the King with the news! O oracles of the 945
Gods, where are you now? It was from this man Oedipus fled, lest
he should be his murderer! And now he is dead, in the course of
nature, and not killed by Oedipus.

(*Enter Oedipus.*)

Oedipus

Dearest Jocasta, why have you sent for me? 950

Jocasta

Listen to this man and when you hear reflect what is the outcome
of the holy oracles of the Gods.

Oedipus

Who is he? What is his message for me?

Jocasta

 He is from Corinth and he tells us that your father Polybus is 955
 dead and gone.

Oedipus

 What's this you say, sir? Tell me yourself.

Messenger

 Since this is the first matter you want clearly told: Polybus has
 gone down to death. You may be sure of it.

Oedipus

 By treachery or sickness?   960

Messenger

 A small thing will put old bodies asleep.

Oedipus

 So he died of sickness, it seems,—poor old man!

Messenger

 Yes, and of age—the long years he had measured.

Oedipus

 Ha! Ha! O dear Jocasta, why should one
 look to the Pythian hearth? Why should one look   965
 to the birds screaming overhead? They prophesied
 that I should kill my father! But he's dead,
 and hidden deep in earth, and I stand here
 who never laid a hand on spear against him,—
 unless perhaps he died of longing for me,
 and thus I am his murderer. But they,   970
 the oracles, as they stand—he's taken them
 away with him, they're dead as he himself is,
 and worthless.

Jocasta

       That I told you before now.

Oedipus

 You did, but I was misled by my fear.

Jocasta

 Then lay no more of them to heart, not one   975

Oedipus
But surely I must fear my mother's bed?

Jocasta
Why should man fear since chance is all in all
for him, and he can clearly foreknow nothing?
Best to live lightly, as one can, unthinkingly.
As to your mother's marriage bed,—don't fear it.   980
Before this, in dreams too, as well as oracles,
many a man has lain with his own mother.
But he to whom such things are nothing bears
his life most easily.

Oedipus
All that you say would be said perfectly
if she were dead; but since she lives I must   985
still fear, although you talk so well, Jocasta.

Jocasta
Still in your father's death there's light of comfort?

Oedipus
Great light of comfort; but I fear the living.

Messenger
Who is the woman that makes you afraid?

Oedipus
Merope, old man, Polybus' wife.   990

Messenger
What about her frightens the queen and you?

Oedipus
A terrible oracle, stranger, from the Gods.

Messenger
Can it be told? Or does the sacred law
forbid another to have knowledge of it?

Oedipus
O no! Once on a time Loxias said
that I should lie with my own mother and   995

take on my hands the blood of my own father.
And so for these long years I've lived away
from Corinth; it has been to my great happiness;
but yet it's sweet to see the face of parents.

Messenger
This was the fear which drove you out of Corinth?   1000

Oedipus
Old man, I did not wish to kill my father.

Messenger
Why should I not free you from this fear, sir,
since I have come to you in all goodwill?

Oedipus
You would not find me thankless if you did.

Messenger
Why, it was just for this I brought the news,—   1005
to earn your thanks when you had come safe home.

Oedipus
No, I will never come near my parents.

Messenger
                     Son,
it's very plain you don't know what you're doing.

Oedipus
What do you mean, old man? For God's sake, tell me.

Messenger
If your homecoming is checked by fears like these.   1010

Oedipus
Yes, I'm afraid that Phoebus may prove right.

Messenger
The murder and the incest?

Oedipus
                     Yes, old man;
that is my constant terror.

Messenger
Do you know

that all your fears are empty?

Oedipus
How is that,

if they are father and mother and I their son?

1015

Messenger
Because Polybus was no kin to you in blood.

Oedipus
What, was not Polybus my father?

Messenger
No more than I but just so much.

Oedipus
How can

my father be my father as much as one
that's nothing to me?

Messenger
Neither he nor I

1020

begat you.

Oedipus
Why then did he call me son?

Messenger
A gift he took you from these hands of mine.

Oedipus
Did he love so much what he took from another's hand?

Messenger
His childlessness before persuaded him.

Oedipus
Was I a child you bought or found when I
was given to him?

1025

Messenger
On Cithaeron's slopes

in the twisting thickets you were found.

Oedipus
And why
were you a traveller in those parts?

Messenger
I was
in charge of mountain flocks.

Oedipus
You were a shepherd?
A hireling vagrant?

Messenger
Yes, but at least at that time   1030
the man that saved your life, son.

Oedipus
What ailed me when you took me in your arms?

Messenger
In that your ankles should be witnesses.

Oedipus
Why do you speak of that old pain?

Messenger
I loosed you;
the tendons of your feet were pierced and fettered,—

Oedipus
My swaddling clothes brought me a rare disgrace.   1035

Messenger
So that from this you're called your present name.

Oedipus
Was this my father's doing or my mother's?
For God's sake, tell me.

Messenger
I don't know, but he
who gave you to me has more knowledge than I.

Oedipus
You yourself did not find me then? You took me
from someone else?

Messenger
Yes, from another shepherd.   1040

Oedipus
Who was he? Do you know him well enough
to tell?

Messenger
He was called Laius' man.

Oedipus
You mean the king who reigned here in the old days?

Messenger
Yes, he was that man's shepherd.

Oedipus
Is he alive   1045
still, so that I could see him?

Messenger
You who live here
would know that best.

Oedipus
Do any of you here
know of this shepherd whom he speaks about
in town or in the fields? Tell me. It's time   1050
that this was found out once for all.

Chorus
I think he is none other than the peasant
whom you have sought to see already; but
Jocasta here can tell us best of that.

Oedipus
Jocasta, do you know about this man
whom we have sent for? Is he the man he mentions?   1055

Jocasta
Why ask of whom he spoke? Don't give it heed;
nor try to keep in mind what has been said.
It will be wasted labour.

Oedipus
With such clues
I could not fail to bring my birth to light.

Jocasta
I beg you—do not hunt this out—I beg you,   1060
if you have any care for your own life.
What I am suffering is enough.

Oedipus
Keep up
your heart, Jocasta. Though I'm proved a slave,
thrice slave, and though my mother is thrice slave,
you'll not be shown to be of lowly lineage.

Jocasta
O be persuaded by me, I entreat you;
do not do this.

Oedipus
I will not be persuaded to let be   1065
the chance of finding out the whole thing clearly.

Jocasta
It is because I wish you well that I
give you this counsel—and it's the best counsel.

Oedipus
Then the best counsel vexes me, and has
for some while since.

Jocasta
O Oedipus, God help you!
God keep you from the knowledge of who you are!

Oedipus
Here, some one, go and fetch the shepherd for me;
and let her find her joy in her rich family!   1070

Jocasta
O Oedipus, unhappy Oedipus!
that is all I can call you, and the last thing
that I shall ever call you.

(Exit.)

Chorus

 Why has the queen gone, Oedipus, in wild
 grief rushing from us? I am afraid that trouble   1075
 will break out of this silence.

Oedipus

 Break out what will! I at least shall be
 willing to see my ancestry, though humble.
 Perhaps she is ashamed of my low birth,
 for she has all a woman's high-flown pride.
 But I account myself a child of Fortune,   1080
 beneficent Fortune, and I shall not be
 dishonoured. She's the mother from whom I spring;
 the months, my brothers, marked me, now as small,
 and now again as mighty. Such is my breeding,
 and I shall never prove so false to it,   1085
 as not to find the secret of my birth.

Chorus

 Strophe

 If I am a prophet and wise of heart
 you shall not fail, Cithaeron,   1090
 by the limitless sky, you shall not!—
 to know at tomorrow's full moon
 that Oedipus honours you,
 as native to him and mother and nurse at once;
 and that you are honoured in dancing by us, as finding favour in
    sight of our king.
 Apollo, to whom we cry, find these things pleasing!

 Antistrophe

 Who was it bore you, child? One of   1098
 the long-lived nymphs who lay with Pan—
 the father who treads the hills?
 Or was she a bride of Loxias, your mother? The grassy slopes
 are all of them dear to him. Or perhaps Cyllene's king   1104
 or the Bacchants' God that lives on the tops

of the hills received you a gift from some
one of the Helicon Nymphs, with whom he mostly plays?

(*Enter an old man, led by Oedipus' servants.*)

Oedipus

If some one like myself who never met him   1110
may make a guess,—I think this is the herdsman,
whom we were seeking. His old age is consonant
with the other. And besides, the men who bring him
I recognize as my own servants. You   1115
perhaps may better me in knowledge since
you've seen the man before.

Chorus
                        You can be sure
I recognize him. For if Laius
had ever an honest shepherd, this was he.

Oedipus
You, sir, from Corinth, I must ask you first,
is this the man you spoke of?   1120

Messenger
                        This is he
before your eyes.

Oedipus
                        Old man, look here at me
and tell me what I ask you. Were you ever
a servant of King Laius?

Herdsman
                        I was,—
no slave he bought but reared in his own house.

Oedipus
What did you do as work? How did you live?

Herdsman
Most of my life was spent among the flocks.   1125

Oedipus
In what part of the country did you live?

Herdsman

Cithaeron and the places near to it.

Oedipus

And somewhere there perhaps you knew this man?

Herdsman

What was his occupation? Who?

Oedipus

          This man here,   1130
have you had any dealings with him?

Herdsman

             No—
not such that I can quickly call to mind.

Messenger

That is no wonder, master. But I'll make him remember what he
does not know. For I know, that he well knows the country of
Cithaeron, how he with two flocks, I with one kept company for   1135
three years—each year half a year—from spring till autumn time
and then when winter came I drove my flocks to our fold home
again and he to Laius' steadings. Well—am I right or not in what   1140
I said we did?

Herdsman

You're right—although it's a long time ago.

Messenger

Do you remember giving me a child
to bring up as my foster child?

Herdsman

             What's this?
Why do you ask this question?

Messenger

             Look old man,   1145
here he is—here's the man who was that child!

Herdsman

Death take you! Won't you hold your tongue?

Oedipus
                              No, no,
do not find fault with him, old man. Your words
are more at fault than his.

Herdsman
                              O best of masters,
    how do I give offense?

Oedipus
                              When you refuse   1150
    to speak about the child of whom he asks you.

Herdsman
    He speaks out of his ignorance, without meaning.

Oedipus
    If you'll not talk to gratify me, you
    will talk with pain to urge you.

Herdsman
                              O please, sir,
    don't hurt an old man, sir.

Oedipus (to the servants)
                              Here, one of you,
    twist his hands behind him.

Herdsman
                              Why, God help me, why?   1155
    What do you want to know?

Oedipus
                              You gave a child
    to him,—the child he asked you of?

Herdsman
                              I did.
    I wish I'd died the day I did.

Oedipus
                              You will
    unless you tell me truly.

Herdsman

And I'll die

far worse if I should tell you.

Oedipus

This fellow 1160

is bent on more delays, as it would seem.

Herdsman

O no, no! I have told you that I gave it.

Oedipus

Where did you get this child from? Was it your own or did you get it from another?

Herdsman

Not

my own at all; I had it from some one.

Oedipus

One of these citizens? or from what house?

Herdsman

O master, please—I beg you, master, please 1165

don't ask me more.

Oedipus

You're a dead man if I

ask you again.

Herdsman

It was one of the children

of Laius.

Oedipus

A slave? Or born in wedlock?

Herdsman

O God, I am on the brink of frightful speech.

Oedipus

And I of frightful hearing. But I must hear. 1170

Herdsman

The child was called his child; but she within,
your wife would tell you best how all this was.

Oedipus
  She gave it to you?

Herdsman
                    Yes, she did, my lord.

Oedipus
  To do what with it?

Herdsman
                    Make away with it.

Oedipus
  She was so hard—its mother?   1175

Herdsman
                    Aye, through fear
  of evil oracles.

Oedipus
                    Which?

Herdsman
                    They said that he
  should kill his parents.

Oedipus
                    How was it that you
  gave it away to this old man?

Herdsman
                    O master,
  I pitied it, and thought that I could send it
  off to another country and this man
  was from another country. But he saved it   1180
  for the most terrible troubles. If you are
  the man he says you are, you're bred to misery.

Oedipus
  O, O, O, they will all come,
  all come out clearly! Light of the sun, let me
  look upon you no more after today!
  I who first saw the light bred of a match
  accursed, and accursed in my living
  with them I lived with, cursed in my killing.   1185

                    (*Exeunt all but the Chorus.*)

Chorus

   Strophe

O generations of men, how I
count you as equal with those who live
not at all!
What man, what man on earth wins more   1190
of happiness than a seeming
and after that turning away?
Oedipus, you are my pattern of this,
Oedipus, you and your fate!
Luckless Oedipus, whom of all men
I envy not at all.   1196

   Antistrophe

In as much as he shot his bolt
beyond the others and won the prize
of happiness complete—
O Zeus—and killed and reduced to nought
the hooked taloned maid of the riddling speech,
standing a tower against death for my land:
hence he was called my king and hence
was honoured the highest of all
honours; and hence he ruled
in the great city of Thebes.

   Strophe

But now whose tale is more miserable?   1204
Who is there lives with a savager fate?
Whose troubles so reverse his life as his?

O Oedipus, the famous prince
for whom a great haven
the same both as father and son
sufficed for generation,
how, O how, have the furrows ploughed
by your father endured to bear you, poor wretch,
and hold their peace so long?

Antistrophe

Time who sees all has found you out   1213
against your will; judges your marriage accursed,
begetter and begot at one in it.

O child of Laius,
would I had never seen you.
I weep for you and cry
a dirge of lamentation.

To speak directly, I drew my breath
from you at the first and so now I lull   1222
my mouth to sleep with your name.

                              (*Enter a second messenger.*)

Second Messenger

O Princes always honoured by our country,
what deeds you'll hear of and what horrors see,
what grief you'll feel, if you as true born Thebans   1225
care for the house of Labdacus's sons.
Phasis nor Ister cannot purge this house,
I think, with all their streams, such things
it hides, such evils shortly will bring forth
into the light, whether they will or not;   1230
and troubles hurt the most
when they prove self-inflicted.

Chorus

What we had known before did not fall short
of bitter groaning's worth; what's more to tell?

Second Messenger

Shortest to hear and tell—our glorious queen   1235
Jocasta's dead.

Chorus

                              Unhappy woman! How?

Second Messenger

By her own hand. The worst of what was done
you cannot know. You did not see the sight.
Yet in so far as I remember it

you'll hear the end of our unlucky queen. 1240
When she came raging into the house she went
straight to her marriage bed, tearing her hair
with both her hands, and crying upon Laius 1245
long dead—Do you remember, Laius,
that night long past which bred a child for us
to send you to your death and leave
a mother making children with her son?
And then she groaned and cursed the bed in which
she brought forth husband by her husband, children 1250
by her own child, an infamous double bond.
How after that she died I do not know,—
for Oedipus distracted us from seeing.
He burst upon us shouting and we looked
to him as he paced frantically around,
begging us always: Give me a sword, I say, 1255
to find this wife no wife, this mother's womb,
this field of double sowing whence I sprang
and where I sowed my children! As he raved
some god showed him the way—none of us there.
Bellowing terribly and led by some 1260
invisible guide he rushed on the two doors,—
wrenching the hollow bolts out of their sockets,
he charged inside. There, there, we saw his wife
hanging, the twisted rope around her neck.
When he saw her, he cried out fearfully 1265
and cut the dangling noose. Then, as she lay,
poor woman, on the ground, what happened after,
was terrible to see. He tore the brooches—
the gold chased brooches fastening her robe—
away from her and lifting them up high
dashed them on his own eyeballs, shrieking out 1270
such things as: they will never see the crime
I have committed or had done upon me!
Dark eyes, now in the days to come look on
forbidden faces, do not recognize

those whom you long for—with such imprecations
he struck his eyes again and yet again   1275
with the brooches. And the bleeding eyeballs gushed
and stained his beard—no sluggish oozing drops
but a black rain and bloody hail poured down.

So it has broken—and not on one head   1280
but troubles mixed for husband and for wife.
The fortune of the days gone by was true
good fortune—but today groans and destruction
and death and shame—of all ills can be named   1285
not one is missing.

Chorus
Is he now in any ease from pain?

Second Messenger
            He shouts
for some one to unbar the doors and show him
to all the men of Thebes, his father's killer,
his mother's—no I cannot say the word,
it is unholy—for he'll cast himself,
out of the land, he says, and not remain   1290
to bring a curse upon his house, the curse
he called upon it in his proclamation. But
he wants for strength, aye, and some one to guide him;
his sickness is too great to bear. You, too,
will be shown that. The bolts are opening.   1295
Soon you will see a sight to waken pity
even in the horror of it.
                (Enter the blinded Oedipus.)

Chorus
This is a terrible sight for men to see!
I never found a worse!
Poor wretch, what madness came upon you!   1300
What evil spirit leaped upon your life
to your ill-luck—a leap beyond man's strength!
Indeed I pity you, but I cannot

look at you, though there's much I want to ask
and much to learn and much to see.   1305
I shudder at the sight of you.

Oedipus
    O, O,
    where am I going? Where is my voice   1310
    borne on the wind to and fro?
    Spirit, how far have you sprung?

Chorus
    To a terrible place whereof men's ears
    may not hear, nor their eyes behold it.

Oedipus
    Darkness!
    Horror of darkness enfolding, resistless, unspeakable visitant sped
        by an ill wind in haste!   1315
    madness and stabbing pain and memory
    of evil deeds I have done!

Chorus
    In such misfortunes it's no wonder
    if double weighs the burden of your grief.   1320

Oedipus
    My friend,
    you are the only one steadfast, the only one that attends on me;
    you still stay nursing the blind man.
    Your care is not unnoticed. I can know   1325
    your voice, although this darkness is my world.

Chorus
    Doer of dreadful deeds, how did you dare
    so far to do despite to your own eyes?
    what spirit urged you to it?

Oedipus
    It was Apollo, friends, Apollo,
    that brought this bitter bitterness, my sorrows to completion.   1330
    But the hand that struck me

was none but my own.
Why should I see
whose vision showed me nothing sweet to see?   1335

Chorus
    These things are as you say.

Oedipus
    What can I see to love?
    What greeting can touch my ears with joy?
    Take me away, and haste—to a place out of the way!   1340
    Take me away, my friends, the greatly miserable,
    the most accursed, whom God too hates   1345
    above all men on earth!

Chorus
    Unhappy in your mind and your misfortune,
    would I had never known you!

Oedipus
    Curse on the man who took
    the cruel bonds from off my legs, as I lay in the field.   1350
    He stole me from death and saved me,
    no kindly service.
    Had I died then
    I would not be so burdensome to friends.   1355

Chorus
    I, too, could have wished it had been so.

Oedipus
    Then I would not have come
    to kill my father and marry my mother infamously.
    Now I am godless and child of impurity,   1360
    begetter in the same seed that created my wretched self.
    If there is any ill worse than ill,   1365
    that is the lot of Oedipus.

Chorus
    I cannot say your remedy was good;
    you would be better dead than blind and living.

Oedipus

What I have done here was best done—don't tell me   1370
otherwise, do not give me further counsel.
I do not know with what eyes I could look
upon my father when I die and go
under the earth, nor yet my wretched mother—
those two to whom I have done things deserving
worse punishment than hanging. Would the sight   1375
of children, bred as mine are, gladden me?
No, not these eyes, never. And my city,
its towers and sacred places of the Gods,
of these I robbed my miserable self   1380
when I commanded all to drive *him* out,
the criminal since proved by God impure
and of the race of Laius.
To this guilt I bore witness against myself—
with what eyes shall I look upon my people?   1385
No. If there were a means to choke the fountain
of hearing I would not have stayed my hand
from locking up my miserable carcase,
seeing and hearing nothing; it is sweet   1390
to keep our thoughts out of the range of hurt.

Cithaeron, why did you receive me? why
having received me did you not kill me straight?
And so I had not shown to men my birth.

O Polybus and Corinth and the house,
the old house that I used to call my father's—   1395
what fairness you were nurse to, and what foulness
festered beneath! Now I am found to be
a sinner and a son of sinners. Crossroads,
and hidden glade, oak and the narrow way
at the crossroads, that drank my father's blood   1400
offered you by my hands, do you remember
still what I did as you looked on, and what
I did when I came here? O marriage, marriage!

you bred me and again when you had bred
bred children of your child and showed to men 1405
brides, wives and mothers and the foulest deeds
that can be in this world of ours.

Come—it's unfit to say what is unfit
to do.—I beg of you in God's name hide me 1410
somewhere outside your country, yes, or kill me,
or throw me into the sea, to be forever
out of your sight. Approach and deign to touch me
for all my wretchedness, and do not fear.
No man but I can bear my evil doom. 1415

Chorus
   Here Creon comes in fit time to perform
   or give advice in what you ask of us.
   Creon is left sole ruler in your stead.

Oedipus
   Creon! Creon! What shall I say to him?
   How can I justly hope that he will trust me? 1420
   In what is past I have been proved towards him
   an utter liar.

                                   (Enter Creon.)

Creon
                     Oedipus, I've come
   not so that I might laugh at you nor taunt you
   with evil of the past. But if you still
   are without shame before the face of men
   reverence at least the flame that gives all life, 1425
   our Lord the Sun, and do not show unveiled
   to him pollution such that neither land
   nor holy rain nor light of day can welcome.

                                 (To a servant.)

   Be quick and take him in. It is most decent 1430
   that only kin should see and hear the troubles
   of kin.

Oedipus

     I beg you, since you've torn me from
my dreadful expectations and have come
in a most noble spirit to a man
that has used you vilely—do a thing for me.
I shall speak for your own good, not for my own.

Creon

What do you need that you would ask of me?   1435

Oedipus

Drive me from here with all the speed you can
to where I may not hear a human voice.

Creon

Be sure, I would have done this had not I
wished first of all to learn from the God the course
of action I should follow.

Oedipus

     But his word   1440
has been quite clear to let the parricide,
the sinner, die.

Creon

     Yes, that indeed was said.
But in the present need we had best discover
what we should do.

Oedipus

     And will you ask about
a man so wretched?

Creon

     Now even you will trust   1445
the God.

Oedipus

    So. I command you—and will beseech you—
to her that lies inside that house give burial
as you would have it; she is yours and rightly
you will perform the rites for her. For me—

never let this my father's city have me   1450
living a dweller in it. Leave me live
in the mountains where Cithaeron is, that's called
my mountain, which my mother and my father
while they were living would have made my tomb.
So I may die by their decree who sought
indeed to kill me. Yet I know this much: 1455
no sickness and no other thing will kill me.
I would not have been saved from death if not
for some strange evil fate. Well, let my fate
go where it will.

                    Creon, you need not care   1460
about my sons; they're men and so wherever
they are, they will not lack a livelihood.
But my two girls—so sad and pitiful—
whose table never stood apart from mine,
and everything I touched they always shared—   1465
O Creon, have a thought for them! And most
I wish that you might suffer me to touch them
and sorrow with them.

     (*Enter Antigone and Ismene, Oedipus' two daughters.*)
O my lord! O true noble Creon! Can I   1470
really be touching them, as when I saw?
What shall I say?
Yes, I can hear them sobbing—my two darlings!
and Creon has had pity and has sent me
what I loved most?
Am I right?   1475

Creon

    You're right: it was I gave you this
because I knew from old days how you loved them
as I see now.

Oedipus

                God bless you for it, Creon,
and may God guard you better on your road
than he did me!

O children,   1480
where are you? Come here, come to my hands,
a brother's hands which turned your father's eyes,
those bright eyes you knew once, to what you see,
a father seeing nothing, knowing nothing,
begetting you from his own source of life.   1485
I weep for you—I cannot see your faces—
I weep when I think of the bitterness
there will be in your lives, how you must live
before the world. At what assemblages
of citizens will you make one? to what   1490
gay company will you go and not come home
in tears instead of sharing in the holiday?
And when you're ripe for marriage, who will he be,
the man who'll risk to take such infamy
as shall cling to my children, to bring hurt   1495
on them and those that marry with them? What
curse is not there? "Your father killed his father
and sowed the seed where he had sprung himself
and begot you out of the womb that held him."
These insults you will hear. Then who will marry you?   1500
No one, my children; clearly you are doomed
to waste away in barrenness unmarried.
Son of Menoeceus, since you are all the father
left these two girls, and we, their parents, both   1505
are dead to them—do not allow them wander
like beggars, poor and husbandless.
They are of your own blood.
And do not make them equal with myself
in wretchedness; for you can see them now
so young, so utterly alone, save for you only.
Touch my hand, noble Creon, and say yes.   1510
If you were older, children, and were wiser,
there's much advice I'd give you. But as it is,
let this be what you pray: give me a life

wherever there is opportunity
to live, and better life than was my father's.

Creon
Your tears have had enough of scope; now go within the house.   1515

Oedipus
I must obey, though bitter of heart.

Creon
In season, all is good.

Oedipus
Do you know on what conditions I obey?

Creon
                              You tell me them,
and I shall know them when I hear.

Oedipus
                              That you shall send me out
to live away from Thebes.

Creon
                    That gift you must ask of the God.

Oedipus
But I'm now hated by the Gods.

Creon
                    So quickly you'll obtain your prayer.

Oedipus
You consent then?   1520

Creon
                    What I do not mean, I do not use to say.

Oedipus
Now lead me away from here.

Creon
                    Let go the children, then, and come.

Oedipus
Do not take them from me.

Creon

        Do not seek to be master in everything,
for the things you mastered did not follow you throughout your
    life.

                    (As Creon and Oedipus go out.)

Chorus

    You that live in my ancestral Thebes, behold this Oedipus,—
    him who knew the famous riddles and was a man most masterful;   1525
    not a citizen who did not look with envy on his lot—
    see him now and see the breakers of misfortune swallow him!
    Look upon that last day always. Count no mortal happy till
    he has passed the final limit of his life secure from pain.   1530

OEDIPUS AT COLONUS

Translated by David Grene

CHARACTERS

Oedipus

Antigone

A Stranger

Ismene

Theseus

Creon

Polyneices

A Messenger

Chorus

OEDIPUS AT COLONUS

(Enter Oedipus, now a very old man, accompanied by
his daughter Antigone.)

Oedipus

I am blind and old, Antigone, my child.
What country have we come to? Whose is this city?
Who will today receive the wandering
Oedipus, with the scantiest of gifts?
It's little I ask for, and still less I get,
yet it is enough for me.
My sufferings have taught me to endure—
and how long these sufferings have lasted!—
and my high breeding teaches me the same.

Child, do you see anywhere I could sit,   10
either on the common ground or in the groves
belonging to the god? Set me there securely,
that we may find out where we are; we have come to be learners
as foreigners from citizens, to do as we are told.

Antigone

My poor suffering father, Oedipus!
there are towers here that protect the city; they look,
to my eyes, far off. This place is sacred—
as I would guess—it's thick with laurel,
with olives and with vines; the nightingales are singing,
thick-feathered, happily, inside the grove.   20
Here's a rough rock; bend and sit down on it.
This has been a long journey for an old man like you.

Oedipus

Set me now in place, watch over the blind man.

Antigone
> I do not need to learn that now;
> time has seen to that.

Oedipus
> Can you tell me where we are?

Antigone
> Athens—that much I know—but not this place.

Oedipus
> Yes, Athens; every traveler has told us that.

Antigone
> Shall I go and try to find which this place is?

Oedipus
> Yes, child, if indeed there are people in it.   30

Antigone
> People there are; I think I need do nothing.
> I see a man now, near us.

Oedipus
> Are you sure? Is he really coming this way?

Antigone
> He is, indeed—here with us. Whatever you have
> that is suitable to say, say it; the man is here.

Oedipus
> Sir, I have heard her say—
> she has eyes for both of us—that you have come
> to inquire about us. Very opportunely
> you come to clear up our uncertainty.

Stranger
> Before you ask any more—up from this place   40
> where you are sitting! This is no ground to tread on.

Oedipus
> What is this place? What god is thought to possess it?

Stranger
It is inviolable, none may live in it. The Goddesses
most dreadful, the daughters of Earth and Darkness, possess it.

Oedipus
May I hear their sacred name to pray to them?

Stranger
The all-seeing Eumenides, the people here call them,
but they have other fair names elsewhere.

> *(A silence, broken by Oedipus' words.)*

Oedipus
May they be gracious and receive their suppliant.
For I will never go from this land—from *this* place in it!

Stranger
What can you mean?   50

Oedipus
                                        I have heard
the watchword of my destiny.

Stranger
No—I would certainly never have the boldness
to drive you out, without the city's sanction,
until I tell them what I am doing.

Oedipus
Sir, for God's sake, do not do me such dishonor—
poor wanderer that I am—to deny me
what I would beg you tell me.

Stranger
Then speak. I *shall* not do you such dishonor.

Oedipus
What *is* this place on which I have set foot?   60

Stranger
If you listen, I will tell you, whatever it is
I know myself. All of this place is sacred;

our holy lord Poseidon holds it. In it
there dwells Prometheus the Titan, fire-bearing god.
Within this land the spot you tread on
is the Bronze Road—so it is called—
it is the founding stone of Athens; the neighboring acres
boast that their ruler is the Knight Colonus
and all the people here bear his name in common.
That is how things are, sir; here is no mere honor in word;   70
the honor comes of living with the place, as theirs.

Oedipus

There are some, then, that live within this place?

Stranger

Yes, surely, those that are called by the god's name.

Oedipus

Have they a sovereign, or does the word rest with the people?

Stranger

They are ruled by the city's king.

Oedipus

                                        And who is he
that is so mighty both in power and word?

Stranger

His name is Theseus, son of Aegeus, that was.

Oedipus

Can a messenger go from you to him?

Stranger

                                 What for?   80
To tell him what, to urge his coming here?

Oedipus

That by small help he may reap great gains.

Stranger

Can a blind man give such help?

Oedipus

There shall be sight in all the words I say.

Stranger

    Let me tell you, sir, how you will make no mistake;
    You are noble—anyone can see that—in all but fortune.
    Remain here where I first saw you, until I go
    and tell my fellow citizens; not those in the city,
    but citizens of *this* place. They are those to judge
    whether you should stay here or again take the road.   90

Oedipus

    Child, is the stranger gone?

Antigone

                    Yes, he is gone;
    so, father, you may freely say everything,
    for only I am by.

        (Oedipus turns towards the grove and addresses those in it.)

Oedipus

    O solemn, dreadful-faced Ones,
    since first in this land with you I found my resting place
    and bent the knee there, be not unmindful
    of Phoebus and of me!
    For Phoebus when he prophesied those horrors,
    those many horrors for me, yet said that at the last   100
    I should find rest here, in this final country,
    when I should gain the haunt of the Dread Goddesses,
    a place of hospitality for strangers.
    There I should round my wretched life's last lap,
    a gain for those that settled me, received me,
    but a curse to those that drove me out.
    As warranty of this there should come signs,
    earthquakes and thunder, Zeus' lightning.
    Now I know well that I can trust your omen
    that guided me to this grove! Never, else, surely,   110
    had I in my traveling met with *you* first of all,
    I dry-mouthed, you that use no wine. Nor had I
    sat on this sacred undressed rock. But, Goddesses,

as Phoebus' mouth has spoken, give my life ending
at last, some consummation of my course,
unless I seem to you inconsequential,
a slave to toils, the greatest in the world.
Come, you sweet daughters of ancient Darkness,
come, city, called after great Pallas,
Athens, most full of honor of any city,   120
pity this wretched shade of the man Oedipus;
the body that once was Oedipus is no more.

Antigone
Hush! Here are some old men coming
to spy out where we are resting.

Oedipus
I will be silent.
Do you conceal me in the grove, out of the way,
till I can find out what they will say; if we only hear,
we can be cautious in our actions.

Chorus of old men, nobles of Athens
Look! Who was he? And where?
Where has he disappeared? Where has he hurried,   130
man of most impious daring? Look for him, search for him,
inquire everywhere! Some wandering tramp
he must be, not from hereabouts; else he had never
set foot within this sacred grove
of those violent virgins whom we tremble to name,
whose dwelling place we pass
with no eyes to look, and without voice to speak,
with silent guard on lips, that no words
may a pious mouth sound forth.

But now the story goes that someone has come   140
who shows no reverence at all,
and search as I may I cannot discover
who he may be.

Oedipus
    I am he; for I see
    by the sound of a voice, as the proverb runs.

Chorus
    Someone terrible to see,
    terrible to hear.

Oedipus
    Do not see me as a lawbreaker—
    that I entreat you.

Chorus
    Zeus the Defender, who can this old man be?   150

Oedipus
    Surely no one to congratulate
    on prime good fortune, guardians of this land.
    I can be clear on that; else others' eyes
    would not so guide my erring steps,
    else had my greatness not found its anchor
    on those that are but little.

Chorus
    Woe for your blinded eyes! Were you so from birth?
    Old and unfortunate
    is how you look to us.
    But at least if it lies with me,   160
    you should not add another curse on yourself.
    You advance too far, too far! Take heed
    lest you stumble on that grassy stretch
    where the mixing bowl
    mixes its water with the stream that runs
    sweetened with honey.
    Unlucky stranger, watch heedfully. Away!
    Step right away! He is too far away to hear!
    Do you hear, you sorrowful wanderer?

If you want to speak and answer us,   170
leave that forbidden place and speak
where all may speak. Till then be silent.

Oedipus

Daughter, what should one think of this?

Antigone

Father, we must do as other citizens here,
yielding in what is dutiful, hearing with obedience.

Oedipus

Reach out your hand to me.

Antigone

Here do I reach it out.

Oedipus

Sirs, let me not meet with injustice
now I have trusted you and moved my ground.

Chorus

Old man, no one shall lead you   180
against your will, from where you rest at present.

Oedipus

Must I go further still?

Chorus

Still further.

Oedipus

Still further?

Chorus

Lead him, girl,
somewhat further. *You* are listening to me.

[*R. C. Jebb, the main English commentator on Sophocles, thinks
that here there are three lines lost, in interchanges between Oedipus and
Antigone.*]

Antigone
Follow me then, follow me
with your blind steps; follow where I lead you.

[*Jebb thinks that a line is lost here also.*]

Chorus
You are a stranger in a strange land,
poor man. Make your mind up   190
to reject what this city dislikes,
and reverence what she loves.

Oedipus
Lead me on, child,
to where, my feet once more on pious footing,
I may speak and hear.
We must not fight against necessity.

Chorus
Here, do not bend your steps
beyond this block of natural stone.

Oedipus
Is this as you want it?

Chorus
Far enough, I tell you.   200

Oedipus
May I sit?

Chorus
Yes, sideways, on the edge of the rock,
crouch low.

Antigone
Father, let me help you—this is my task—
step evenly with me.
Lean your old body on my arm that loves it.

(*Oedipus groans.*)

Oedipus
  Oh, for the mischief that haunts my mind!

Chorus
  Poor man, now that you rest,
  tell me—who are you?
  Who are you that is led so sorrowfully?   210
  May we ask what is your country?

Oedipus
  Sirs, I have no city; please do not—

Chorus
  Do not do what, old man?

Oedipus
  Do not ask who I am; do not push further
  in your inquiry.

Chorus
  Why so?

Oedipus
  My breeding is full of terror.

Chorus
  Tell me.

Oedipus
  Daughter, what am I to say?

                              (He breaks into a sob.)

Chorus
  Tell me what stock you are of, sir, and your father.   220

Oedipus (sobbing)
  What will become of me, child?

Antigone
  Tell them. You are as far as you can go.

Oedipus
  I will tell them, then. Indeed, I cannot hide it.

Chorus
You are slow and hesitant. Be quick and tell us.

Oedipus
Do you know a son
of Laius?

Chorus
Oh, yes, yes!

Oedipus
He was of the family of the Labdacids.

Chorus
O Zeus!

Oedipus
The miserable Oedipus.   230

Chorus
And you are *he*?

Oedipus
Do not be so terrified
at what I say.

Chorus
(*cries out*)

Oedipus
A doomed man.

Chorus
(*cries out*)

Oedipus
Daughter,
what will become of me *now*?

Chorus
Out of this place, out of it!

Oedipus

And your promise? What will that be? 240

Chorus

Punishment is not the due lot of anyone
who but requites what is already done to him.
Trickery matching others' trickery gives
pain and not pleasure in return.
Up from this place!—and from this country where
you have found an anchorage!
Do not fix upon my city
some further debt to bear.

Antigone

Sirs, you have honor in your hearts,
but you cannot bear with my father, old and blind, 250
because you have heard the tale
of acts done in unconsciousness!
Yet, sirs, take pity on my wretched self;
I who beg you for my father only.
I beg you, with eyes not blinded, facing your eyes,
as though I came of your own blood,
that he, in his unhappiness, win your mercy.
What happens to us lies in your hands,
as though you were a god.
Come, grant me a favor—though I scarce look for it— 260
I entreat you by all that is dear to you—
by child or wife, by duty or by god.
No matter where you look, you will find no man
who can escape if a god leads him on.

Chorus

Why, know, you child of Oedipus, that you and he
both win our pity for your calamity.
But we dread judgment from the gods. We cannot
say more than what we have said to you already.

Oedipus

What is the good of a glorious reputation

if it is like an idly flowing stream? 270
They say that Athens is the holiest of cities,
say that she always rescues the injured stranger,
that she alone is able to defend him.
Where are these things for me? You moved me out
from the safety of this rock; then drive me out
forth from your country—fearing my name alone!
Surely not what I am nor what I have done.
Indeed, what I have done
is suffering rather than doing, if I were to tell you
the story of both my parents, which makes you dread me. 280
That I know well. How can my nature be evil,
when all I did was matching others' actions?
Even had I done what I did full consciously,
even so, I would not have been evil.
But the truth is, I knew nothing
when I came where I did. Yet *they* knew—
those by whom I suffered—knew what they did.
It was meant to be my death.
Therefore, sirs, I beseech you by the gods,
since you took me from my place of safety, save me now. 290
Do not, as honoring the gods, fail to give those gods
their dues of recognition. Think that they look
upon those that respect the gods and those
who do not so—among all men in the world.
Never yet has the wicked man got clear away,
escaping them. Take the side of those gods, do not dim the glory
of Athens by serving deeds of wickedness.
Rescue me, guard me; do not see the ugliness
of my face to its dishonor.
I am here as sacred and pious both, 300
and bringing benefit to your citizens.
When your lord comes here—whoever is your leader—
you shall hear all and understand it all.
In the time between these words and his arrival
do not turn villains.

Chorus

>We needs must fear, old man, those haunted thoughts
>coming from you; the words that clothe them are not light.
>It is enough for me that this land's princes
>shall know the matter through and through.

Oedipus

>Sirs, where is the ruler of this land? 310

Chorus

>He is in his father's city, in our country.
>The man who sent me here has gone to fetch him.

Oedipus

>Do you believe that he will care so much
>to give a thought to a blind man—that he will come
>himself to see me?

Chorus

>He surely will when he has heard your name.

Oedipus

>Who is there that will bring *that* word to him?

Chorus

>It is a long road here; there are many travelers
>and many tales of theirs; these he will hear
>and come; do not trouble for that. Your name, old man, 320
>has pierced the ears of many; were he asleep
>or slow to move, yet when he hears
>of *you,* he will come quickly to this place.

Oedipus

>Well, may he come, with good luck for this city,
>and for me, too! For what good man is there
>who is no friend to himself?

Antigone

>Zeus, what shall I say? What am I to think, father?

Oedipus

>What is it, Antigone, my child?

Antigone
> I see a girl
> coming towards us riding an Etnean horse;   330
> on her head is a Thessalian bonnet
> which shields her from the sun. What do I say?
> Is it really she? or not? does my mind cheat me?
> It is—it isn't—I cannot tell—
> It *is* she and no other. Her eyes are all aglow
> as she comes to welcome me. That shows it is she—
> she and no other, Ismene, my darling!

Oedipus
> What is it you say, child?

Antigone
> That I see your daughter,
> my own sister. Soon you will know,   340
> hearing her voice.

Ismene
> Dear father and sister—how sweet are both those names!
> How hard it was to find you, and now you are found,
> how hard, again, to see you, for my tears!

Oedipus
> You have really come, my child?

Ismene
> Father—how hard to see you so!

Oedipus
> You are really there, child!

Ismene
> Yes, though it was hard to come here.

Oedipus
> Touch me, my child.

Ismene
> I touch you both alike.   350

Oedipus
　　Sisters. True sisters both!

Ismene
　　How wretched this life of ours.

Oedipus
　　You mean, her life and mine?

Ismene
　　Yes, and mine too.

Oedipus
　　Why have you come?

Ismene
　　Through care of you.

Oedipus
　　Because you longed to see me?

Ismene
　　Yes, and to tell you things
　　with my own tongue. My companion here
　　was the only trusty servant that I have.　　　　　　360

Oedipus
　　Where are those brothers of your blood
　　to do us service now?

Ismene
　　They are where they are.
　　This is a terrible time for them.

Oedipus
　　Those two are like in everything
　　to the ways of Egypt,
　　both in their nature and in how they live.
　　For in that country the men sit within doors
　　working at the loom, while the wives go out
　　to get the daily bread.　　　　　　370
　　So, children, those two brothers of yours, who should

bear the stress and strain, keep house within, like girls,
and you, in their stead, struggle to bear my troubles.
You, Antigone, since you ceased to be a child,
and had grown strong enough, wandered with me always,
to your unhappiness, guiding an old man's steps.
Many a time you strayed in the wild woods,
without a bite to eat and barefoot;
many a wet day, many a burning sunlight
you toiled through; you never thought   380
of home or comfort in comparison
with the need to earn your father the means to live.
And you, Ismene, in the old time came to me
unknown to the Cadmeans, with all their oracles
that spoke about this carcass of mine.
You were my trusty guard when I was hunted
out of Theban land.
But now again what tale have you to tell me,
your father? What mission started you from your home?
I am very sure you are not empty-handed,   390
but carry with you some terror affecting me.

Ismene

What I endured in looking for you, father—
in trying to find where you were living—
let me leave alone. I do not want to suffer
twice over, in the doing and telling both.
But I have come here to declare to you
the evils that befell your unhappy sons.

At first their passionate wish—as it was Creon's—
was to leave the throne to him, and not pollute
the city further. They looked sensibly   400
at the old destruction that lay on their breeding,
which indeed beset your unlucky house.
But now stirred by some god
and by some sinfulness of mind themselves,

a deadly spirit of competition
has entered these thrice unhappy beings
to grasp the government and the monarchy;
and the younger born, his hot blood up,
would rob his elder brother Polyneices
of the throne and has banished him the country.   410
The elder, as rumor multiplied declares,
went into exile in hollow Argos,
and there took to himself a new marriage tie
and for new friends new fellow spearmen,
his aim that Argos should possess in honor
the land of Thebes or else exalt to heaven
the Theban power by the defeat of Argos.
This is no empty sum of words, my father;
they are deeds and terrible. At what point the gods
will pity your tribulations I cannot guess.   420

Oedipus

Did you really hope the gods would take any heed
of me, enough some day to rescue me?

Ismene

I do, my father, from these present oracles.

Oedipus

And what are they? What has been prophesied,
my child?

Ismene

That you shall one day be desired
by Thebes, yes, living and dead you *shall* be,
for their own welfare's sake.

Oedipus

How can anyone's welfare depend
on such as I am?   430

Ismene

With you, they say, there rests
their victory.

Oedipus
When I *am* no longer
then am I a man?

Ismene
Yes, father, for today the gods exalt you;
then they destroyed you.

Oedipus
It is a poor thing to exalt the old
when he fell in his youth.

Ismene
Still, you must know that Creon
for these very causes is coming here,   440
and shortly, without loss of time.

Oedipus
What would he do,
my daughter? Explain that to me.

Ismene
They want to place you near the land of Thebes,
to own you, still not letting your foot tread
within the borders of their country.

Oedipus
What good can I do, lying outside their doors?

Ismene
The place you lie in—if it suffer wrong—
will be a heavy curse on them.

Oedipus
One needs no god to have the knowledge of that.   450

Ismene
Well, that is why they want to have you as an ally,
near to their land, but not as your own master.

Oedipus
Will they let the shadowing dust of Thebes lie on me?

Ismene

No, for the guilt of family bloodletting
debars it, father.

Oedipus

Then they will never own me.

Ismene

So shall there be a heavy weight of sorrow
upon the Thebans.

Oedipus

In what conjunction, child, shall this come to pass?

Ismene

When your anger strikes them, as they stand on your grave.　460

Oedipus

What you say now—from whom did you hear that?

Ismene

The sacred envoys when they came back from Delphi.

Oedipus

And that was, truly, what Phoebus said about me?

Ismene

So the men said that came to Thebes from Delphi.

Oedipus

Did either of my sons know this about me?

Ismene

Both of them equally; both knew it well.

Oedipus

And then those villains, when they heard of it,
longed for me less than for this throne of theirs?

Ismene

I hate to hear that said, but I must bear it.

Oedipus

Then may the gods never quench their fated quarrel　470
and may it lie in *my* hands to determine

the end of the fight, which now they seek so eagerly
with their raised spears. If that shall happen
neither he that presently holds throne and scepter
shall remain where he is; nor he the exile
shall return home. I am their father
and when I was dishonored and driven out
from my own land, they never hindered it,
nor helped defend me; as far as they could do it,
it was those two expelled me; by them I was proclaimed exile.   480
You might say that *then* I also willed it so,
and that the city granted me that gift.
This is not so; for on the day itself
when my spirit seethed, and death was dearest to me,
yes, death by stoning, no one would help me to it.
But when time had gone by,
and all the agony had mellowed,
when I felt my agony had outrun itself
in punishing my former sins—it was then and then
the city drove me out—after all that time!—   490
in my despite—and these, these sons of mine,
could have helped me, their father, but they would not.
No, for the lack of one short word from them
I was banished, a beggar, to wander forever.
But it was from *these,* girls as they are,
as far as their nature could, I had my sustenance,
and ground to tread on without fear,
and the support of kinfolk.
Those other two, above their father's claims
chose sovereignty, wielding the scepter,   500
and their land's lordship. No, they will never win me
to be their ally, nor shall there ever come
profit to them from their reign in Thebes:
that I know well, both from Ismene's oracles,
which I now hear, and when I recollect
those of old days which Phoebus has accomplished
now in this time.

So let them send Creon to fetch me in,
or anyone else of power within their city,
for if you, my foreign friends, are willing,   510
backed by those solemn goddesses
that are your champions, to grant me your protection,
you will win for your city
a mighty service and for enemies, trouble.

Chorus

Oedipus, you certainly deserve pity,
yourself and your daughters; and since you add to the count
that you will be the savior of our country,
may I suggest to you thoughts perhaps useful?

Oedipus

Dear friend: do but be my champion,
and be assured I will do all you tell me.   520

Chorus

Make an atonement to those deities
you came to first, when you trespassed on their ground.

Oedipus

In what fashion shall I do it? Tell me, sirs.

Chorus

First bring a sacred draught from the everlasting
springs there; and let the hands that bring it be pure.

Oedipus

And when I take this draught unsullied—what then?

Chorus

There are bowls there, work of a skillful maker;
crown the top of each, and the handles at either side.

Oedipus

With twigs or flocks of wool—or how shall I do it?

Chorus

With a flock of wool, new shorn, from a ewe lamb.   530

Oedipus
Very well; after that what must I do?

Chorus
Pour your offerings, with your face towards the first dawn.

Oedipus
Shall I pour them from the vessels that you speak of?

Chorus
Yes, in three streams; the last must empty the bowl.

Oedipus
What shall I fill the third with before I set it?
Tell me that, too.

Chorus
With water and with honey.
Do not bring wine near it.

Oedipus
And when the dark-shading earth has drunk of it?

Chorus
Then with both hands, taking nine sprigs of olive,   540
lay them on it; and say this prayer over them.

Oedipus
That I would hear—that is the greatest thing!

Chorus
"As we call these the Kindly Ones, with kindly
hearts may they welcome this suppliant for his saving."
So pray, or those who speak for you.
But say the words inaudibly; do not raise your voice.
Then go away—and do not look behind you.
If you do this, I will stand by your side and welcome.
Otherwise, sir, I will fear on your behalf.

Oedipus
My children, you have heard the strangers who live here?   550

Antigone
We have heard; do you but tell us what to do.

Oedipus
> I cannot go myself; I fail in strength
> and sight, my double weakness.
> One of you must go and do this thing,
> for I think that one soul—be it but a well-wisher's—
> can pay the debt for tens of thousands.
> Quickly now; but do not leave me alone.
> My body cannot move, lonely of help,
> nor without guidance.

Ismene
> I will go to do it.   560
> But I must know where I should find the place.

Chorus
> On the other side of the grove, girl. If you need anything,
> a man lives there who will tell you.

Ismene
> I will go to my task; Antigone,
> stay here and guard our father; for a parent's sake,
> whatever trouble there is—if there is any—
> does not count.

Chorus
> It is a dreadful thing, sir,
> to awaken again an old ill that lies quiet.
> Yet still I long to know—   570

Oedipus
> What? What do you mean?

Chorus
> Of the pain that besets your life,
> so remediless, so wretched—

Oedipus
> Do not, I beg you—
> I am your guest; you were kind to me.
> Do not lay bare my sufferings;
> they are beyond shame.

Chorus
> It is a story that has spread far;
> it doesn't die out. I would like to hear the right of it.

Oedipus
> *(moans)*   580

Chorus
> Endure the pain, I say.

Oedipus
> Oh, oh.

Chorus
> Do as I beg you. I gave you what *you* asked.

Oedipus
> I bore the worst of sufferings—but for deeds—
> be God my witness!—done without knowledge.
> In all this there was nothing of conscious choice.

Chorus
> How was it?

Oedipus
> It was the city bound me,
> in utter ignorance, in a deadly marriage,
> in fated ruin, that came with my wife.   590

Chorus
> Was it then, as I hear,
> that you filled your bed
> with your mother to your infamy?

Oedipus
> Oh, it is death to hear it said,
> strangers. These two girls of mine—

Chorus
> You mean—

Oedipus
> Yes, my children, they are the two
> curses upon me.

Chorus

Zeus!

Oedipus

They sprang from the womb that bore me also.   600

Chorus

Then they are your children and—

Oedipus

Their father's sisters, too.

[*The passage that follows is difficult to understand. The Chorus has from the first, on hearing Oedipus' name, seemed to know the story. Apparently this may not be the case—at least the story in its entirety. There is another version of the myth, a fragment of Theban epic known to Pausanias, the very much later author of the geography of Greece, according to which the children of Oedipus here, Ismene and Antigone, are the children of his second wife, Euryganeia. Odyssey XI 271 is not explicit on this, but there are other aspects of its difference from our version—e.g., after Jocasta killed herself, Oedipus went on ruling Thebes. R. C. Jebb thinks it was the Attic dramatists who first introduced into the story the bearing of the incest on the daughters (Jebb, Commentary on O.C. 534). If this is right, the Chorus in the passage following this does make a genuinely new discovery from Oedipus. They may have been following till then the other and older version of the myth. The half lines of each speaker, each completing the statement, is far from anything we find dramatic. The whole is written in semi-lyrical meters and was probably delivered in a semi-ritualized manner, a kind of singsong interchange, almost like a dirge. It is of course extremely difficult for a translator to render tolerably.*]

Chorus

Oh, oh!

Oedipus

Ten thousand horrors sweep back upon me.

Chorus

You have suffered—

Oedipus
>   What I can never forget.

Chorus
  But you *did*—

Oedipus
>   I *did* nothing.

Chorus
  How can that be?

Oedipus
>   I received a gift   610
for serving the city—would to God I had never won it!—
for my heart is broken.

Chorus
  Unhappy man! But you did a murder.

Oedipus
  How a murder? What is it you would know?

Chorus
  Your father's murder.

Oedipus
  You strike me again, wound upon wound.

Chorus
  But you killed him.

Oedipus
  Yes, I killed him, but he had from me—

Chorus
  What?

Oedipus
  Something of justice.   620

Chorus
  How can that be?

Oedipus

    I will tell you.
    Those that I killed would have killed me.
    So in law I am innocent and came to all this
    in ignorance.

Chorus

    Here is our king, Theseus, son of Aegeus,
    to do what the news of you summoned him to do.

Theseus

    In time past, son of Laius, I have heard from many
    of the bloody blinding of your eyes—and I recognized you.
    Now as I heard more on my journey here   630
    I am in greater certainty.
    The clothes you wear and your unhappy face
    show us clearly who you are. Because you have
    my pity, unfortunate Oedipus, I would ask you
    what is this supplication you urge on Athens
    and on myself—you and the poor girl beside you?
    Tell me. You must tell me something dreadful indeed
    to make me turn away from you.
    For my part I know what it means,
    myself, to be brought up in exile,   640
    as you are in exile. I too in a foreign country
    wrestled with dangers to my life, more than anyone else.
    So there is surely no stranger, such as you,
    from whom I would turn my face, nor help to save.
    For I am very certain I am but a man:
    as such, I have of tomorrow no greater share
    than you have.

Oedipus

    Theseus, your nobleness in one short speech
    has left me the necessity of saying little.
    You have said about me all that is true—   650
    who I am, from what father born, from what country come.

All that is left me to say is what I want,
and then the story is told.

Theseus
Tell me; let me know.

Oedipus
I come to give you this wretched carcass of mine,
a gift to you; to look at, no great matter,
but no beautiful body will give you such gains as it will.

Theseus
What is this gain you claim to bring with you?

Oedipus
In time you will know—but the time is not yet, I think.

Theseus
When will your benefit be shown?   660

Oedipus
When I die and you shall have been my burial man.

Theseus
You ask about the last moments of your life;
what lies between this and then
you either forget or have no heed of.

Oedipus
Yes:
when that is given, my whole harvest is in.

Theseus
The favor you ask me lies in small compass, then?

Oedipus
Watch that; it is no easy fight to win.

Theseus
Do you mean between your sons and me?

Oedipus
Yes.   670
They wish to carry me away to Thebes.

Theseus
　　Well, if you are willing—
　　exile is not a fine thing.

Oedipus
　　When I myself was willing they would not let me.

Theseus
　　You are being foolish; anger does not sit well
　　with folk in trouble.

Oedipus
　　Rebuke me when you understand, and not till then.

Theseus
　　Then tell me. True, without knowledge I should not speak.

Oedipus
　　I have suffered, Theseus, terribly, evils upon evils.

Theseus
　　You mean what befell your family from of old?　　　　680

Oedipus
　　No. That is the talk of everyone in Greece.

Theseus
　　What then is your suffering beyond all men's endurance?

Oedipus
　　This is how it is. I was banished from my own country
　　by my own sons, return forever denied me,
　　because I killed my father.

Theseus
　　How then would they send for you
　　if it is but to settle you apart?

Oedipus
　　It is the mouth of God will force them to it.

Theseus
　　What is it, then, they fear foretold in oracles?

Oedipus
  That they must be smitten by this land of yours.   690

Theseus
  But how should there be bitterness between
  them and myself?

Oedipus
  O dearest son of Aegeus:
  only the gods know neither age nor death;
  everything else all-mastering time confounds.
  The strength of earth, the strength of body, dies;
  trust dies, distrust comes into blossoming.
  The same breath does not blow from man to man,
  constant in friendship, nor in city towards city.
  It may be now, it may be later, sometime   700
  the sweet turns bitter, and then again to friendship.
  If now the day is bright betwixt you and Thebes,
  uncounted time in course will breed uncounted
  nights and days, shattering with the spear
  those right hands presently clasped in harmony.
  The cause will be so slight!
  At that time my body hidden in earth and sleeping
  will coldly drink their hot blood,
  if Zeus be still Zeus and if Zeus' son
  Phoebus speak clearly.   710
  But it is not pleasant
  to speak the words that should lie undisturbed.
  Let me stop where I began; do you only keep
  the pledge you gave me and you will never say
  that you received as dweller in this land,
  a worthless fellow, Oedipus—
  unless the gods shall cheat me.

Chorus
  My lord, this man has talked like this before,
  as though he would do something for our country.

Theseus

Who would reject goodwill in such a man?   720
In the first place, forever a hearth between us
speaks of guest-friendship and a spear alliance.
And then he has come a suppliant of these Goddesses,
and promises to this land and myself
no inconsiderable recompense.
These matters claim my reverence and so
I will not reject his claim upon my gratitude.
I will make him our citizen. If it be his pleasure,
this stranger's, to remain here I will charge you
to guard him. (*Turning to Oedipus.*)   730
            Or, if you please to come with me,
Oedipus, I submit to your judgment.
It shall be as you choose.

Oedipus

May God send blessings on such men as you!

Theseus

What would you, then? Will you come to my home?

Oedipus

I would—if it were lawful. But this place here—

Theseus

What would you do in "this place"? I will not oppose you.

Oedipus

It is *here* I will conquer those that cast me out.

Theseus

This would be a great gift of your staying here.

Oedipus

If you stand fast by what you said and do it.   740

Theseus

You need not fear for me. I will not fail you.

Oedipus

I will not put you on your oath like someone base.

Theseus
  No oath will give you more than my bare word.

Oedipus
  What will you do then—

Theseus
                    What is it you fear most?

Oedipus
  Some will come here—

Theseus
                    My friends will take care of *that*.

Oedipus
  See you do not fail me—

Theseus
                    Do not tell me my duty.

Oedipus
  It is inevitable that I should fear.   750

Theseus
                              I do not fear.

Oedipus
  You do not know the threats—

Theseus
                        I do know that no one
  will take you out of here against my will.
  There are many threats, and many threatening words
  issue out of anger. When the mind is master of itself,
  the threats have vanished.
  Perhaps these people had strength enough to speak
  dreadful things of your carrying off, but *I* know
  the sea to sail between us will seem long,   760
  poor prospects for a voyage. I would say to you
  "Be of good cheer" even without my judgment,
  since Phoebus sent you hither. Even though *I* were not here,
  my *name* will guard you against ill-usage.

Chorus

Here are the fairest homesteads of the world,
here in this country, famed for its horses, stranger,
where you have come:
Here to Colonus, gleaming white,
where the nightingale in constant trilling song
cries from beneath the green leaves,   770
where she lives in the wine dark ivy
and the dark foliage of ten thousand berries,
safe from the sun, safe from the wind
of every storm, god's place, inviolable.
Where Dionysus the reveler paces
thronged by the nymphs his nurses.

Here there blooms, fed by heaven's dew,
daily and ever, the lovely-clustered narcissus,
the ancient crown of the Great Goddesses,
and also the golden gleaming crocus.   780
Nor fail the wandering springs
that feed the streams of Cephisus,
but daily and ever the river
with his pure waters gives increase
over the swelling bosom of the land.
This country the bands of the Muses
have not disdained
nor yet Aphrodite of the Golden Reins.
There is a thing too, of which no other like
I have heard in Asian land,   790
nor as ever grown in the great Dorian
island of Pelops,
a plant unconquered and self-renewing,
a terror that strikes the spear-armed enemy,
a plant that flourishes greatest here,
leaf of gray olive,
nourishing our children.

It shall not be rendered impotent
by the young nor by him that lives with old age,
destroying it with violence,   800
for the ever-living eye of Morian Zeus
looks upon it—and gray-eyed Athene also.

Yet another matter of praise have I
for this my mother city,
gift of a great god, our land's great boast,
that it is horse master, colt breaker, master of the sea.
Son of Cronus, Lord Poseidon,
you it is who have set her in that glory.
For you are the one who in these roads first
established the bit to control the horse,   810
and the oar, too, well fitted to the hand
leaps marvelously in the sea,
following the hundred-footed Nereids.

Antigone
Land with praises richly celebrated,
now be it yours to make those praises shine.

Oedipus
What is there new, child?

Antigone
Creon draws near.
Here he is—and with followers.

Oedipus (to the Chorus)
Old men,
my friends, now manifest, I beg you,   820
the last goal of my safety.

Chorus
Courage!
That safety shall be yours. If *I* am old,
the strength of Attica has not grown old.

Creon

    Sirs, noble gentlemen of this land,
    I see your eyes have suddenly taken fright
    at my intrusion. I beg you, do not fear
    nor speak ill words to me.
    I have come with no determination
    to offer any violence. I am old myself   830
    and know I have come to a city powerful
    as any is in Greece.
    I was sent, old as I am, to urge this man
    to come with me to Thebes.
    No single person sent me. I have my orders
    from the whole commonality. They sent *me*
    because it was I who was most concerned
    (because of our relationship) to sorrow,
    most of all within our city, for *his* troubles.

    Unhappy Oedipus, hear me and come home!   840
    All the Cadmean people summon you, and rightly,
    and most of all do I, in the proportion
    that I must be the worst of scoundrels
    if I felt no pain at these your sufferings.
    I see you an unfortunate wretch, a foreigner,
    a beggar always and your sightless journeyings
    propped on this one girl only. I could not believe
    that she could fall to such a depth of misery
    as this unhappy child here, tending you
    and your life in daily beggary, young as she is,   850
    but with no part in marriage, a ready victim
    to be seized and raped by anyone.
    It *is* a miserable reproach, is it not?,
    that I have cast on you—and on me and all our breed.
    There is no hiding it. It's plain.
    But, Oedipus, it is you—I beg you—by our fathers' gods, *you*,
    listen to my words! it is *you* should hide it,
    by willingness to come to your own city

and to the house that was your fathers'.
Greet this city kindly—of course she has deserved it!—   860
but your own country should be honored more,
in justice, for she bred you up at first.

Oedipus

You would dare anything; from every plea of justice
you can extract some means of trickery.
Why do you try so? Why do you want
to catch me once again, when the catching will hurt most?
In the old time I was so sick in my troubles
that it had been my pleasure to be exiled;
but then when I was willing, you were not
to give me any such favor. But when my anger   870
was sated of itself, when living in that house
had become sweet to me, you threw me out,
you banished me. In that day this kinship you speak of
was no way dear to you.
And now again, when you see this city friendly
to my staying, when you see all the people friendly,
you try to tear me out, the harshness of your message
so softly rendered!
Yet, what pleasure can you have in showing kindness
to those that will not welcome it? It is as if   880
one begged for something, but was given nothing,
nor was there wish to help; but when the spirit
was sated with what one had sought for, then only,
one got the gift, when the grace carried no grace.
Surely this is an empty pleasure you gain.
And that indeed is what you have given me,
where the words are good and the substance evil.
I will show these people what a villain you are.
You have come to bring me, yes, but *not* to bring me home
but to set me in a dwelling apart—but near you,   890
so there will be no trouble with Athens for your city.
You will not succeed, no, instead

my spirit shall dwell forever, a curse,
a curse upon your country.
For these sons of mine, this is my prayer—
so much of their father's earth as to make their graves.
Am I not wiser than you in Theban matters?
Far wiser, for I learn from clearer speakers,
Phoebus and Zeus himself, that is his father.
But you have come here, a mouth suborned, 900
but with a right sharp tongue. For all that, in your speaking
you will win more harm than safety.
However, I know I am not persuading you.
Get gone!
Let us live here; even as it is
we would live well enough
if we are content.

Creon

Who do you think has had the worst of it
in this discussion? I in respect to you
or you towards yourself? 910

Oedipus

What I find most pleasant is your failure
to persuade me or these men here.

Creon

You miserable creature, clearly you haven't
been able to grow wise, with all your years.

Oedipus

You have a clever tongue, but I never knew a just man
speak equally well on every plea.

Creon

Saying much is one thing, seasonableness another.

Oedipus

As though *your* words were few but very seasonable!

Creon

Not seasonable, of course, for one so clever
as you are.   920

Oedipus

Away with you! I will speak on these men's behalf;
do not watch and hem me in; this is where I live.

Creon

I call these men to witness, not you, for what you have answered
to those of us who are your family. If ever I catch you—

Oedipus

How will you catch me in despite of these allies?

Creon

I can hurt you enough without such action.

Oedipus

What lies behind these threats of yours?

Creon

                                   You have
two daughters, one of whom I have seized
and sent away. The other I will take soon.   930

Oedipus

O God!

Creon

Soon you will have more reason to cry out.

Oedipus

You have my child?

Creon

                              And will have *this* one soon.

Oedipus

Sirs, what will you do? Will you betray your trust?
Will you not get rid of this unholy wretch?

Chorus

Here, you, sir, off with you! What you are doing
is utterly unjust. So is what you *have* done.

Creon (to his servants)

It is high time for you to lead her off.
If she won't go willingly, force her! 940

Antigone

What refuge have I? What help can I find
from god or man?

Chorus

What are you about, sir?

Creon

I will not take the man, but *she* is mine.

Oedipus

O, princes of this country!

Chorus

Sir, this is injustice!

Creon

No, it is just.

Chorus

How can it be just?

Creon

I take my own.

Oedipus

O city of Athens! 950

Chorus

What are you doing, sir? Release her at once.
If not—a trial of strength between us!

Creon

Give way!

Chorus

Not to you while this is your purpose.

Creon
You will fight with Thebes, if you do me an injury.

Oedipus
Did I not say
this is how it would be?

Chorus
Release that girl at once.

Creon
      Do not give orders
that you cannot enforce.   960

Chorus
I tell you take your hands off her!

Creon
          I tell you
take a walk!

Chorus
Come, countrymen of ours, come here, come here!
The city is made nothing of, our city,
by this violence. Come here, come here to us!

Antigone
Friends, I am dragged away.

Oedipus
       Where are you, child?

Antigone
They are forcing me away!

Oedipus
Reach me your hands!   970

Antigone
I cannot I cannot.

Creon (to the servants)
Bring her away, you!

Oedipus
  O God, O God!

Creon
  Well, on these crutches you will not travel again.
  But since you are determined to beat your country,
  and your family at whose command I do
  what I do—although I am their sovereign lord as well—
  enjoy your victory. In time you will know,
  I am certain, that what you do to yourself at present
  is nothing good, nor what you did before,   980
  when in the teeth of your friends you yielded to temper.
  It is your temper which constantly ruins you.

Chorus
  Stop right there, sir.

Creon
                                      I warn you, do not touch me.

Chorus
  Give back the girls. Else you will not go from here.

Creon
  You will soon give my city a greater prize
  for our security. I will take more than these.

Chorus
  What will you do next?

Creon
                                      I will take and carry *him* off.

Chorus
  An outrageous threat!   990

Creon
  It shall be executed.

Chorus
  Unless this country's ruler thwarts you.

Oedipus
  A shameless thing to say! Will you seize me indeed?

Creon
Hold your tongue!

Oedipus
May the gods of this place
not take away my tongue from uttering this curse!
You villain: after the violence to my onetime eyes,
you have wrenched from me the one poor eye I had left.
May the Sun-God that sees all give you and your seed
an old age like this of mine!   1000

Creon
Do you see that, you people of this country?

Oedipus
They see both you and me; they understand
I am wronged in deeds, my defense, words only.

Creon
I'll not hold back my anger. I will bring him away by force,
although I am alone and slow with age.

Oedipus
(*cries out*)

Chorus
You have a bold spirit, sir, to think to come here,
and do as you do.

Creon
Yes, I believe I have.

Chorus
If you are right, I will no longer think   1010
Athens a city.

Creon
With a just cause the weak subdue the strong.

Oedipus
Do you hear what he says?

Chorus

But he will not act it—
Zeus knows!

Creon

Zeus maybe knows—not you.

Chorus

The insolence of this!

Creon

Insolence you must put up with.

Chorus

You people, and the rulers of this state, come here to us!
Come quickly. These men will cross the border. 1020

(Theseus enters.)

Theseus

What is this noise about? What has happened here?
You have stopped me in my sacrifice to the sea-god,
lord of Colonus here: I was at the altar.
What fear made you do that? Tell me. I want
to know it all, why I have been made to hasten
faster than I liked to this place here.

Oedipus

Dearest of men, I recognize your voice. I have suffered
dreadfully, right now, at this man's hands.

Theseus

What happened? Who has injured you? Speak!

Oedipus

Creon here, before your eyes, has taken my two 1030
children, all that I had.

Theseus

What is this you say?

Oedipus
You have heard what he did to me.

Theseus (points to his servants)
Here, quickly, one of you go to the altars,
urge all the people to leave the sacrifice
and hurry, on horseback and on foot,
at a full gallop to that place hereabouts
where the two traveled roads combine,
so that the girls won't get across and I,
worsted by violence, become a mockery   1040
to my guest-friend.
Away you go! Quickly! As I told you.
For you, Creon, if I went as far in anger
as you deserve, you would not go without
marks of my hands upon you.
However, such laws as he imported here
shall be made to fit him—these and no others.

                    (He speaks directly to Creon.)

You shall not leave this country until you bring here
these girls for me to see. What you have done
is a disgrace to me, and your own blood,   1050
and to your country. You came within this city
that makes a practice of justice and determines
nothing without a law. You then throw aside
her lawful institutions by your invasion.
You take what you want, making them yours by force.
Apparently you thought this city quite unmanned
or some slave place, and me a nobody.
Yet it is not Thebes has taught you to be so bad.
They do not usually rear men as wrongdoers,
nor would the Thebans praise you if they heard   1060
you had violated what are mine and the gods' possessions,
dragging out the helpless creatures that are their suppliants.
I certainly never would have put foot on your soil—

not if I had the justest cause in the world—
without permission of the governors, whoever.
I would not have harried and plundered; I would have known
how I ought—a foreigner among citizens—
to conduct myself. But you dishonor
a city that has not merited dishonor—
your own city; and your years, so many,   1070
show you an old man still empty of wisdom.
So I tell you now what I have said before;
let someone bring those girls here—quickly, too—
unless you want to be a resident alien
of Athens, under constraint, not voluntarily.
That is what I have to say. It comes from my full meaning,
not simply from my tongue.

Chorus

You see what you have come to, sir. You appear
to be of those who are just, but what you do
is found to be evil.   1080

Creon

Of course I did not think this city unmanned,
son of Aegeus, nor yet without wisdom as you claim,
when I did this thing I did. I thought
that no one would ever feel such eager love
for those that are my kinfolk that they would keep them
against my wishes! I knew you would not accept
a man who is his father's killer, unholy,
nor one whose marriage is found accursed,
a union of mother and son.
I knew the Areopagus, that grave council   1090
which belongs to this country, would not permit
such outcasts as these to live within its realm.
It was because I was confident of this
that I laid my hands upon this quarry.
Even then I would not have done so had he not cursed me

myself with bitter curses, and my breed.
This is what he did to me, and I determined
to give as good again. Anger knows no old age,
except in death. No sting touches the dead.
That is the case; do as you will about it.   1100
However just my cause, I am all alone;
that makes me weak; but yet as you shall act,
old as I am, I will try to act against you.

Oedipus

Spirit lost to shame, whom does the insult light on,
on you or me since both of us are old?
Your mouth is wide with taunts against me—murders,
and incest and calamity, which I bore,
poor wretch, involuntarily: the gods' pleasure!
Perhaps they were angry against my people of old.
You cannot find in me, taken by myself,   1110
an offense to reproach me with of such a greatness
to occasion such dreadful sins as I committed
against me and mine.

Tell me this:
if some god-utterance came to my father
given by oracles, that he should die by the hand
of his son, how can you justly taunt me with that,
who then owned neither father's seed nor mother's womb,
but was a creature still unborn?
If then I appeared, as I did to my sorrow,   1120
and came to blows with my father and murdered him,
knowing nothing of what I did, nor who he was,
how can you be right to blame that unknowing action?
For my mother's marriage, how can you be so shameless,
villain that you are, to make me speak of this?
She was your sister. But what that marriage was
I will say now. I will not hold my tongue,
when you have gone so far in impious speech.

She bore me, yes, she bore me—evil on evil—
she knowing no more than I did, and having borne me 1130
brought forth, to her shame, those children to her son.
One thing I do know: *you* know what you do,
when you speak ill of her and me for this;
but when I married her *I* did not know
nor chose; nor, as I speak of it now,
do I choose willingly to speak.
Even in this marriage I will not be reviled,
nor accept the bitter blame of father-killer
with which you have belabored me incessantly.
Answer me only one of my questions—this one. 1140
If someone here and now should stand beside you
trying to kill you—such a just man as you!—
would you ask the would-be killer was he your father,
or would you pay him back for the blow at once?
I think you would, if you love your life, pay back
the man who did it; you would not look around for justice.
Into such evil I entered, for the gods
guided me to it. I do not think
that my father's spirit, alive, would gainsay that.
But you, you are no just man—you think it right 1150
to say everything, things not to be spoken,
as well as those proper to speech; you taunt me
before these people here. You speak flatteringly
of Theseus' glorious name.
You say how nobly Athens is administered.
With all your lavish praise you forget this:
that if there is a land that understands
how to worship the gods in honor, this land excels.
This is the city, I am the suppliant, old,
and you tried to steal me from it; you laid your hands 1160
upon my daughters and made off with them.
For these your actions I call upon these Goddesses,
I beseech them, I entreat them with my prayers

to come as helpers and allies; so you shall learn
indeed what sort of government guards this city.

Chorus

My lord the stranger is a good man; what has happened to him
is all in all destructive; we should help him.

Theseus

We have talked enough; those who have done this deed
are hurrying away, while we the victims stand here.

Creon

What would you have me do? I am quite helpless.   1170

Theseus

I want you to lead the way on their tracks, and I
must go as your escort; if you have these girls
still in my country, you may show them to me yourself.
If those who have them are in flight, we may spare our trouble,
for we have others to chase them. They will not escape
and fleeing from this country bless their gods for it!
Lead the way, you. Know, the taker is taken.
You were the hunter; Fortune has hunted you down.
What is gained by craft, unjustly, is not kept safely.
You need not look for anyone else to help you—   1180
for I am sure that you were not alone
nor unprovided, seeing that you have reached
such recklessness and daring.
You must have some accomplice in whom you trusted.
I must look to all of this, nor make my city
weaker than a single man. Do you understand
anything of all this? Or are my words spoken in vain
as those were that were said to you when you planned this act?

Creon

I will not fault anything you say to me
when I am here. At home they will know what to do.   1190

Theseus

    Threaten—but go on! For you, Oedipus,
    stay here at your ease, with absolute confidence
    that if I do not die first, I will not rest
    until I make your children yours again.

Oedipus

    God bless you, Theseus, for your nobleness
    and for the justice of your care for me!

Chorus

    I would I were where the wheeling charge
    of foemen soon will join
    in fight to the clash of bronze,
    on Pythian shores or the torch-lighted strand   1200
    where the Sacred Ones cherish
    their solemn rites for mortal men,
    on whose tongues the golden key rested
    of the ministrant Eumolpidae.

    There, I think, they shall reunite—
    our Theseus, rouser of battles,
    and the two captive sister maids,
    in the midst of the warring of men strong to save,
    still within Attic bounds.

    But perhaps it is where they approach   1210
    the pastures of the west
    of Oea's rock, snow-clad,
    the prisoners riding or carried in chariots,
    pushed to racing speed.

    Creon will lose. Terrible is the might
    of those that neighbor Colonus,
    and terrible the might
    of Theseus' folk.
    Every bit shines, like a lightning flash.
    Each horseman in eagerness rides,   1220
    with loosened bridle rein.

They are the horsemen who honor
Athene, goddess of horsemanship,
and the Sea Lord, Earth shaker,
dear son of Rhea.
Is the action started, or yet to come?
My mind gives me hints of hope
soon again to see the two girls
so cruelly tried,
so cruelly suffering   1230
at the hands of their kinfolk.
Zeus will bring something to pass;
he will—and on this day.
I am the prophet
of happy outcome.
I would I were a dove in the sky,
quick of wing,
to reach a cloud over the fight
with eyes lifted above the fight.

O supreme ruler of Gods,   1240
Zeus who sees everything,
grant that those who hold this land
may achieve triumph, may win the prize
with strength victorious.

Holy daughter of Zeus,
Pallas Athene, grant it,
and you Apollo, the hunter,
and your sister, the follower
of dappled deer. I beg you
for help to come doubly—   1250
for this land and for its citizens.

Stranger and wanderer, you will not say
that I who watched on your behalf
was a false prophet. For I see
the girls returning here, and escorted, too.

Oedipus
Where? Where? What are you saying? How can it be?

Antigone
Father, O father! that some god would grant you
to see this noble man who brought us home!

Oedipus
My dear, are you both here?

Antigone

         Yes, for the hands   1260
of Theseus and his dear servants rescued us.

Oedipus
Come to your father, child, and let me touch
that body I never hoped would come again!

Antigone
You shall have your wish. What you beg of us
is all our longing, too.

Oedipus
Where, oh where are you?

Antigone

        Here, we are right beside you.

Oedipus
Dear children!

Antigone

       All a father's love is there.

Oedipus
You loves, that have supported me!   1270

Antigone

      Poor daughters, and poor father!

Oedipus
I have what I love most. Were I still to die now,
I would not be wholly wretched,

for now I have you two beside me.
Press on me, you on this side, you on that,
clinging to your father; rest yourselves now
from all the old wandering, lonely and unhappy.
And tell me, but as shortly as you can
what has happened. For girls like you
a short tale suffices.   1280

Antigone

Here is the man who rescued us. Hear him, father.
He did it all—so shall my telling
be brief enough.

Oedipus

Sir, do not wonder that with seeming obstinacy
I prolong this conversation with my children;
so utterly unexpected is what has happened!
But I know well that from none else than you
my joy in these has come to pass. You, you
it is that saved me, you and no other man.
May the gods grant all that I wish for you,   1290
for you and for this country! Only in this people
of yours have I found piety towards the gods,
and human feeling and no hypocrisy.
I know all this—and with these words alone
do I requite what you have done. I have
all that I have through you and no one else.
My lord, reach me your right hand; let me touch it
and let me kiss your head—if that is lawful.

What am I saying? How can a wretched being,
such as I have become, wish to touch *you*,   1300
a man in whom no single stain of evil
has dwelling place? I and you cannot do so.
Nor will I suffer it to be. The possibility
of sharing in my misery is only
for those already in it.
Stand where you are. God bless you where you stand!

In the days to come may you look after me
with the justice you have shown me in this hour!

Theseus

Even if you had extended your words longer,
I would not have wondered—for your delight in your children.　1310
Nor would I, if you preferred their words to mine.
I have no weight of vexation at that.
I would have my life one of distinction,
not so much in words—rather by deeds achieved.
I let you see that what I swore to you
old man, I have not proved false to—not in anything.
For here I come, bringing your girls with me,
alive, untouched by all the threats against them.
How the fight was won, why should I boast pointlessly?
You yourself from these two will know all.　1320

But there *is* something of question that has happened to me
as I came here; let me have your counsel on it.
It is little to tell, but remarkable. No man
should treat of anything as insignificant.

Oedipus

What is it, son of Aegeus? Tell me.
I do not know what it is you ask about.

Theseus

They say there is a man, no countryman
of yours, but of your kinfolk,
who had, it would seem, thrown himself down before
the altar of Poseidon, has taken his station there. It was　1330
where I was sacrificing, when I came here to you.

Oedipus

What countryman is he? What does he want,
that he sits there as suppliant?

Theseus

　　　　　　　　I only know one thing.
He asks some little speech with you. This is no great matter.

Oedipus
> What can it be? His suppliant seat there does not
> suggest some trivial matter.

Theseus
> > > What they say
> is that he asks only to talk with you
> and go away without suffering for coming here.   1340

Oedipus
> Who can he be that makes this supplication?

Theseus
> Reflect if there be anyone in Argos
> akin to you, that he might ask this favor.

Oedipus
> Dearest of friends, stop right where you are!

Theseus
> What is it?

Oedipus
> Do not beg this of me.

Theseus
> What is it, that I should not?

Oedipus
> As I hear you, I know who this suppliant is.

Theseus
> And who is he that I should find fault with him?

Oedipus
> He is my son, prince, he is my hated son,   1350
> whose words would hurt my ears more than all others.

Theseus
> What is this? Surely it's possible
> to listen and not do what you do not want?
> Why should it be so bitter to you to *hear* him?

Oedipus

His voice, prince, has become a thing most hateful
to me his father; do not constrain me
to yield in this.

Theseus

Consider if it be not his suppliancy
that makes your yielding a necessity.
Perhaps regard for the god should make you careful.   1360

Antigone

Father, let me persuade you, though I am young to advise.
Suffer the king here to gratify his own heart
and give the god what the prince would have you give him.
For our sake *(pointing to her sister),* suffer our brother to come here.
He will not tear you from your resolution—
do not fear that—if he pleads what is unfit.
What harm is there in hearing what he says?
Evil contrivings are best revealed in speech.
You begot him; even if what he does to you
is the most impious of all that is vile,   1370
you ought not, father, to match him in evil.
No, let him come. Other men have had bad sons,
and have had sharp tempers.
But when they were schooled by friends' enchanting voices
their natures yield to the might of them. You,
look to that other time—not now—
the father-and-mother evils that you suffered.
If you look at that other time, I am sure,
you will know the evil end of anger, the evil
which comes to climax in it. What your heart tells you then   1380
are not slight things—when you lost those eyes, now sightless.
Yield to us all; it is not right
that those who ask what is just should have to be
importunate; nor that the man himself
who has had good treatment should not know how
to pay requital for it.

Oedipus
> My child, when you win me with your words,
> it is a bitter pleasure to yield. Let it be so,
> as you will have it. Only, sir, if he comes here
> let no one have the disposal of my life.   1390

Theseus
> Once is enough for that. I do not need to hear it twice,
> old man; I do not want to boast, but you,
> you know you are safe—if a god keeps *me* safe.

Chorus
> Whoever it is that seeks to have
> a greater share of life,
> letting moderation slip out of his thoughts,
> I count him a fool, a persistent fool;
> I am clear in my mind of that.

> Indeed, the long days store up many things
> that are nearer to sorrow than joy,   1400
> and the whereabouts of delight
> you will not find, once you have fallen
> into the region beyond your due term.
> The Helper still is the same for all,
> the same Consummator,
> Death at the last,
> the appearance of Death in Doom.
> He comes to no sound of wedding joy,
> no lyre, no dances.

> Not to be born is best of all;   1410
> when life is there, the second best
> to go hence where you came,
> with the best speed you may.
> For when his youth with its gift of light heart
> has come and gone, what grievous stroke
> is spared to a man, what agony
> is he without? Envy, and faction,

strife and fighting and murders are his,
and yet there is something more that claims him,
old age at the last, most hated,   1420
without power, without comrades, and friends,
when every ill, all ills,
take up their dwelling with him.
So, he is old—this old man here—
I am not alone in that,
as the wave-lashed cape that faces north,
in the wintertime,
the din of the winds on every side,
the din of the mischiefs encompass him utterly,
like the breaking crests of the waves forever,   1430
some from the setting sun,
some from his rising,
and some from the place of his midday beams,
and some from the northern mountains of night.

Antigone
  Here he is, it seems, this stranger,
  alone, my father, weeping his tears in floods,
  as he comes here.

Oedipus
  Who is it?

Antigone
                  He whom we always held in mind
  that it would be; here is Polyneices.   1440

Polyneices
  O, what shall I do?
  Shall I cry for my own troubles, first of all,
  my sisters? Or his, my old father's,
  as I see them before me?
  Here I find him in a foreign country,
  an exile banished here, with clothes upon him
  where the foul ancient dirt has lived so long

that it infects his old body,
and his uncombed hair floats in the wind
about his eyeless face.   1450
The food he carries to fill his belly,
is, I should guess, akin to what he wears.
I learn all this too late, wretch that I am!
I will bear witness against myself, as the world's villain,
for not supporting him. You need not learn
from others what I am.
But yet there is Mercy; in everything
she shares the throne of Zeus. Let her stand by you
too, father. Why are you silent?
Say something!   1460
Do not turn away from me giving no answer,
sending me hence dishonored by your silence,
not even telling me why you are angry.
You children of this father, blood of my blood,
will you try at least to make him open his mouth
that now denies approach, in implacable silence?
So may he not dismiss me in dishonor—
a god's suppliant that I am—with never a word.

Antigone
    Speak yourself, unhappy man, say what you come to seek.
    The flood of words may give some kind of pleasure: 1470
    They may make angry or just bring some pity;
    still, somehow, they give a voice to what is voiceless.

Polyneices
    Then I will speak; your advice is good.
    First, here I make the god my helper
    from whose altar the prince of this country raised me up
    to come to you. He granted me permission
    to speak, and hear, and a safe-conduct home.
    These things I would have from you, my foreign friends,
    and from my sisters and my father.

Father, I want to tell you why I came here.   1480
I have been banished from my country, made an exile,
because I claimed my right as the elder born
to sit upon your sovereign throne. For this,
my younger brother, Eteocles, drove me out.
He did not have the best of me in words,
nor in the proof of hand or deed. It was the city
which he persuaded. The chief reason, I think,
was the curse, *your* curse, that lay upon the house.
That is what I hear also from the soothsayers.

When I came to the Dorian land of Argos   1490
Adrastus gave me his daughter to wife.
Then I swore to my side all
that were reputed best and honored most
for skill in warfare in the Apian land,
that I might gather from these a seven-fold band
of spearmen against Thebes; then with justice on my side
either die—or banish those that had done me wrong.
Very well, then; why have I come to you?
To bring, my father, my suppliant prayers, for myself
and for my allies, who with seven hosts   1500
behind their seven spears encompass about
the entire plain of Thebes.

There is the spearman, Amphiareus, supreme
master in war, supreme in knowledge of omens;
the second is the Aetolian, son of Oeneus,
Tydeus; third Eteoclus, born an Argive;
the fourth Hippomedon, sent by his father Talaos;
the fifth Capaneus, who has vowed to burn
the city of Thebes into the ground; the sixth
Parthenopaeus, the Arcadian, hastens to the war,   1510
his name recalling his mother, long a virgin
but brought at last to travail by the trusty
son of Atalanta;
and then myself, yours but not yours, begotten

of an evil fate, yet called at least your son,
I lead the fearless host of Argos to Thebes.

We all entreat you, by these your children, by
your life, my father, remit your heavy anger
against me, as I set forth to punish my brother
who thrust me out, despoiled me of my country.   1520
For if there is any trust to be placed in oracles,
they have said the victory shall come to those
whose side you join.
Then, by our fountains, and our race's gods,
I beg you to be persuaded and to yield.
We are beggars and foreigners both—and so are you!
We live by flattering others, both you and I.
We have drawn the selfsame lot in life.
But he is a prince, at home—oh wretched me!—
and laughs at both of us, in luxury.   1530
If you will stand a helper to my purpose
I will shake him out of it with little trouble
and quick enough, so that I can place you again
in your own house and place myself there too,
once I have driven him out and forcefully.
I may make this my boast if you stand by me,
without you I have no strength, even to survive.

Chorus
    Oedipus, as to this man,
    out of consideration for him that sent him here,
    say what is proper and send him on his way.   1540

Oedipus
    Yes, public guardians of this land, I will.
    If he that sent him to me had not been
    Theseus, who thought it right that he should hear
    words of mine, he never would have heard my voice.
    But now he will go hence, having been thought worthy
    and heard from me such words as never will
    gladden his life.

You scoundrel, you, with your scepter and your throne—
held now by your blood brother in Thebes—
you chased me out, your father, made me cityless;   1550
these are the clothes *you* made me wear,
the sight of which now brings tears to your eyes,
when *you* have come to the same stress of misery.
I may not weep, *I* must put up with it
as long as I live remembering my murderer;
you have contrived my rearing in agony;
you drove me out. It is because of you
I am a wanderer begging my daily bread.
Had I not begotten these children to be my nurses
I had been dead, for all you did to help.   1560
Now it is they who save me, these very nurses.
They are men, not women, in bearing troubles with me.
You are no sons of mine, you are someone else's.
Therefore the Evil Spirit has eyes upon you,
although, by and by, those eyes will be still fiercer,
if these hosts are really moving towards Thebes.
That city you will not destroy—no, before that
you will fall yourself, polluted with blood, and equally
your brother. Such are the curses I sent forth
in days gone by, against you two. And now   1570
I summon those curses to come to me as allies,
that you two, brothers, may know to reverence parents,
and not dishonor a father because he was blind—
and got such men as you for sons. These girls
have done none of this.
Therefore my curses overcome
your suppliant seat, and that, your throne, in Thebes,
as sure as Justice, claimed of old time, is sharer
in Zeus' throne, by the might of the old laws.
Get you gone! I spit you from me. I am no father   1580
of yours, you worst of villains! Pack away
all of these curses that I invoke against you.
You shall not conquer by spear your native land;

you shall not come again to hollow Argos;
you are to die by a brother's hand, and kill him
by whom you were exiled.
There are my curses on you! And I summon
your father's hateful darkness of Tartarus
to give you a new dwelling place. I call
upon the spirits there, I call on Ares,   1590
that thrust upon you both this dreadful hatred.

That is what you have heard. Now, off with you and tell
all the Cadmeans and your trusty allies
that such are the honors Oedipus divided
between those sons of his!

Chorus
    I had no pleasure, Polyneices,
    in your past journeyings. Now, speedily back again!

Polyneices
    Woe for my journey! woe for its ill success!
    Woe for my comrades! what an end this road had
    when we set out from Argos! woe is me!   1600
    such an end that I cannot tell to any
    of those comrades, nor yet turn *them* home again!
    but, saying nothing, go on to meet my fortune.
    Sisters—for you *are* my sisters, although his daughters—
    since you have heard my father's dreadful curses,
    I pray you two, by the gods, if the day come
    when his curses come to pass, and you have somehow
    come home again, do not dishonor me,
    but lay me in a grave with funeral rites.
    You have praise now, for the pains that you took,   1610
    in caring for this old man; you will earn no less
    besides for helping me.

Antigone
    Polyneices, I entreat you,
    do the thing that I ask you.

Polyneices
>   Dearest Antigone,
>   what is it? Tell me.

Antigone
>   Turn your army
>   back to Argos speedily. Do not
>   destroy yourself and the city both.

Polyneices
>   I cannot   1620
>   do this. How can I lead this selfsame army
>   back again when I have once
>   proved myself coward?

Antigone
>   Why must you, brother, fall to anger again?
>   If you destroy your own country, what do you gain?

Polyneices
>   Exile is shameful, and shameful that one elder
>   be so mocked by his brother.

Antigone
>   Do you see, then,
>   how right our father's prophecies come out
>   when he spoke of the mutual murder of you two?   1630

Polyneices
>   That is what *he* wants. But I must not yield.

Antigone
>   Wretched that I am! But who, once he has heard
>   our father's prophecies, will dare to follow you?

Polyneices
>   I will not tell bad news. That is good generalship—
>   to tell one's strengths and not one's weaknesses.

Antigone
>   Then, brother, you are truly so determined?

Polyneices
Do not stop me. Now this must be my care,
this road of mine, ill-omened and terrible,
made so by my father and those Furies of his;
but may Zeus prosper *your* road, if you fulfill   1640
my wishes, at my death. For me in life
there is nothing you can do. Let me go now,
and, both of you, goodbye. You will never again
see me alive.

Antigone
My heart is broken!

Polyneices
Do not mourn for me.

Antigone
Brother, how can anyone
not mourn, seeing you set out
to death so clear before you?

Polyneices   1650
If die I must, I'll die.

Antigone
Do not, dearest;
do as I say.

Polyneices
Do not try to persuade me
to fail my duty.

Antigone
Then I am utterly
destroyed if I must lose you.

Polyneices
All of that
whether for good or ill, Fortune determines.
But for you two, I pray the gods that never

you meet with ill. In all men's judgment   1660
you should not suffer misfortune.

Chorus

> Here are other new ills that have come
> just now, of evil doom,
> from the blind stranger—
> unless Fate is somehow at work.
> For I cannot call any decision of God
> a vain thing.
> Time watches constantly those decisions;
> Some fortunes it destroys, and others,
> on the day following, lifts up again.   1670
>
> There is the thunder! Zeus!

Oedipus

My children, children, please can someone go
and fetch for me Theseus that best of men?

Antigone

Father, what is the occasion of your summons?

Oedipus

The winged thunder of Zeus will carry me
straightway to death. Send and send quickly!

Chorus

Look at it! rolling down, crashing,
the thunderbolt unspeakable, hurled by Zeus.
Terror has raised the hair on my head;
my heart is trembling.   1680
There, again, is the flash of the lightning!
It burns in the sky. What event will it yield?
I am all fear. It is not for nothing
when it lightens so; there will be issue of it.
O, the great sky! O Zeus!

Oedipus

Children, there has come to me, as the gods said,
my end of life. There is no more turning away.

Antigone

    How do you know? What makes you think it?

Oedipus

    I know it well. But, quickly, someone go
    and summon here this country's prince.   1690

Chorus

    See, there again, around us
    the piercing thunder!
    Be merciful, God, if you are bringing
    some black-night thing
    to this land, our mother.
    May I find you gracious.
    Because I have looked on a man accursed
    may I not have a share in a graceless grace!
    Lord Zeus, to you I cry.

Oedipus

    Is the man near? And children, will he find me   1700
    still alive and my wits not astray?

Antigone

    What confidence would you implant in his mind?

Oedipus

    That, for the kindness he has shown me, the requital,
    as I once promised, now is duly paid.

Chorus

    My son, come here,
    or if in the innermost recess of the glade
    you are hallowing Poseidon's altar
    with sacrifice of cattle, come still.
    For the stranger claims to make return
    to you, and the city and his friends,   1710
    a just return for a just kindness done.

Theseus

    What is this public summons from all of you,
    clearly from my people, clearly from this stranger?

Is it the thunder of Zeus or rushing hail?
One can indeed conjecture anything
when Zeus sends such a storm.

Oedipus

My lord, I have longed for you and you have come.
Some god has made for you a happy blessing
from this coming.

Theseus

What new thing is it, son of Laius?   1720

Oedipus

The balance of my life's scale has come down.
I will not choose to fail my promises
to you and the city, now, before I die.

Theseus

What evidence have you of this impending death?

Oedipus

The gods are their own messengers to me;
they are not false to the signs they have arranged.

Theseus

What signs? Make this clear, old man.

Oedipus

The long continued thunder, the massive lightning
hurled from the hand that never knew defeat.

Theseus

I believe you; for I have seen you prophesy   1730
much, and falsely never. Tell me what to do.

Oedipus

Yes; I will direct you, son of Aegeus,
in what shall be a treasure for this city.
Old age shall not decay it. Immediately
I will show the way without a hand to guide me
to the place where I must die.
And you, describe this to no man, ever,

neither where it is hidden nor in what region,
that doing so may make you a defense
beyond the worth of many shields, or many neighbors' help.   1740
The things within this ban, not to be uttered,
yourself shall learn, when you come there alone,
for I shall not declare them to anyone
of these citizens, nor to my daughters, dear though I hold them.
Keep them yourself always, and when you come
to the end of life reveal them only
to him that is nearest to you, and he in turn
to his successor.
So you shall hold this city undevastated
by the Sown Men. Ten thousand states   1750
have committed violence on one another,
despite their rulers' excellent government.
For the gods are careful watchers at the last
but slow in action, when one dismissing gods' will
has turned to madness. Never
let that befall you, son of Aegeus.
But I will not school you in such things; you know them.
Let us now go to the place—a pressing summons
from the god forces me—and delay no more.
My children, follow me—so. In a strange way   1760
I have become your guide; you were once mine.
Come on, but touch me not. Suffer me to find
my sacred grave where it is fated
that I shall be hidden in this country's earth.
This way, this way, like this! For this way Hermes,
the Conductor, leads me, and the goddess of the dead.
O light, no light though you were once a light
to me! now for the last time touch my body.
For I creep along to hide my last of life
in Hades. You dearest of friends *(to Theseus)*   1770
yourself, this land and these your citizens—
blessings upon you! and in your blessedness
remember me, the dead! Live blessed forever.

Chorus

　　　　If it be lawful, it is mine
　　　　to adore with prayers the Goddess Unseen
　　　　and you, my lord of the Creatures of Night,
　　　　Aidoneus, Aidoneus,
　　　　that our stranger friend may pass to his end
　　　　untroubled and free of the tears
　　　　attendant on a grievous doom;　　　　　　　　　　　1780
　　　　that he may come to the world below,
　　　　that hides all within itself,
　　　　to the land of the dead, the Stygian house.
　　　　Many the ills that were his, all uncalled for;
　　　　may God in justice exalt him again!

　　　　O goddesses of that Underworld,
　　　　and Form of the Hound Unconquered
　　　　who keeps his lair at the guest-haunted gate,
　　　　and sleeps and snuffles from out his cave,
　　　　the guardian in death's house, unsubdued—　　　　1790
　　　　thus is always the story told.

　　　　O son of Earth and Tartarus
　　　　I pray that that Hound may give a clear path
　　　　to our friend coming down
　　　　to dead men's country;
　　　　You, Giver of Sleep Everlasting,
　　　　I call on You.

Messenger

　　Citizens: to speak most briefly and truthfully,
　　Oedipus is gone. But what has happened,
　　the tale of that cannot be told so briefly,　　　　　1800
　　for the acts there were not brief.

Chorus

　　The unhappy man is gone!

Messenger
    You must think of him
    as of one truly parted out of life.

Chorus
    How was it? By God's chance and painlessly
    the poor man ended?

Messenger
    That is wonderful indeed.
    How he moved from here with no guidance of friends,
    you yourselves know. For I think you were here.
    He was himself the guide to all of us.   1810
    When he came to the steep road, rooted in earth
    by brazen steps, he stood in one of the many
    branching paths, near the hollow basin
    where is, forever confident, the memorial
    to Theseus' and Peirithous' compact.
    Where he stood, he was midway between
    that basin and the Thorician rock,
    the hollow pear tree and the grave of stone.

    Then he sat down and loosed his filthy robes,
    cried loudly to his daughters to bring him water   1820
    from some stream, to wash and make drink offerings.
    They hurried to Demeter's hill, in front of them,
    guardian of tender plants; they brought what he ordered;
    and then with lustral washing and with clothes
    equipped him in the customary fashion.
    When he had his pleasure of all he did,
    and nothing that he sought was scanted, Zeus
    of the Underworld thundered. They fell at their father's knees
    and cried, ceaselessly, beating their breasts,
    and with unending long laments. But he,   1830
    when he heard the sudden bitter cries from them,
    folded his hands upon them; then said "My children,
    this is the day when you become fatherless.
    All that was me has perished; now no more

for you the heavy task of tending me.
It was a cruel task, children, that I know,
but there's a single word that overthrows
all tasks of work. My love you had; no one
could love you more. That is the love you lose now
and must pass through the rest of life without it."   1840
They embraced and sobbed shrilly, all three of them.
When they came to the end of their mourning
and not another cry rose, there, in the stillness,
there was a voice of someone, summoning him,
and suddenly in their terror, all hair stood up.
It was the god who called him, over and over,
"You, Oedipus, Oedipus, why are you hesitating
to go our way? You have been too slow, too long."
When he understood that calling of the god,
he cried to this country's ruler, Theseus,   1850
to come to him, and when he came, he said:
"You that I love, give me your hand's sworn pledge
to these my children, and you, my children, to him.
Promise me that you will never consciously
forsake them, but perform whatever you judge
will be for their advantage always."
He, noble man that he is, gave him his promise
and with no word of sorrow swore he would do
that, for his friend.
When he had finished, suddenly Oedipus   1860
touching his children with blind hands said "Both, my children,
be brave and noble of mind, and leave this place.
Do not seek to know what is forbidden,
nor hear it from others' speaking.
Quickly, away with you; only let Theseus
stay to understand what is to be done."

That was what he said; we listened all,
and with the girls in tears and lamentations,
followed them away. When we departed,

in a few moments we looked back and saw that   1870
Oedipus, yes, Oedipus, was no longer there,
but the king by himself, holding his hand
before his face, to shade his eyes, as though
some deadly terror had appeared to him
that sight could not endure.
Then just a little afterwards, we saw him
bow to salute the earth and the gods' Olympus
united in the same prayer at once.
But by what manner of doom that other died
no mortal man can say, save our lord Theseus.   1880
It was no fiery thunderbolt of God
that made away with him, nor a sea hurricane
rising; no, it was some messenger
sent by the gods, or some power of the dead
split open the fundament of earth, with good will,
to give him painless entry. He was sent on his way
with no accompaniment of tears, no pain of sickness;
if any man ended miraculously,
this man did. If I seem to talk nonsense,
I would not try to win over such as think so.   1890

Chorus
    Where are the girls? And where their escorting friends?

Messenger
    Not far away. The sounds of their mourning voices
    show they are coming here.

Antigone
    Now it belongs to both of us,
    unhappy beings, to sorrow
    for the curse that inheres
    in our father's blood;
    not for this part, yes, and for that part, no—
    totally.
    For him we have borne in his life   1900
    a great burden unrelieved,

but now at the end we will have to speak
of things beyond reason's scope,
what we saw, what we suffered.

Chorus
    What is it?

Antigone
    My friends, we can only guess.

Chorus
    He has gone?

Antigone
    As you would have him go.
    What else can be said of one
    whom neither the War God,   1910
    nor the sea encountered,
    but the unseen fields of the world of Death
    snatched away in some doom invisible?
    On us two destruction's night
    has settled on our eyes.
    How shall we wander, how find
    a bitter living in distant lands
    or on the waves of the sea?

Ismene
    I do not know.
    Let murdering Hades   1920
    take me and join me in death with him,
    my father in his old age.
    The life that will henceforth be mine
    is a life that cannot be lived.

Chorus
    You two are the best of children;
    you must bear what the god gives to bear.
    No more fire of grief. You cannot truly
    sorrow for what has happened.

Antigone

> There can be a love
> even of suffering;
> for that which is anything but dear itself
> could still be dear,
> while I still had him in these hands of mine.
> Father, dear one, you that forever
> have put on the darkness of underground,
> even there you shall not be unloved,
> by me and by my sister.

1930

Chorus

> His end?

Antigone

> His end is what he wished.

Chorus

> What end?

1940

Antigone

> And he died in a foreign land,
> but one he yearned for. He has his bed
> below in the shadowy grass
> forever.
> He has left behind him a mourning sorrow—
> these eyes of mine with their tears
> bewail you. I do not know how
> in my misery I should cast out
> such a weight of sorrow.
> Yes, you chose in a foreign land
> to die. I find it a lonely death.

1950

Ismene

> What further destiny awaits
> you and me, dear one, alone as we are?

Chorus
My dears, the end of his life was blessed;
do not keep sorrowing. No one
is hard for misfortune to capture.

Antigone
Let us hurry back, sister.

Ismene
What to do?

Antigone
Desire possesses me—

Ismene
What desire?   1960

Antigone
To see where he lies in earth.

Ismene
Who lies?

Antigone
Our father—Oh, misery!

Ismene
How can that be lawful?
Do you not see?

Antigone
Why do you blame me for this?

Ismene
And this again—

Antigone
What is *this* again?

Ismene
Where he fell, there *is* no grave—
and he was quite alone.   1970

Antigone
   Bring me where he was,
   and then kill me.

Ismene
   Where now so lonely,
   so helpless, shall *I* live?

Chorus
   Friends, do not be afraid!

Antigone
   But where to find refuge?

Chorus
   You *have* found refuge.

Antigone
   From what?

Chorus
   From misfortune, refuge for you both.

Antigone
   I understand.   1980

Chorus
   What is it you are thinking?

Antigone
   I cannot tell
   how I can come home.

Chorus
   Do not seek to go home.

Antigone
   Trouble is upon us.

Chorus
   It has pursued you before.

Antigone
   Desperate then, but now still worse.

Chorus

    Yes, yours was a sea of sorrow.

Antigone

    Where shall we go, O God?
    To what of hope now   1990
    can Fate drive us?

                                    (Theseus enters.)

Theseus

    Cease your mourning, children; for those
    to whom the grace of the Underworld Gods
    has been stored as a treasure, to the quick and the dead,
    for them there shall be no mourning.
    Else the gods may be angry.

Antigone

    Son of Aegeus, we beg you—

Theseus

    What would you have me grant, children?

Antigone

    We would ourselves see the grave
    of our father.   2000

Theseus

    No, this is not lawful.

Antigone

    What do you mean, king of Athens?

Theseus

    He
    has forbidden approach to the place,
    nor may any voice invoke
    the sacred tomb where he lies.
    He said, if I truly did this,
    I should have forever a land unharmed.

These pledges the God heard from me
and Oath, Zeus' servant, all seeing.   2010

Antigone
    If this was, then, the mind of Him,
    the dead, I must be content.
    Send us, then, to our ancient Thebes
    that perhaps we may prevent
    the murder that comes to our brothers.

Theseus
    That I will do and whatever else
    shall profit yourselves and pleasure both you
    and the man under earth who is newly gone—
    for him I must spare no pains.

Chorus
    Now cease lamentation, nor further prolong   2020
    your dirge. All of these matters
    have found their consummation.

ANTIGONE

Translated by David Grene

CHARACTERS

Antigone

Ismene

Chorus of Theban Elders

Creon

A Sentry

Haemon

Teiresias

A Messenger

Eurydice

Second Messenger

ANTIGONE

(The two sisters Antigone and Ismene meet in front of the palace gates in Thebes.)

Antigone

Ismene, my dear sister,
whose father was my father, can you think of any
of all the evils that stem from Oedipus
that Zeus does not bring to pass for us, while we yet live?
No pain, no ruin, no shame, and no dishonor
but I have seen it in our mischiefs,
yours and mine.
And now what is the proclamation that they tell of
made lately by the commander, publicly,
to all the people? Do you know it? Have you heard it?   10
Don't you notice when the evils due to enemies
are headed towards those we love?

Ismene

Not a word, Antigone, of those we love,
either sweet or bitter, has come to me since the moment
when we lost our two brothers,
on one day, by their hands dealing mutual death.
Since the Argive army fled in this past night,
I know of nothing further, nothing
of better fortune or of more destruction.

Antigone

I knew it well; that is why I sent for you   20
to come outside the palace gates
to listen to me, privately.

Ismene

What is it? Certainly your words
come of dark thoughts.

Antigone

Yes, indeed; for those two brothers of ours, in burial
has not Creon honored the one, dishonored the other?
Eteocles, they say he has used justly
with lawful rites and hid him in the earth
to have his honor among the dead men there.
But the unhappy corpse of Polyneices   30
he has proclaimed to all the citizens,
they say, no man may hide
in a grave nor mourn in funeral,
but leave unwept, unburied, a dainty treasure
for the birds that see him, for their feast's delight.
That is what, they say, the worthy Creon
has proclaimed for you and me—for me, I tell you—
and he comes here to clarify to the unknowing
his proclamation; he takes it seriously;
for whoever breaks the edict death is prescribed,   40
and death by stoning publicly.
There you have it; soon you will show yourself
as noble both in your nature and your birth,
or yourself as base, although of noble parents.

Ismene

If things are as you say, poor sister, how
can I better them? how loose or tie the knot?

Antigone

Decide if you will share the work, the deed.

Ismene

What kind of danger is there? How far have your thoughts gone?

Antigone

Here is this hand. Will you help it to lift the dead man?

Ismene

Would you bury him, when it is forbidden the city?   50

Antigone

At least he is my brother—and yours, too,
though you deny him. *I* will not prove false to him.

Ismene

You are so headstrong. Creon has forbidden it.

Antigone

It is not for him to keep me from my own.

Ismene

O God!
Consider, sister, how our father died,
hated and infamous; how he brought to light
his own offenses; how he himself struck out
the sight of his two eyes;
his own hand was their executioner.   60
Then, mother and wife, two names in one, did shame
violently on her life, with twisted cords.
Third, our two brothers, on a single day,
poor wretches, themselves worked out their mutual doom.
Each killed the other, hand against brother's hand.
Now there are only the two of us, left behind,
and see how miserable our end shall be
if in the teeth of law we shall transgress
against the sovereign's decree and power.
You ought to realize we are only women,   70
not meant in nature to fight against men,
and that we are ruled, by those who are stronger,
to obedience in this and even more painful matters.
I do indeed beg those beneath the earth
to give me their forgiveness,
since force constrains me,
that I shall yield in this to the authorities.
Extravagant action is not sensible.

Antigone

I would not urge you now; nor if you wanted
to act would I be glad to have you with me.   80
Be as you choose to be; but for myself
I myself will bury him. It will be good
to die, so doing. I shall lie by his side,

loving him as he loved me; I shall be
a criminal—but a religious one.
The time in which I must please those that are dead
is longer than I must please those of this world.
For there I shall lie forever. You, if you like,
can cast dishonor on what the gods have honored.

Ismene

I will not put dishonor on them, but   90
to act in defiance of the citizenry,
my nature does not give me means for that.

Antigone

Let that be your excuse. But I will go
to heap the earth on the grave of my loved brother.

Ismene

How I fear for you, my poor sister!

Antigone

Do not fear for me. Make straight your own path to destiny.

Ismene

At least do not speak of this act to anyone else;
bury him in secret; I will be silent, too.

Antigone

Oh, oh, no! shout it out. I will hate you still worse
for silence—should you not proclaim it,   100
to everyone.

Ismene

You have a warm heart for such chilly deeds.

Antigone

I know I am pleasing those I should please most.

Ismene

If you can do it. But you are in love
with the impossible.

Antigone
  No. When I can no more, then I will stop.

Ismene
  It is better not to hunt the impossible
  at all.

Antigone
  If you will talk like this I will loathe you,
  and you will be adjudged an enemy—   110
  justly—by the dead's decision. Let me alone
  and my folly with me, to endure this terror.
  No suffering of mine will be enough
  to make me die ignobly.

Ismene
  Well, if you will, go on.
  Know this; that though you are wrong to go, your friends
  are right to love you.

Chorus
        Sun's beam, fairest of all
        that ever till now shone
        on seven-gated Thebes;   120
        O golden eye of day, you shone
        coming over Dirce's stream;
        You drove in headlong rout
        the whiteshielded man from Argos,
        complete in arms;
        his bits rang sharper
        under your urging.

        Polyneices brought him here
        against our land, Polyneices,
        roused by contentious quarrel;   130
        like an eagle he flew into our country,
        with many men-at-arms,
        with many a helmet crowned with horsehair.

He stood above the halls, gaping with murderous lances,
encompassing the city's
seven-gated mouth.
But before his jaws would be sated
with our blood, before the fire,
pine fed, should capture our crown of towers,
he went hence—   140
such clamor of war stretched behind his back,
from his dragon foe, a thing he could not overcome.

For Zeus, who hates the most
the boasts of a great tongue,
saw them coming in a great tide,
insolent in the clang of golden armor.
The god struck him down with hurled fire,
as he strove to raise the victory cry,
now at the very winning post.

The earth rose to strike him as he fell swinging.   150
In his frantic onslaught, possessed, he breathed upon us
with blasting winds of hate.
Sometimes the great god of war was on one side,
and sometimes he struck a staggering blow on the other;
the god was a very wheel horse on the right trace.

At seven gates stood seven captains,
ranged equals against equals, and there left
their brazen suits of armor
to Zeus, the god of trophies.
Only those two wretches born of one father and mother   160
set their spears to win a victory on both sides;
they worked out their share in a common death.

Now Victory, whose name is great, has come
to Thebes of many chariots
with joy to answer her joy,
to bring forgetfulness of these wars;
let us go to all the shrines of the gods

and dance all night long.
Let Bacchus lead the dance,
shaking Thebes to trembling.   170

But here is the king of our land,
Creon, son of Menoeceus;
in our new contingencies with the gods,
he is our new ruler.
He comes to set in motion some design—
what design is it? Because he has proposed
the convocation of the elders.
He sent a public summons for our discussion.

Creon

Gentlemen: as for our city's fortune,
the gods have shaken her, when the great waves broke,   180
but the gods have brought her through again to safety.
For yourselves, I chose you out of all and summoned you
to come to me, partly because I knew you
as always loyal to the throne—at first,
when Laïus was king, and then again
when Oedipus saved our city and then again
when he died and you remained with steadfast truth
to their descendants,
until they met their double fate upon one day,
striking and stricken, defiled each by a brother's murder.   190
Now here I am, holding all authority
and the throne, in virtue of kinship with the dead.

It is impossible to know any man—
I mean his soul, intelligence, and judgment—
until he shows his skill in rule and law.
I think that a man supreme ruler of a whole city,
if he does not reach for the best counsel for her,
but through some fear, keeps his tongue under lock and key,   200
him I judge the worst of any;
I have always judged so; and anyone thinking
another man more a friend than his own country,

I rate him nowhere. For my part, God is my witness,
who sees all, always, I would not be silent
if I saw ruin, not safety, on the way
towards my fellow citizens. I would not count
any enemy of my country as a friend—
because of what I know, that she it is
which gives us our security. If she sails upright
and we sail on her, friends will be ours for the making.
In the light of rules like these, I will make her greater still.   210

In consonance with this, I here proclaim
to the citizens about Oedipus' sons.
For Eteocles, who died this city's champion,
showing his valor's supremacy everywhere,
he shall be buried in his grave with every rite
of sanctity given to heroes under earth.
However, his brother, Polyneices, a returned exile,
who sought to burn with fire from top to bottom
his native city, and the gods of his own people;
who sought to taste the blood he shared with us,   220
and lead the rest of us to slavery—
I here proclaim to the city that this man
shall no one honor with a grave and none shall mourn.
You shall leave him without burial; you shall watch him
chewed up by birds and dogs and violated.
Such is my mind in the matter; never by me
shall the wicked man have precedence in honor
over the just. But he that is loyal to the state
in death, in life alike, shall have my honor.

Chorus

Son of Menoeceus, so it is your pleasure   230
to deal with foe and friend of this our city.
To use any legal means lies in your power,
both about the dead and those of us who live.

Creon

I understand, then, you will do my bidding.

Chorus
    Please lay this burden on some younger man.

Creon
    Oh, watchers of the corpse I have already.

Chorus
    What else, then, do your commands entail?

Creon
    That you should not side with those who disagree.

Chorus
    There is none so foolish as to love his own death.

Creon
    Yes, indeed those are the wages, but often greed   240
    has with its hopes brought men to ruin.

[*The sentry whose speeches follow represents a remarkable experiment in Greek tragedy in the direction of naturalism of speech. He speaks with marked clumsiness, partly because he is excited and talks almost colloquially. But also the royal presence makes him think apparently that he should be rather grand in his show of respect. He uses odd bits of archaism or somewhat stale poetical passages, particularly in catch phrases. He sounds something like lower-level Shakespearean characters, e.g. Constable Elbow, with his uncertainty about benefactor and malefactor.*]

Sentry
    My lord, I will never claim my shortness of breath
    is due to hurrying, nor were there wings in my feet.
    I stopped at many a lay-by in my thinking;
    I circled myself till I met myself coming back.
    My soul accosted me with different speeches.
    "Poor fool, yourself, why are you going somewhere
    when once you get there you will pay the piper?"
    "Well, aren't you the daring fellow! stopping again?
    and suppose Creon hears the news from someone else—   250

don't you realize that you will smart for that?"
I turned the whole matter over. I suppose I may say
"I made haste slowly" and the short road became long.
However, at last I came to a resolve:
I must go to you; even if what I say
is nothing, really, still I shall say it.
I come here, a man with a firm clutch on the hope
that nothing can betide him save what is fated.

Creon

What is it then that makes you so afraid?

Sentry

No, I want first of all to tell you my side of it.   260
I didn't do the thing; I never saw who did it.
It would not be fair for me to get into trouble.

Creon

You hedge, and barricade the thing itself.
Clearly you have some ugly news for me.

Sentry

Well, you know how disasters make a man
hesitate to be their messenger.

Creon

For God's sake, tell me and get out of here!

Sentry

Yes, I *will* tell you. Someone just now
buried the corpse and vanished. He scattered on the skin
some thirsty dust; he did the ritual,   270
duly, to purge the body of desecration.

Creon

What! Now who on earth could have done that?

Sentry

I do not know. For there was there no mark
of axe's stroke nor casting up of earth
of any mattock; the ground was hard and dry,

unbroken; there were no signs of wagon wheels.
The doer of the deed had left no trace.
But when the first sentry of the day pointed it out,
there was for all of us a disagreeable
wonder. For the body had disappeared;   280
not in a grave, of course; but there lay upon him
a little dust as of a hand avoiding
the curse of violating the dead body's sanctity.
There were no signs of any beast nor dog
that came there; he had clearly not been torn.
There was a tide of bad words at one another,
guard taunting guard, and it might well have ended
in blows, for there was no one there to stop it.
Each one of us was the criminal but no one
manifestly so; all denied knowledge of it.   290
We were ready to take hot bars in our hands
or walk through fire, and call on the gods with oaths
that we had neither done it nor were privy
to a plot with anyone, neither in planning
nor yet in execution.
At last when nothing came of all our searching,
there was one man who spoke, made every head
bow to the ground in fear. For we could not
either contradict him nor yet could we see how
if we did what he said we would come out all right.   300
His word was that we must lay information
about this matter to yourself; we could not cover it.
This view prevailed and the lot of the draw chose me,
unlucky me, to win that prize. So here
I am. I did not want to come,
and you don't want to have me. I know that.
For no one likes the messenger of bad news.

Chorus
   My lord: I wonder, could this be God's doing?
   This is the thought that keeps on haunting me.

Creon

Stop, before your words fill even me with rage,   310
that you should be exposed as a fool, and you so old.
For what you say is surely insupportable
when you say the gods took forethought for this corpse.
Is it out of excess of honor for the man,
for the favors that he did them, they should cover him?
This man who came to burn their pillared temples,
their dedicated offerings—and this land
and laws he would have scattered to the winds?
Or do you see the gods as honoring
criminals? This is not so. But what I am doing   320
now, and other things before this, some men disliked,
within this very city, and muttered against me,
secretly shaking their heads; they would not bow
justly beneath the yoke to submit to me.
I am very sure that these men hired others
to do this thing. I tell you the worse currency
that ever grew among mankind is money. This
sacks cities, this drives people from their homes,
this teaches and corrupts the minds of the loyal
to acts of shame. This displays   330
all kinds of evil for the use of men,
instructs in the knowledge of every impious act.
Those that have done this deed have been paid to do it,
but in the end they will pay for what they have done.

It is as sure as I still reverence Zeus—
know this right well—and I speak under oath—
if you and your fellows do not find this man
who with his own hand did the burial
and bring him here before me face to face,
your death alone will not be enough for me.   340
You will hang alive till you open up this outrage.
That will teach you in the days to come from what
you may draw profit—safely—from your plundering.

It's not from anything and everything
you can grow rich. You will find out
that ill-gotten gains ruin more than they save.

Sentry

Have I your leave to say something—or should I
just turn and go?

Creon

Don't you know your talk is painful enough already?

Sentry

Is the ache in your ears or in your mind?   350

Creon

Why do you dissect the whereabouts of my pain?

Sentry

Because it is he who did the deed who hurts
your mind. I only hurt your ears that listen.

Creon

I am sure you have been a chatterbox since you were born.

Sentry

All the same, I did not do this thing.

Creon

You might have done this, too, if you sold your soul.

Sentry

It's a bad thing if one judges and judges wrongly.

Creon

You may talk as wittily as you like of judgment.
Only, if you don't bring to light those men
who have done this, you will yet come to say   360
that your wretched gains have brought bad consequences.

Sentry (aside)

It were best that he were found, but whether
the criminal is taken or he isn't—
for that chance will decide—one thing is certain,

you'll never see me coming here again.
I never hoped to escape, never thought I could.
But now I have come off safe, I thank God heartily.

Chorus

Many are the wonders, none
is more wonderful than what is man.
This it is that crosses the sea   370
with the south winds storming and the waves swelling,
breaking around him in roaring surf.
He it is again who wears away
the Earth, oldest of gods, immortal, unwearied,
as the ploughs wind across her from year to year
when he works her with the breed that comes from horses.

The tribe of the lighthearted birds he snares
and takes prisoner the races of savage beasts
and the brood of the fish of the sea,
with the close-spun web of nets.   380
A cunning fellow is man. His contrivances
make him master of beasts of the field
and those that move in the mountains.
So he brings the horse with the shaggy neck
to bend underneath the yoke;
and also the untamed mountain bull;
and speech and windswift thought
and the tempers that go with city living
he has taught himself, and how to avoid
the sharp frost, when lodging is cold   390
under the open sky
and pelting strokes of the rain.
He has a way against everything,
and he faces nothing that is to come
without contrivance.
Only against death
can he call on no means of escape;
but escape from hopeless diseases

he has found in the depths of his mind.
With some sort of cunning, inventive   400
beyond all expectation
he reaches sometimes evil,
and sometimes good.

If he honors the laws of earth,
and the justice of the gods he has confirmed by oath,
high is his city; no city
has he with whom dwells dishonor
prompted by recklessness.
He who is so, may he never
share my hearth!   410
may he never think my thoughts!

Is this a portent sent by God?
I cannot tell.
I know her. How can I say
that this is not Antigone?
Unhappy girl, child of unhappy Oedipus,
what is this?
Surely it is not you they bring here
as disobedient to the royal edict,
surely not you, taken in such folly.   420

Sentry
She is the one who did the deed;
we took her burying him. But where is Creon?

Chorus
He is just coming from the house, when you most need him.

Creon
What is this? What has happened that I come
so opportunely?

Sentry
My lord, there is nothing
that a man should swear he would never do.

Second thoughts make liars of the first resolution.
I would have vowed it would be long enough
before I came again, lashed hence by your threats. 430
But since the joy that comes past hope, and against all hope,
is like no other pleasure in extent,
I have come here, though I break my oath in coming.
I bring this girl here who has been captured
giving the grace of burial to the dead man.
This time no lot chose me; this was my jackpot,
and no one else's. Now, my lord, take her
and as you please judge her and test her; I
am justly free and clear of all this trouble.

Creon

This girl—how did you take her and from where? 440

Sentry

She was burying the man. Now you know all.

Creon

Do you know what you are saying? Do you mean it?

Sentry

She is the one; I saw her burying
the dead man you forbade the burial of.
Now, do I speak plainly and clearly enough?

Creon

How was she seen? How was she caught in the act?

Sentry

This is how it was. When we came there,
with those dreadful threats of yours upon us,
we brushed off all the dust that lay upon
the dead man's body, heedfully 450
leaving it moist and naked.
We sat on the brow of the hill, to windward,
that we might shun the smell of the corpse upon us.

Each of us wakefully urged his fellow
with torrents of abuse, not to be careless
in this work of ours. So it went on,
until in the midst of the sky the sun's bright circle
stood still; the heat was burning. Suddenly
a squall lifted out of the earth a storm of dust,
a trouble in the sky. It filled the plain,   460
ruining all the foliage of the wood
that was around it. The great empty air
was filled with it. We closed our eyes, enduring
this plague sent by the gods. When at long last
we were quit of it, why, then we saw the girl.

She was crying out with the shrill cry
of an embittered bird
that sees its nest robbed of its nestlings
and the bed empty. So, too, when she saw
the body stripped of its cover, she burst out in groans,   470
calling terrible curses on those that had done that deed;
and with her hands immediately
brought thirsty dust to the body; from a shapely brazen
urn, held high over it, poured a triple stream
of funeral offerings; and crowned the corpse.
When we saw that, we rushed upon her and
caught our quarry then and there, not a bit disturbed.
We charged her with what she had done, then and the first time.
She did not deny a word of it—to my joy,
but to my pain as well. It is most pleasant   480
to have escaped oneself out of such troubles
but painful to bring into it those whom we love.
However, it is but natural for me
to count all this less than my own escape.

Creon
    You there, that turn your eyes upon the ground,
    do you confess or deny what you have done?

Antigone

Yes, I confess; I will not deny my deed.

Creon (to the Sentry)

You take yourself off where you like.
You are free of a heavy charge.
Now, Antigone, tell me shortly and to the point,   490
did you know the proclamation against your action?

Antigone

I knew it; of course I did. For it was public.

Creon

And did you dare to disobey that law?

Antigone

Yes, it was not Zeus that made the proclamation;
nor did Justice, which lives with those below, enact
such laws as that, for mankind. I did not believe
your proclamation had such power to enable
one who will someday die to override
God's ordinances, unwritten and secure.
They are not of today and yesterday;   500
they live forever; none knows when first they were.
These are the laws whose penalties I would not
incur from the gods, through fear of any man's temper.

I know that I will die—of course I do—
even if you had not doomed me by proclamation.
If I shall die before my time, I count that
a profit. How can such as I, that live
among such troubles, not find a profit in death?
So for such as me, to face such a fate as this
is pain that does not count. But if I dared to leave   510
the dead man, my mother's son, dead and unburied,
that would have been real pain. The other is not.
Now, if you think me a fool to act like this,
perhaps it is a fool that judges so.

Chorus

    The savage spirit of a savage father
    shows itself in this girl. She does not know
    how to yield to trouble.

Creon

    I would have you know the most fanatic spirits
    fall most of all. It is the toughest iron,
    baked in the fire to hardness, you may see   520
    most shattered, twisted, shivered to fragments.
    I know hot horses are restrained
    by a small curb. For he that is his neighbor's slave cannot
    be high in spirit. This girl had learned her insolence
    before this, when she broke the established laws.
    But here is still another insolence
    in that she boasts of it, laughs at what she did.
    I swear I am no man and she the man
    if she can win this and not pay for it.
    No; though she were my sister's child or closer   530
    in blood than all that my hearth god acknowledges
    as mine, neither she nor her sister should escape
    the utmost sentence—death. For indeed I accuse her,
    the sister, equally of plotting the burial.
    Summon her. I saw her inside, just now,
    crazy, distraught. When people plot
    mischief in the dark, it is the mind which first
    is convicted of deceit. But surely I hate indeed
    the one that is caught in evil and then makes
    that evil look like good.   540

Antigone

    Do you want anything
    beyond my taking and my execution? .

Creon

    Oh, nothing! Once I have that I have everything.

Antigone
Why do you wait, then? Nothing that you say
pleases me; God forbid it ever should.
So my words, too, naturally offend you.
Yet how could I win a greater share of glory
than putting my own brother in his grave?
All that are here would surely say that's true,
if fear did not lock their tongues up. A prince's power   550
is blessed in many things, not least in this,
that he can say and do whatever he likes.

Creon
You are alone among the people of Thebes
to see things in that way.

Antigone
No, these do, too,
but keep their mouths shut for the fear of you.

Creon
Are you not ashamed to think so differently
from them?

Antigone
There is nothing shameful in honoring my brother.

Creon
Was not he that died on the other side your brother?   560

Antigone
Yes, indeed, of my own blood from father and mother.

Creon
Why then do you show a grace that must be impious
in *his* sight?

Antigone
That other dead man
would never bear you witness in what you say.

Creon

    Yes he would, if you put him only on equality
    with one that was a desecrator.

Antigone

    It was his brother, not his slave, that died.

Creon

    He died destroying the country the other defended.

Antigone

    The god of death demands these rites for both.   570

Creon

    But the good man does not seek an *equal* share only,
    with the bad.

Antigone

                Who knows
    if in that other world this is true piety?

Creon

    My enemy is still my enemy, even in death.

Antigone

    My nature is to join in love, not hate.

Creon

    Go then to the world below, yourself, if you
    must love. Love *them*. When I am alive no woman shall rule.

Chorus

    Here before the gates comes Ismene
    shedding tears for the love of a brother.   580
    A cloud over her brow casts shame
    on her flushed face, as the tears wet
    her fair cheeks.

Creon

    You there, who lurked in my house, viper-like—
    secretly drawing its lifeblood; I never thought

that I was raising two sources of destruction,
two rebels against my throne. Come tell me now,
will you, too, say you bore a hand in the burial
or will you swear that you know nothing of it?

Ismene

   I did it, yes—if she will say I did it   590
   I bear my share in it, bear the guilt, too.

Antigone

   Justice will not allow you what you refused
   and I will have none of your partnership.

Ismene

   But in your troubles I am not ashamed
   to sail with you the sea of suffering.

Antigone

   Where the act was death, the dead are witnesses.
   I do not love a friend who loves in words.

Ismene

   Sister, do not dishonor me, denying me
   a common death with you, a common honoring
   of the dead man.   600

Antigone

   Don't die with me, nor make your own
   what you have never touched. I that die am enough.

Ismene

   What life is there for me, once I have lost you?

Antigone

   Ask Creon; all your care was on his behalf.

Ismene

   Why do you hurt me, when you gain nothing by it?

Antigone

   I am hurt by my own mockery—if I mock you.

Ismene
Even now—what can I do to help you still?

Antigone
Save yourself; I do not grudge you your escape.

Ismene
I cannot bear it! Not even to share your death!

Antigone
Life was your choice, and death was mine.   610

Ismene
You cannot say I accepted that choice in silence.

Antigone
You were right in the eyes of one party, I in the other.

Ismene
Well then, the fault is equally between us.

Antigone
Take heart; you are alive, but my life died
long ago, to serve the dead.

Creon
Here are two girls; I think that one of them
has suddenly lost her wits—the other was always so.

Ismene
Yes, for, my lord, the wits that they are born with
do not stay firm for the unfortunate.
They go astray.   620

Creon
       Certainly yours do,
when you share troubles with the troublemaker.

Ismene
What life can be mine alone without her?

Creon
           Do not
speak of *her. She* isn't, anymore.

Ismene

Will you kill your son's wife to be?

Creon

Yes, there are other fields for him to plough.

Ismene

Not with the mutual love of him and her.

Creon

I hate a bad wife for a son of mine.

Antigone

Dear Haemon, how your father dishonors you.   630

Creon

There is too much of you—and of your marriage!

Chorus

Will you rob your son of this girl?

Creon

Death—it is death that will stop the marriage for me.

Chorus

Your decision it seems is taken: she shall die.

Creon

Both you and I have decided it. No more delay.

(He turns to the servants.)

Bring her inside, you. From this time forth,
these must be women, and not free to roam.
For even the stout of heart shrink when they see
the approach of death close to their lives.

Chorus

    Lucky are those whose lives   640
    know no taste of sorrow.
    But for those whose house has been shaken by God
    there is never cessation of ruin;
    it steals on generation after generation

within a breed. Even as the swell
is driven over the dark deep
by the fierce Thracian winds
I see the ancient evils of Labdacus' house
are heaped on the evils of the dead.
No generation frees another, some god   650
strikes them down; there is no deliverance.
Here was the light of hope stretched
over the last roots of Oedipus' house,
and the bloody dust due to the gods below
has mowed it down—that and the folly of speech
and ruin's enchantment of the mind.

Your power, O Zeus, what sin of man can limit?
All-aging sleep does not overtake it,
nor the unwearied months of the gods; and you,
for whom time brings no age,   660
you hold the glowing brightness of Olympus.

For the future near and far,
and the past, this law holds good:
nothing very great
comes to the life of mortal man
without ruin to accompany it.
For Hope, widely wandering, comes to many of mankind
as a blessing,
but to many as the deceiver,
using light-minded lusts;   670
she comes to him that knows nothing
till he burns his foot in the glowing fire.
With wisdom has someone declared
a word of distinction:
that evil seems good to one whose mind
the god leads to ruin,
and but for the briefest moment of time
is his life outside of calamity.

Here is Haemon, youngest of your sons.
Does he come grieving 680
for the fate of his bride to be,
in agony at being cheated of his marriage?

Creon

Soon we will know that better than the prophets.
My son, can it be that you have not heard
of my final decision on your betrothed?
Can you have come here in your fury against your father?
Or have I your love still, no matter what I do?

Haemon

Father, I am yours; with your excellent judgment
you lay the right before me, and I shall follow it.
No marriage will ever be so valued by me 690
as to override the goodness of your leadership.

Creon

Yes, my son, this should always be
in your very heart, that everything else
shall be second to your father's decision.
It is for this that fathers pray to have
obedient sons begotten in their halls,
that they may requite with ill their father's enemy
and honor his friend no less than he would himself.
If a man have sons that are no use to him,
what can one say of him but that he has bred 700
so many sorrows to himself, laughter to his enemies?
Do not, my son, banish your good sense
through pleasure in a woman, since you know
that the embrace grows cold
when an evil woman shares your bed and home.
What greater wound can there be than a false friend?
No. Spit on her, throw her out like an enemy,
this girl, to marry someone in Death's house.
I caught her openly in disobedience
alone out of all this city and I shall not make 710

myself a liar in the city's sight. No, I will kill her.
So let her cry if she will on the Zeus of kinship;
for if I rear those of my race and breeding
to be rebels, surely I will do so with those outside it.
For he who is in his household a good man
will be found a just man, too, in the city.
But he that breaches the law or does it violence
or thinks to dictate to those who govern him
shall never have my good word.
The man the city sets up in authority   720
must be obeyed in small things and in just
but also in their opposites.
I am confident such a man of whom I speak
will be a good ruler, and willing to be well ruled.
He will stand on his country's side, faithful and just,
in the storm of battle. There is nothing worse
than disobedience to authority.
It destroys cities, it demolishes homes;
it breaks and routs one's allies. Of successful lives
the most of them are saved by discipline.   730
So we must stand on the side of what is orderly;
we cannot give victory to a woman.
If we must accept defeat, let it be from a man;
we must not let people say that a woman beat us.

Chorus
    We think, if we are not victims of Time the Thief,
    that you speak intelligently of what you speak.

Haemon
    Father, the natural sense that the gods breed
    in men is surely the best of their possessions.
    I certainly could not declare you wrong—
    may I never know how to do so!—Still there might   740
    be something useful that some other than you might think.
    It is natural for me to be watchful on your behalf
    concerning what all men say or do or find to blame.

Your face is terrible to a simple citizen;
it frightens him from words you dislike to hear.
But what *I* can hear, in the dark, are things like these:
the city mourns for this girl; they think she is dying
most wrongly and most undeservedly
of all womenkind, for the most glorious acts.
Here is one who would not leave her brother unburied,   750
a brother who had fallen in bloody conflict,
to meet his end by greedy dogs or by
the bird that chanced that way. Surely what she merits
is golden honor, isn't it? That's the dark rumor
that spreads in secret. Nothing I own
I value more highly, father, than your success.
What greater distinction can a son have than the glory
of a successful father, and for a father
the distinction of successful children?
Do not bear this single habit of mind, to think   760
that what you say and nothing else is true.
A man who thinks that he alone is right,
or what he says, or what he *is* himself,
unique, such men, when opened up, are seen
to be quite empty. For a man, though he be wise,
it is no shame to learn—learn many things,
and not maintain his views too rigidly.
You notice how by streams in wintertime
the trees that yield preserve their branches safely,
but those that fight the tempest perish utterly.   770
The man who keeps the sheet of his sail tight
and never slackens capsizes his boat
and makes the rest of his trip keel uppermost.
Yield something of your anger, give way a little.
If a much younger man, like me, may have
a judgment, I would say it were far better
to be one altogether wise by nature, but,
as things incline not to be so, then it is good
also to learn from those who advise well.

Chorus
    My lord, if he says anything to the point,   780
    you should learn from him, and you, too, Haemon,
    learn from your father. Both of you
    have spoken well.

Creon
    Should we that are my age learn wisdom
    from young men such as he is?

Haemon
    Not learn injustice, certainly. If I am young,
    do not look at my years but what I do.

Creon
    Is what you do to have respect for rebels?

Haemon
                                I

    would not urge you to be scrupulous   790
    towards the wicked.

Creon
    Is *she* not tainted by the disease of wickedness?

Haemon
    The entire people of Thebes says no to that.

Creon
    Should the city tell me how I am to rule them?

Haemon
    Do you see what a young man's words these are of yours?

Creon
    Must I rule the land by someone else's judgment
    rather than my own?

Haemon
                  There is no city
    possessed by one man only.

Creon
    Is not the city thought to be the ruler's?   800

Haemon

You would be a fine dictator of a desert.

Creon

It seems this boy is on the woman's side.

Haemon

If you are a woman—my care is all for you.

Creon

You villain, to bandy words with your own father!

Haemon

I see your acts as mistaken and unjust.

Creon

Am I mistaken, reverencing my own office?

Haemon

There is no reverence in trampling on God's honor.

Creon

Your nature is vile, in yielding to a woman.

Haemon

You will not find me yield to what is shameful.

Creon

At least, your argument is all for her.   810

Haemon

Yes, and for you and me—and for the gods below.

Creon

You will never marry her while her life lasts.

Haemon

Then she must die—and dying destroy another.

Creon

Has your daring gone so far, to threaten me?

Haemon

What threat is it to speak against empty judgments?

Creon

    Empty of sense yourself, you will regret
    your schooling of me in sense.

Haemon

                       If you were not
    my father, I would say you are insane.

Creon

    You woman's slave, do not try to wheedle me.   820

Haemon

    You want to talk but never to hear and listen.

Creon

    Is that so? By the heavens above you will not—
    be sure of that—get off scot-free, insulting,
    abusing me.

                       (He speaks to the servants.)

            You people bring out this creature,
    this hated creature, that she may die before
    his very eyes, right now, next her would-be husband.

Haemon

    Not at my side! Never think that! She will not
    die by my side. But you will never again
    set eyes upon my face. Go then and rage   830
    with such of your friends as are willing to endure it.

Chorus

    The man is gone, my lord, quick in his anger.
    A young man's mind is fierce when he is hurt.

Creon

    Let him go, and do and think things superhuman.
    But these two girls he shall not save from death.

Chorus

    Both of them? Do you mean to kill them both?

Creon

No, not the one that didn't do anything.
You are quite right there.

Chorus

And by what form of death do you mean to kill her?

Creon

I will bring her where the path is loneliest,   840
and hide her alive in a rocky cavern there.
I'll give just enough of food as shall suffice
for a bare expiation, that the city may avoid pollution.
In that place she shall call on Hades, god of death,
in her prayers. That god only she reveres.
Perhaps she will win from him escape from death
or at least in that last moment will recognize
her honoring of the dead is labor lost.

Chorus

Love undefeated in the fight,
Love that makes havoc of possessions,   850
Love who lives at night in a young girl's soft cheeks,
Who travels over sea, or in huts in the countryside—
there is no god able to escape you
nor anyone of men, whose life is a day only,
and whom you possess is mad.

You wrench the minds of just men to injustice,
to their disgrace; this conflict among kinsmen
it is you who stirred to turmoil.
The winner is desire. She gleaming kindles
from the eyes of the girl good to bed.   860
Love shares the throne with the great powers that rule.
For the golden Aphrodite holds her play there
and then no one can overcome her.

Here I too am borne out of the course of lawfulness
when I see these things, and I cannot control
the springs of my tears

when I see Antigone making her way
to her bed—but the bed
that is rest for everyone.

Antigone

You see me, you people of my country,   870
as I set out on my last road of all,
looking for the last time on this light of this sun—
never again. I am alive but Hades who gives sleep to everyone
is leading me to the shores of Acheron,
though I have known nothing of marriage songs
nor the chant that brings the bride to bed.
My husband is to be the Lord of Death.

Chorus

Yes, you go to the place where the dead are hidden,
but you go with distinction and praise.
You have not been stricken by wasting sickness;   880
you have not earned the wages of the sword;
it was your own choice and alone among mankind
you will descend, alive,
to that world of death.

Antigone

But indeed I have heard of the saddest of deaths—
of the Phrygian stranger, daughter of Tantalus,
whom the rocky growth subdued, like clinging ivy.
The rains never leave her, the snow never fails,
as she wastes away. That is how men tell the story.
From streaming eyes her tears wet the crags;   890
most like to her the god brings me to rest.

Chorus

Yes, but she was a god, and god born,
and you are mortal and mortal born.
Surely it is great renown
for a woman that dies, that in life and death
her lot is a lot shared with demigods.

Antigone

You mock me. In the name of our fathers' gods
why do you not wait till I am gone to insult me?
Must you do it face to face?
My city! Rich citizens of my city!   900
You springs of Dirce, you holy groves of Thebes,
famed for its chariots! I would still have you as my witnesses,
with what dry-eyed friends, under what laws
I make my way to my prison sealed like a tomb.
Pity me. Neither among the living nor the dead
do I have a home in common—
neither with the living nor the dead.

Chorus

You went to the extreme of daring
and against the high throne of Justice
you fell, my daughter, grievously.   910
But perhaps it was for some ordeal of your father
that you are paying requital.

Antigone

You have touched the most painful of my cares—
the pity for my father, ever reawakened,
and the fate of all of our race, the famous Labdacids;
the doomed self-destruction of my mother's bed
when she slept with her own son,
my father.
What parents I was born of, God help me!
To them I am going to share their home,   920
the curse on me, too, and unmarried.
Brother, it was a luckless marriage you made,
and dying killed my life.

Chorus

There *is* a certain reverence for piety.
But for him in authority,
he cannot see that authority defied;

it is your own self-willed temper
that has destroyed you.

Antigone
No tears for me, no friends, no marriage. Brokenhearted
I am led along the road ready before me.   930
I shall never again be suffered
to look on the holy eye of the day.
But my fate claims no tears—
no friend cries for me.

Creon (to the servants)
Don't you know that weeping and wailing before death
would never stop if one is allowed to weep and wail?
Lead her away at once. Enfold her
in that rocky tomb of hers—as I told you to.
There leave her alone, solitary,
to die if she so wishes   940
or live a buried life in such a home;
we are guiltless in respect of her, this girl.
But living above, among the rest of us, this life
she shall certainly lose.

Antigone
Tomb, bridal chamber, prison forever
dug in rock, it is to you I am going
to join my people, that great number that have died,
whom in their death Persephone received.
I am the last of them and I go down
in the worst death of all—for I have not lived   950
the due term of my life. But when I come
to that other world my hope is strong
that my coming will be welcome to my father,
and dear to you, my mother, and dear to you,
my brother deeply loved. For when you died,
with my own hands I washed and dressed you all,
and poured the lustral offerings on your graves.

And now, Polyneices, it was for such care of your body
that I have earned these wages.
Yet those who think rightly will think I did right   960
in honoring you. Had I been a mother
of children, and my husband been dead and rotten,
I would not have taken this weary task upon me
against the will of the city. What law backs me
when I say this? I will tell you:
If my husband were dead, I might have had another,
and child from another man, if I lost the first.
But when father and mother both were hidden in death
no brother's life would bloom for me again.
That is the law under which I gave you precedence,   970
my dearest brother, and that is why Creon thinks me
wrong, even a criminal, and now takes me
by the hand and leads me away,
unbedded, without bridal, without share
in marriage and in nurturing of children;
as lonely as you see me; without friends;
with fate against me I go to the vault of death
while still alive. What law of God have I broken?
Why should I still look to the gods in my misery?
Whom should I summon as ally? For indeed   980
because of piety I was called impious.
If this proceeding is good in the gods' eyes
I shall know my sin, once I have suffered.
But if Creon and his people are the wrongdoers
let their suffering be no worse than the injustice
they are meting out to me.

Chorus
   It is the same blasts, the tempests of the soul,
   possess her.

Creon
               Then for this her guards,
   who are so slow, will find themselves in trouble.   990

Antigone (cries out)
    Oh, that word has come
    very close to death.

Creon
    I will not comfort you
    with hope that the sentence will not be accomplished.

Antigone
    O my father's city, in Theban land,
    O gods that sired my race,
    I am led away, I have no more stay.
    Look on me, princes of Thebes,
    the last remnant of the old royal line;
    see what I suffer and who makes me suffer   1000
    because I gave reverence to what claims reverence.

Chorus
        Danae suffered, too, when, her beauty lost, she gave
        the light of heaven in exchange for brassbound walls,
        and in the tomb-like cell was she hidden and held;
        yet she was honored in her breeding, child,
        and she kept, as guardian, the seed of Zeus
        that came to her in a golden shower.
        But there is some terrible power in destiny
        and neither wealth nor war
        nor tower nor black ships, beaten by the sea,   1010
        can give escape from it.

        The hot-tempered son of Dryas, the Edonian king,
        in fury mocked Dionysus,
        who then held him in restraint
        in a rocky dungeon.
        So the terrible force and flower of his madness
        drained away. He came to know the god
        whom in frenzy he had touched with his mocking tongue,
        when he would have checked the inspired women
        and the fire of Dionysus,   1020
        when he provoked the Muses that love the lyre.

By the black rocks, dividing the sea in two,
are the shores of the Bosporus, Thracian Salmydessus.
There the god of war who lives near the city
saw the terrible blinding wound
dealt by his savage wife
on Phineus' two sons.
She blinded and tore with the points of her shuttle,
and her bloodied hands, those eyes
that else would have looked on her vengefully.   1030
As they wasted away, they lamented
their unhappy fate that they were doomed
to be born of a mother cursed in her marriage.
She traced her descent from the seed
of the ancient Erechtheidae.
In far-distant caves she was raised
among her father's storms, that child of Boreas,
quick as a horse, over the steep hills,
a daughter of the gods.
But, my child, the long-lived Fates   1040
bore hard upon her, too.

(Enter Teiresias, the blind prophet, led by a boy.)

Teiresias
My lords of Thebes, we have come here together,
one pair of eyes serving us both. For the blind
such must be the way of going, by a guide's leading.

Creon
What is the news, my old Teiresias?

Teiresias
I will tell you; and you, listen to the prophet.

Creon
Never in the past have I turned from your advice.

Teiresias
And so you have steered well the ship of state.

« 198 »

Creon
    I have benefited and can testify to that.

Teiresias
    Then realize you are on the razor edge   1050
    of danger.

Creon
    What can that be? I shudder to hear those words.

Teiresias
    When you learn the signs recognized by my art
    you will understand.
    I sat at my ancient place of divination
    for watching the birds, where every bird finds shelter;
    and I heard an unwonted voice among them;
    they were horribly distressed, and screamed unmeaningly.
    I knew they were tearing each other murderously;
    the beating of their wings was a clear sign.   1060
    I was full of fear; at once on all the altars,
    as they were fully kindled, I tasted the offerings,
    but the god of fire refused to burn from the sacrifice,
    and from the thighbones a dark stream of moisture
    oozed from the embers, smoked and sputtered.
    The gall bladder burst and scattered to the air
    and the streaming thighbones lay exposed
    from the fat wrapped round them—
    so much I learned from this boy here,
    the fading prophecies of a rite that failed.   1070
    This boy here is my guide, as I am others'.
    This is the city's sickness—and your plans are the cause of it.
    For our altars and our sacrificial hearths
    are filled with the carrion meat of birds and dogs,
    torn from the flesh of Oedipus' poor son.
    So the gods will not take our prayers or sacrifice
    nor yet the flame from the thighbones, and no bird
    cries shrill and clear, so glutted
    are they with fat of the blood of the killed man.

Reflect on these things, son. All men   1080
can make mistakes; but, once mistaken,
a man is no longer stupid nor accursed
who, having fallen on ill, tries to cure that ill,
not taking a fine undeviating stand.
It is obstinacy that convicts of folly.
Yield to the dead man; do not stab him—
now he is gone—what bravery is this,
to inflict another death upon the dead?
I mean you well and speak well for your good.
It is never sweeter to learn from a good counselor   1090
than when he counsels to your benefit.

Creon

Old man, you are all archers, and I am your mark.
I must be tried by your prophecies as well.
By the breed of you I have been bought and sold
and made a merchandise, for ages now.
But I tell you: make your profit from silver-gold
from Sardis and the gold from India
if you will. But this dead man you shall not hide
in a grave, not though the eagles of Zeus should bear
the carrion, snatching it to the throne of Zeus itself.   1100
Even so, I shall not so tremble at the pollution
to let you bury him.

                    No, I am certain
no human has the power to pollute the gods.
They fall, you old Teiresias, those men,
—so very clever—in a bad fall whenever
they eloquently speak vile words for profit.

Teiresias

I wonder if there's a man who dares consider—

Creon

What do you mean? What sort of generalization
is this talk of yours?   1110

Teiresias
How much the best of possessions is the ability
to listen to wise advice?

Creon
As I should imagine that the worst
injury must be native stupidity.

Teiresias
Now that is exactly where your mind is sick.

Creon
I do not like to answer a seer with insults.

Teiresias
But you do, when you say my prophecies are lies.

Creon
Well,
the whole breed of prophets certainly loves money.

Teiresias
And the breed that comes from princes loves to take
advantage—base advantage. 1120

Creon
Do you realize
you are speaking in such terms of your own prince?

Teiresias
I know. But it is through me you have saved the city.

Creon
You are a wise prophet, but what you love is wrong.

Teiresias
You will force me to declare what should be hidden
in my own heart.

Creon
Out with it—
but only if your words are not for gain.

Teiresias

They won't be for *your* gain—that I am sure of.

Creon

But realize you will not make a merchandise   1130
of my decisions.

Teiresias

                              And you must realize
that you will not outlive many cycles more
of this swift sun before you give in exchange
one of your own loins bred, a corpse for a corpse,
for you have thrust one that belongs above
below the earth, and bitterly dishonored
a living soul by lodging her in the grave;
while one that belonged indeed to the underworld
gods you have kept on this earth without due share   1140
of rites of burial, of due funeral offerings,
a corpse unhallowed. With all of this you, Creon,
have nothing to do, nor have the gods above.
These acts of yours are violence, on your part.
And in requital the avenging Spirits
of Death itself and the gods' Furies shall
after *your* deeds, lie in ambush for you, and
in their hands you shall be taken cruelly.
Now, look at this and tell me I was bribed
to say it! The delay will not be long   1150
before the cries of mourning in your house,
of men and women. All the cities will stir in hatred
against you, because their sons in mangled shreds
received their burial rites from dogs, from wild beasts
or when some bird of the air brought a vile stink
to each city that contained the hearths of the dead.
These are the arrows that archer-like I launched—
you vexed me so to anger—at your heart.
You shall not escape their sting. You, boy,

lead me away to my house, so he may discharge   1160
his anger on younger men; so may he come to know
to bear a quieter tongue in his head and a better
mind than that now he carries in him.

Chorus

That was a terrible prophecy, my lord.
The man has gone. Since these hairs of mine grew white
from the black they once were, he has never spoken
a word of a lie to our city.

Creon

I know, I know.
My mind is all bewildered. To yield is terrible.
But by opposition to destroy my very being
with a self-destructive curse must also be reckoned   1170
in what is terrible.

Chorus

You need good counsel, son of Menoeceus,
and need to take it.

Creon

What must I do, then? Tell me; I shall agree.

Chorus

The girl—go now and bring her up from her cave,
and for the exposed dead man, give him his burial.

Creon

That is really your advice? You would have me yield.

Chorus

And quickly as you may, my lord. Swift harms
sent by the gods cut off the paths of the foolish.

Creon

Oh, it is hard; I must give up what my heart   1180
would have me do. But it is ill to fight
against what must be.

Chorus

 Go now, and do this;
 do not give the task to others.

Creon

 I will go,
 just as I am. Come, servants, all of you;
 take axes in your hands; away with you
 to the place you see, there.
 For my part, since my intention is so changed,
 as I bound her myself, myself will free her.   1190
 I am afraid it may be best, in the end
 of life, to have kept the old accepted laws.

Chorus

  You of many names, glory of the Cadmeian
  bride, breed of loud thundering Zeus;
  you who watch over famous Italy;
  you who rule where all are welcome in Eleusis;
  in the sheltered plains of Deo—
  O Bacchus that dwells in Thebes,
  the mother city of Bacchanals,
  by the flowing stream of Ismenus,   1200
  in the ground sown by the fierce dragon's teeth.

  You are he on whom the murky gleam of torches glares,
  above the twin peaks of the crag
  where come the Corycean nymphs
  to worship you, the Bacchanals;
  and the stream of Castalia has seen you, too;
  and you are he that the ivy-clad
  slopes of Nisaean hills,
  and the green shore ivy-clustered,
  sent to watch over the roads of Thebes,   1210
  where the immortal Evoe chant rings out.

  It is Thebes which you honor most of all cities,
  you and your mother both,
  she who died by the blast of Zeus' thunderbolt.

And now when the city, with all its folk,
is gripped by a violent plague,
come with healing foot, over the slopes of Parnassus,
over the moaning strait.
You lead the dance of the fire-breathing stars,
you are master of the voices of the night.   1220
True-born child of Zeus, appear,
my lord, with your Thyiad attendants,
who in frenzy all night long
dance in your house, Iacchus,
dispenser of gifts.

Messenger
You who live by the house of Cadmus and Amphion,
hear me. There is no condition of man's life
that stands secure. As such I would not
praise it or blame. It is chance that sets upright;
it is chance that brings down the lucky and the unlucky,   1230
each in his turn. For men, that belong to death,
there is no prophet of established things.
Once Creon was a man worthy of envy—
of my envy, at least. For he saved this city
of Thebes from her enemies, and attained
the throne of the land, with all a king's power.
He guided it right. His race bloomed
with good children. But when a man forfeits joy
I do not count his life as life, but only
a life trapped in a corpse.   1240
Be rich within your house, yes greatly rich,
if so you will, and live in a prince's style.
If the gladness of these things is gone, I would not
give the shadow of smoke for the rest,
as against joy.

Chorus
What is the sorrow of our princes
of which you are the messenger?

Messenger
Death; and the living are guilty of their deaths.

Chorus
But who is the murderer? Who the murdered? Tell us.

Messenger
Haemon is dead; the hand that shed his blood   1250
was his very own.

Chorus
Truly his own hand? Or his father's?

Messenger
His own hand, in his anger
against his father for a murder.

Chorus
Prophet, how truly you have made good your word!

Messenger
These things are so; you may debate the rest.
Here I see Creon's wife Eurydice
approaching. Unhappy woman!
Does she come from the house as hearing about her son
or has she come by chance?   1260

Eurydice
I heard your words, all you men of Thebes, as I
was going out to greet Pallas with my prayers.
I was just drawing back the bolts of the gate
to open it when a cry struck through my ears
telling of my household's ruin. I fell backward
in terror into the arms of my servants; I fainted.
But tell me again, what is the story? I
will hear it as one who is no stranger to sorrow.

Messenger
Dear mistress, I will tell you, for I was there,
and I will leave out no word of the truth.   1270

Why should I comfort you and then tomorrow
be proved a liar? The truth is always best.

I followed your husband, at his heels, to the end of the plain
where Polyneices' body still lay unpitied,
and torn by dogs. We prayed to Hecate, goddess
of the crossroads, and also to Pluto
that they might restrain their anger and turn kind.
And him we washed with sacred lustral water
and with fresh-cut boughs we burned what was left of him
and raised a high mound of his native earth;   1280
then we set out again for the hollowed rock,
death's stone bridal chamber for the girl.
Someone then heard a voice of bitter weeping
while we were still far off, coming from that unblest room.
The man came to tell our master Creon of it.
As the king drew nearer, there swarmed about him
a cry of misery but no clear words.
He groaned and in an anguished mourning voice
cried "Oh, am I a true prophet? Is this the road
that I must travel, saddest of all my wayfaring?   1290
It is my son's voice that haunts my ear. Servants,
get closer, quickly. Stand around the tomb
and look. There is a gap there where the stones
have been wrenched away; enter there, by the very mouth,
and see whether I recognize the voice of Haemon
or if the gods deceive me." On the command
of our despairing master we went to look.
In the furthest part of the tomb we saw her, hanging
by her neck. She had tied a noose of muslin on it.
Haemon's hands were about her waist embracing her,   1300
while he cried for the loss of his bride gone to the dead,
and for all his father had done, and his own sad love.
When Creon saw him he gave a bitter cry,
went in and called to him with a groan: "Poor son!
what have you done? What can you have meant?

What happened to destroy you? Come out, I pray you!"
The boy glared at him with savage eyes, and then
spat in his face, without a word of answer.
He drew his double-hilted sword. As his father
ran to escape him, Haemon failed to strike him,   1310
and the poor wretch in anger at himself
leaned on his sword and drove it halfway in,
into his ribs. Then he folded the girl to him,
in his arms, while he was conscious still,
and gasping poured a sharp stream of bloody drops
on her white cheeks. There they lie,
the dead upon the dead. So he has won
the pitiful fulfillment of his marriage
within death's house. In this human world he has shown
how the wrong choice in plans is for a man   1320
his greatest evil.

Chorus
What do you make of this? My lady is gone,
without a word of good or bad.

Messenger
                              I, too,
am lost in wonder. I am inclined to hope
that hearing of her son's death she could not
open her sorrow to the city, but chose rather
within her house to lay upon her maids
the mourning for the household grief. Her judgment
is good; she will not make any false step.   1330

Chorus
I do not know. To me this over-heavy silence
seems just as dangerous as much empty wailing.

Messenger
I will go in and learn if in her passionate
heart she keeps hidden some secret purpose.
You are right; there is sometimes danger in too much silence.

Chorus

    Here comes our king himself. He bears in his hands
    a memorial all too clear;
    it is a ruin of none other's making,
    purely his own if one dare to say that.

Creon

    The mistakes of a blinded man   1340
    are themselves rigid and laden with death.
    You look at us the killer and the killed
    of the one blood. Oh, the awful blindness
    of those plans of mine. My son, you were so young,
    so young to die. You were freed from the bonds of life
    through no folly of your own—only through mine.

Chorus

    I think you have learned justice—but too late.

Creon

    Yes, I have learned it to my bitterness. At this moment
    God has sprung on my head with a vast weight
    and struck me down. He shook me in my savage ways;   1350
    he has overturned my joy, has trampled it,
    underfoot. The pains men suffer
    are pains indeed.

Second Messenger

    My lord, you have troubles and a store besides;
    some are there in your hands, but there are others
    you will surely see when you come to your house.

Creon

    What trouble can there be beside these troubles?

Second Messenger

    The queen is dead. She was indeed true mother
    of the dead son. She died, poor lady,
    by recent violence upon herself.   1360

Creon

Haven of death, you can never have enough.
Why, why do you destroy me?
You messenger, who have brought me bitter news,
what is this tale you tell?
It is a dead man that you kill again—
what new message of yours is this, boy?
Is this new slaughter of a woman
a doom to lie on the pile of the dead?

Chorus

You can see. It is no longer
hidden in a corner.   1370

*(By some stage device, perhaps the so-called eccyclema, the inside of
the palace is shown, with the body of the dead Queen.)*

Creon

Here is yet another horror
for my unhappy eyes to see.
What doom still waits for me?
I have but now taken in my arms my son,
and again I look upon another dead face.
Poor mother and poor son!

Second Messenger

She stood at the altar, and with keen whetted knife
she suffered her darkening eyes to close.
First she cried in agony recalling the noble fate of Megareus,
who died before all this,   1380
and then for the fate of this son; and in the end
she cursed you for the evil you had done
in killing her sons.

Creon

I am distracted with fear. Why does not someone
strike a two-edged sword right through me?
I am dissolved in an agony of misery.

Second Messenger
  You were indeed accused
  by her that is dead
  of Haemon's and of Megareus' death.

Creon
  By what kind of violence did she find her end?   1390

Second Messenger
  Her own hand struck her to the entrails
  when she heard of her son's lamentable death.

Creon
  These acts can never be made to fit another
  to free me from the guilt. It was I that killed her.
  Poor wretch that I am, I say it is true!
  Servants, lead me away, quickly, quickly.
  I am no more a live man than one dead.

Chorus
  What you say is for the best—if there be a best
  in evil such as this. For the shortest way
  is best with troubles that lie at our feet.   1400

Creon
  O, let it come, let it come,
  that best of fates that waits on my last day.
  Surely best fate of all. Let it come, let it come!
  That I may never see one more day's light!

Chorus
  These things are for the future. We must deal
  with what impends. What in the future is to care for
  rests with those whose duty it is
  to care for them.

Creon
  At least, all that I want
  is in that prayer of mine.   1410

Chorus

Pray for no more at all. For what is destined
for us, men mortal, there is no escape.

Creon

Lead me away, a vain silly man
who killed you, son, and you, too, lady.
I did not mean to, but I did.
I do not know where to turn my eyes
to look to, for support.
Everything in my hands is crossed. A most unwelcome fate
has leaped upon me.

Chorus

Wisdom is far the chief element in happiness   1420
and, secondly, no irreverence towards the gods.
But great words of haughty men exact
in retribution blows as great
and in old age teach wisdom.

AJAX

Translated and with an Introduction by John Moore

INTRODUCTION TO *AJAX*

THE *Ajax* is probably the earliest of the seven plays by Sophocles which are preserved. The *Antigone* is generally thought to have been produced in 442 or 441 B.C., and the *Ajax* appears to belong to the same period of Sophocles' work. In dramatic technique these plays have not the suppleness of the *Oedipus*, but they are in no sense to be regarded as immature works. At the time he produced the *Antigone*, Sophocles was already fifty-five years old and had been producing tragedies in the Theatre of Dionysus for a quarter of a century. The *Ajax*, too, is the work not of a novice but of a seasoned dramatist. It is a play of very remarkable beauties and likewise of some perplexities.

The subject which Sophocles has chosen is the shame and death of Ajax, which follow on his defeat in the contest for Achilles' armor, and the growth, in and after this shame and death and triumphing over them, of a revealed sense of his heroic virtue and magnanimity. It will be seen that this subject is a single subject: the death of Ajax, taken quite simply in itself, completes nothing; the play's action is complete only when the spectator is brought to an altered estimate of the meaning of Ajax' career and destiny.

Throughout the drama, Ajax remains the central issue and our principal concern. Sophocles' judgment of him is not simple: he sees that Ajax and the Ajax-world of value and aspiration have their limitations in point of sympathy and insight; and the sense of these limitations is in part conveyed to us by means of the figure of Odysseus. Yet to imagine, as some writers have done, that the structure of the play is a polarity, so to speak, between Ajax and Odysseus is surely a distortion. The major dramatic subject, the weight and heft of it, is Ajax. The greatness of his demand upon life is the thing that we must, above all, be made to feel; and Sophocles places this theme before us by the full dramatization he gives of Ajax' suffering and resolution, of the dismay and pathetic dependence of those around him, and of their desolation when his protection is removed.

Sophocles' version of the myth is not original with him; he chose it from among the epic treatments which were already familiar. It is interesting, though, that he chose the version of the story which is most discreditable to Ajax. Pindar, writing a generation before Sophocles, follows a different version in which there is no hint of any attempt by Ajax to murder the Greek chieftains, no lunacy, and no assault upon the livestock. Ajax is simply filled with chagrin because of his disappointment and falls upon his sword. This version suited Pindar's artistic purpose very well: it provided him with a single arresting picture of outraged merit which could serve for a telling allusion and no more. For a dramatist, though, there were richer possibilities in the ghastlier version of the story which emphasized Ajax' criminality and disgrace. In choosing this version Sophocles incurred one serious embarrassment: his hero has *ex hypothesi* been guilty of a foul and treacherous attempt to assassinate the men who have wronged him, and in the prosecution of his plan he has come to grief in a most unseemly way. Sophocles surmounts the difficulty with his usual dexterity. He contrives in the main to make us lose sight of Ajax' criminality, while making of his ignominy a capital dramatic resource. The disclosure of Ajax in his tent, fouled by the animals he has insanely tormented and killed, is more than a powerful *coup de théâtre;* it is a fearful and summary image of total degradation not merely of heroic, but of all human, value. The process by which this image is transformed and Ajax' disaster irradiated by his recovery of heroic strength and human relatedness is the true action of the play.

This process is already well begun by the end of the long scene in which Ajax is disclosed among the slaughtered animals. The scene ends harshly, and, indeed, it is marked throughout by a certain acerbity. Nevertheless, out of his chagrin and misery Ajax is able to reaffirm some part of his former image of himself: rather than endure disgrace, he is resolved to die. There is a moment of tenderness for Eurysaces, none at all for Tecmessa; and even the address to Eurysaces, one feels, is an uncompromising assertion of the quality ot Ajax more than a response to the child.

In the next scene he appears an altered man. Not wholly so: his purpose is unchanged. But he discovers in himself, rather to his surprise, a softening of his former harshness. He is touched now by the plight of his wife and child; they must be deceived, so that he may have an opportunity of doing in peace what he has to do; but he deceives them tenderly, expressing his true intentions, but in ambiguous words which they are bound to misunderstand. Thus the speech is a farewell to them, while at the same time it expresses a new attitude in him. His suicide is not to be a frantic gesture of despair: it will be performed composedly, on the seashore, and, when the act is done, he, or something of him, will be saved (*sesômenon*). The softening of temper which this scene registers is therefore a necessary step in the development of the drama; and the splendid lines in which Ajax compares the softening of his own severity to the yielding of the great stern things in Nature before their gentler opposites have a deep psychological appropriateness.

The scenes which now follow are an impressive example of Sophocles' skill in dramatic organization. As Ajax leaves, sword in hand, bent as we know upon suicide, the Chorus break into an ecstatic song of joy, for they have been deceived by Ajax' words no less than Tecmessa and Eurysaces. At once the messenger arrives with news of the alarming prognostications of Calchas: if Ajax has left his tent, there is no hope for him. Joy and relief are now replaced by terror; Tecmessa understands that she has been deceived; and she and the Chorus in great agitation leave the scene, in haste to forestall Ajax' death.

But Ajax appears, calmly making his preparations (we understand that the scene has changed, as it does sometimes, though rarely, in Greek tragedy—we are now in the place Ajax has chosen by the shore). His death speech is long, eloquent, and handsome. He prays for a quiet death and for his body to be discovered first by Teucer; he calls the Sun-God to carry the news to his home, and the Erinyes to pursue his enemies; and, lastly, he makes his farewell to the world above and his addresses to the world below. Athena is not present by even a mention to disturb the harmonious order of the scene. True, he does not forgive his enemies: to forgive your enemies when you are dying and they surviving is an impulse which lies outside the ethical universe of Sophocles, unless there is a hint of it, and that doubtful, in *Antigone*.

Upon this splendid and now silent solitude Tecmessa and the Chorus urgently break in: the search, the discovery, the broken-hearted cries of grief come rapidly, one upon the other. Those whom Ajax has left are now helpless. They are threatened in every conceivable way; they cannot vindicate Ajax or protect themselves. Only for us Tecmessa's beautiful words (which this translator is helpless to render) may express a portion of the response that seems to be appropriate. Evidently the drama cannot end here; and if Sophocles has not found an entirely happy solution to the problem of how to conclude it, that is not because no conclusion was necessary. Beyond question, we attend to the long wrangle between Teucer and the Atridae with a sense of diminished tragic feeling, not, however, for the reason that the question of Ajax' burial cannot concern us but because the mode selected or enforced upon Sophocles here, that of the set debate, entails a disastrous lowering of tone. The right argument for burial is Odysseus' argument, not Teucer's; and in the *Antigone* the heroine makes no corresponding defense of Polynices.

The *Ajax* has, then, its imperfections and defects. The role of Athena is perplexing, not to say fiendish. Sophocles ignores with perhaps somewhat too ready a skill our repugnance at Ajax' conduct. The wrangle at the end seems unduly prolonged and at times undignified. But all this counts for little in comparison with the admirable and central virtue of the *Ajax*, its sustained and noble affirmation of the heroic in human life, as expressed in Ajax himself, and its rendering in Tecmessa of the beauty of entire devotion.

In making this translation I have followed the text of Sir Richard Jebb.

CHARACTERS

Athena

Odysseus

Ajax

Chorus of Salaminian Sailors

Tecmessa

Messenger

Teucer

Menelaus

Agamemnon

AJAX

SCENE: *Before the "tent" of Ajax, a fairly considerable structure covered with canvas and equipped with a large principal door and a second door on the flank, which gives access to a lower lateral extension of the structure. As the play opens, the goddess Athena is revealed on a high platform which may be conveniently placed over the lateral extension of the tent. Odysseus enters and moves eagerly across the stage as though tracing footprints.*

Athena
> Odysseus, I have always seen and marked you
> Stalking to pounce upon your enemies;
> And now by the tent of Ajax, where he keeps
> Last place upon the shore, I find you busy
> Tracing and scanning these fresh tracks of his,
> New-printed on the sand, to guess if he's inside.
> You've coursed him like a keen Laconian hound.
> In fact, he has just come in. His head is moist with sweat,
> His murderous hands are moistened too. . . . But now   10
> You need not go on peering in—no, tell me,
> What is the reason for your eager search?
> For I have knowledge and can set you right.

Odysseus
> Voice of Athena, dearest utterance
> Of all the gods' to me—I cannot see you,
> And yet how clearly I can catch your words,
> That speak as from a trumpet's throat of bronze!
> You guess my purpose; I have been circling
> Steadily on the trail of a man I hate,
> Shield-bearing Ajax.   20
> He has done a thing—sometime last night it was—
> An act of staggering horror . . . aimed at us,

If it all can be believed; nothing about it
Is surely known—we are floundering in conjecture,
And I have volunteered to search it out.
This much is sure: we found not long ago
Our flocks and herds of captured beasts all ruined
And struck with havoc by some butchering hand.
Their guards were slaughtered with them. Everyone
Puts the blame of it on Ajax. One man saw him
Alone, bounding over the plain and carrying   30
A sword still wet with blood—this man informed me
And set me on the track. I leapt to the scent
At once; and partly I can trace it still,
Though partly, too, I'm baffled. How can these prints be his?
You come just as I need you. Now and always,
As heretofore, your hand shall be my guide.

Athena

I know, Odysseus;
Some time ago I felt your need and came
On the path to guard and help you in your chase.

Odysseus

Tell me, dear mistress: am I working to some purpose?

Athena

Yes, this is the man that did the things you speak of.

Odysseus

What motive, though, prompted that senseless hand?   40

Athena

He was aggrieved, because of Achilles' armor.

Odysseus

But why this wild assault upon the flocks?

Athena

Ah, he thought it was your murder that fouled his hands.

Odysseus

It was a stroke, then, aimed at the whole Greek army?

Athena
A successful one, if I had not been watchful.

Odysseus
What desperate daring nerved him to the thing?

Athena
In the night he was moving upon you, stealthily and alone.

Odysseus
Did he come close? Was he reaching near his goal?

Athena
To the very doors of the two supreme commanders.

Odysseus
And how did he check that hand that yearned for murder?   50

Athena
I checked him; I threw before his eyes
Obsessive notions, thoughts of insane joy,
To fall on the mingled droves of captured livestock,
The undistributed loot which the herdsmen had in charge.
He hit them,
Hewed out a weltering shambles of horned beasts,
Cleaving them down in a circle all around him.
Sometimes he thought he held the sons of Atreus
In his grip to kill them, and then again
His fancy would seize some other of the chiefs.
The man was wandering in diseased delusions;
I pressed him, urged him into the fatal net.
At last, when he was weary of the slaughter,   60
He hobbled the cattle that were still alive,
And the sheep, and brought them to his tent, thinking
It was men he had captured and not poor horned beasts.
And now he has them bound inside the lodge
And is tormenting them. But I shall show you
His madness in plain view. Take note of it;
Then you can publish it to all the Greeks.

(Odysseus shrinks back.)

Get a grip on your nerves and wait. It's no disaster
To see the man. I'll turn his glance away.   70
He'll never see you or know your face. Halloo!
You there, who are binding fast your captives' arms
With fetters, come outside! Ajax! Come out!

Odysseus

Athena, what can you be thinking of?
Don't call him out!

Athena

Quiet, now! No cowardice!

Odysseus

No, no, for heaven's sake!
I'd very much rather he stayed inside.

Athena

What are you afraid of? He was only a man before.

Odysseus

Yes, but he was my enemy and still is.

Athena

But to laugh at your enemies—
What sweeter laughter can there be than that?

Odysseus

It's enough for me if he stays just where he is.   80

Athena

You're afraid, then, to see a madman face to face?

Odysseus

Certainly if he were sane, I should never shrink from him.

Athena

No need to do so now. He will stand near you,
And yet not see you.

Odysseus

How is that possible, if he sees with the same eyes still?

Athena
　I can darken even the most brilliant vision.

Odysseus
　I know that a god's contriving may do anything.

Athena
　Be still, then, and remain right where you are.

Odysseus
　If I must, I must. But I wish I were anywhere but here!

Athena
　Ajax, I call you once again!
　Is this how much you care for your old ally?　　　　　90

> (*Ajax enters through the principal door of the tent, carrying a
> two-thonged leather whip.*)

Ajax
　Hail, Athena! Daughter of Zeus,
　Hail and welcome! How well you have stood by me!
　I shall deck you with trophies all of gold
　From the spoils of this hunting, in thanksgiving.

Athena
　Excellent. But tell me, did you dip
　Your blade well in the Greeks' blood?

Ajax
　I think I may boast as much. I don't deny it.

Athena
　Did you move your weaponed hand against the generals?

Ajax
　I don't think they will slight Ajax again.

Athena
　The men are dead, if I understand you correctly.

Ajax
　Dead they are. Let them rob my armor now!　　　　　100

Athena
> Tell me, please, what happened to Laertes' son?
> He didn't escape you?

Ajax
> Oho, that villainous sneak! You want to know where *he* is?

Athena
> Yes. Your adversary, you know. Odysseus.

Ajax
> He's sitting there inside, my sweetest prisoner.
> I don't intend for him to die just yet.

Athena
> What are you going to do first?

Aiax
> First bind him to the pole that props my barrack.

Athena
> Poor miserable man! What treatment will you give him?

Ajax
> Crimson his back with this whip first, then kill him.   110

Athena
> Poor wretch! In pity don't mistreat him so!

Ajax
> Have your way, goddess, in all else, and welcome.
> But that man's punishment shall not be changed.

Athena
> Well, then, if your good pleasure wills it so,
> Do execution, carry out all you have in mind.

Ajax
> I must be at my work. Goddess, I grant you this:
> Stand always my ally as you have today.

> > > > > > > > *(Exit.)*

Athena
> Do you see, Odysseus, how great the gods' power is?

Who was more full of foresight than this man,
Or abler, do you think, to act with judgment?   120

Odysseus

None that I know of. Yet I pity
His wretchedness, though he is my enemy,
For the terrible yoke of blindness that is on him.
I think of him, yet also of myself;
For I see the true state of all us that live—
We are dim shapes, no more, and weightless shadow.

Athena

Look well at this, and speak no towering word
Yourself against the gods, nor walk too grandly
Because your hand is weightier than another's,
Or your great wealth deeper founded. One short day   130
Inclines the balance of all human things
To sink or rise again. Know that the gods
Love men of steady sense and hate the proud.

                                                  (*Exeunt.*)
                        (*Enter the Chorus of Salaminian sailors.*)

Chorus

Son of Telamon, lord of the firm floor
Of Salamis, where the sea chafes and swirls,
Ajax, my lord,
When you are fortunate, I too feel gladness;
But when the fury of Zeus or the virulent
Slur of the Greeks' slander
Strikes you, I shrink in fear, and my eye
Like a bird's, like a dove's, shows terror.   140
Now out of this fading night
Come huge oppressive rumors of dismay,
Wretched and shameful;
For you, they say, in the dark went striding out
Over the horse-delighting grassland,
Swinging your bright sword, slaughtering and wasting
All that remained of booty,

Flocks and herds belonging to the host.
Such tales as these, whisperings and fabrications,
Odysseus is supplying to every ear,
And many believe him. For as he speaks of you,   150
His words win credit, and each new hearer
More than the teller relishes his chance
To insult at your distress.
Strike at a great man, and you will not miss;
But if one should bend such slander at me,
None would believe him. Envy stalks
After magnates of wealth and power;
Yet humble men without their princes
Are a frail prop for a fortress. They
Should be dependent upon the great,   160
And the great be upheld by lesser ones.
But the shallow cannot be taught these things—
They raise instead an ignorant clamor;
And against it we have no defense, my lord,
But you. When once they are out of your sight,
They screech like a gaggle of angry birds;
But fear of the huge falcon,
All of a sudden, I think,
If you should only appear,   170
Would make them cower and be still.

Strophe

Can it have been wild, bull-consorting Artemis
   That stirred you, evil Tale,
Mother of my disgrace, to move against the flocks?
   Was she angered perhaps for victory-dues unpaid,
   Or disappointed of rich captured arms,
   Or hunting recompense for a stag slain?
Or was it Enyalios, the bronze-cased Lord of War
   That blamed *our* lord's co-operant spear,
And spitefully paid him out in the night's error?   180

Antistrophe

For never, son of Telamon, of your own heart's prompting,
Would you so far have strayed
To fall upon the flocks. Yet Frenzy comes
When the gods will. Apollo and Zeus forfend
These tales be true that the Greeks are spreading!
·Yet if the high kings
Or Sisyphus' execrated son
Weave with false art a supposititious tale,   190
Guard us from that false speech—
Hide not, so, your face in your tent beside the sea.

Epode

Rise, up from the place
Where you sit so obdurate, forbearing to fight your cause,
While ruin flares toward heaven,
And your enemies' bold outrage
Freshens through all the glades
In a blast of ringing laughter and hard spite.
But I am fixed in my grief.   200

(*Enter Tecmessa from the tent.*)

Tecmessa

Mariners who serve with Ajax,
Our prince of the old and kingly line
Sprung from Athenian earth, we
Who care for him and his father's far-off home
Have cause indeed for grief;
For he, our great grim man of power, lies low,
And a troubling flood is on him.

Chorus

But what, succeeding to yesterday's
Load of wretchedness, has this night brought?
Tell us, daughter of Phrygian Teleutas;   210
For the valiant Ajax loves you,
And honors his spear-won bride—
Being near him, perhaps you have knowledge and can speak.

Tecmessa

But how shall I speak a thing that appalls my speech?
You shall hear too clearly of an accident
Awful as death.
Madness has seized our noble Ajax;
He has come to ignominy in the night.
What a sight is to be seen within the tent!
Victims, slain with his own hand, deep in blood,
As for an oracle, speakingly reveal him.   220

Chorus

   Strophe

You have vouched it true, then, that report of our fiery chief,
That tale we cannot bear, yet may not escape:
Huge it grows, and authoritative voices
Give it huge reinforcement. Oh, I fear
For that which is moving upon us. He will be done to death,
Our glorious prince, because
With frenzied hands and a dark sword he slew   230
Herds and their mounted guardians in a heap.

Tecmessa

Alas, then, it can only have been from there
That he brought those bound beasts home!
And some he slew on the tent's floor
Cleanly with a neck-cut; others he hacked asunder
With slashes at their ribs. But two special
White-footed rams he lifted up, shore off
One's head and the tip of its tongue, and cast them from him;
The other he bound upright against a pillar,   240
Seized a stout length of harness, made from it
A singing whip, two-thonged, to lash him with,
And, mid the blows, poured forth such awful curses
As no man, but some demon, must have taught him.

Chorus

   Antistrophe

Now is the time for a man to muffle his head

And over the land to urge his stealthy way,
Or else, sitting the thwarts to row,
To trust his life to a ship's swift course on the deep—   250
Such are the threats that the sons of Atreus, two in power,
Stir toward us. I am in dread to share
With him the blows and hurt of the killing stone;
For an awful thing to be near is the doom that holds him.

Tecmessa

No longer so. After the lightning
Flash and leap of the storm-wind,
He is calm. But now, being clear in mind,
He is freshly miserable. It is a painful thing
To look at your own trouble and know   260
That you yourself and no one else has made it.

Chorus

But still, if his fit is past, I should think he was lucky;
A seizure, once it is done with, matters less.

Tecmessa

If someone posed the question, which would you choose:
To grieve your friends while feeling joy yourself,
Or to be wretched with them, shares alike?

Chorus

The last, lady, is twice as bad a thing.

Tecmessa

We are ill no longer now, but merely ruined.

Chorus

What do you mean? I cannot understand you.   270

Tecmessa

Ajax, so long as the mad fit was on him,
Himself felt joy at all his wretchedness,
Though we, his sane companions, grieved indeed.
But now that he's recovered and breathes clear,
His own anguish totally masters him,

While we are no less wretched than before.
Is not this a redoubling of our grief?

Chorus

You are quite right. Lady, I wonder
If a fearful blow of God's anger may have hit him.
It is strange that he feels no happier sane than raving.   280

Tecmessa

Strange, perhaps. But the facts are as they are.

Chorus

How at the start did this catastrophe
Swoop down? Tell us: we share the pain of it.

Tecmessa

Indeed, you are partners and shall hear it all.
In the depth of night, after the evening flares
Had all gone out, Ajax, with sword in hand,
Went slowly groping toward the door, intent
Upon some pointless errand. I objected,
And said, "Ajax, what are you doing? Why
Do you stir? No messenger has summoned you: 290
You have heard no trumpet. Why, the whole army now's
    asleep!"
He answered briefly in a well-worn phrase,
"Woman, a woman's decency is silence."
I heard, and said no more; he issued forth alone.
I don't know what horrors occurred outside,
But when he came back in, he brought with him
A mass of hobbled bulls and shepherd dogs
And woolly captives. He struck the heads off some;
Others' he severed with an upward cut;
And some, held fast in bonds, he kept abusing
With words and blows, as though they were human beings—
And all the while he was vexing poor dumb beasts.   300
At length he darted out the door and spoke
Wild, rending words, directed toward some phantom,
Exulting with a harsh laugh *how he'd paid them,*
Odysseus and the sons of Atreus. Then

He sprang back in again, and somehow, slowly,
By painful stages came to his right mind.
And when he saw his dwelling full of Ruin,
He beat his head and bellowed. There he sat,
Wreckage himself among the wreck of corpses,
The sheep slaughtered; and in an anguished gripe
Of fist and fingernail he clutched his hair.   310
He sat so, without speaking, for some time;
Then finally spoke those fearful, threatening words—
What should befall me if I failed to say
What had befallen him: he asked me where he stood.
Friends, I was terrified by all he'd done,
And told him, simply, everything I knew.
Then he cried out—long wails of shattering pain,
Like none I ever heard from him before;
He always used to say such cries were base,
Marks of an abject spirit. His own way   320
Was not to cry aloud in his distress,
But low and muffled, like a roaring bull.
Now, though, quite overcome by his misfortune,
Refusing food and drink, he sits there motionless,
Relapsed among the beasts his iron brought down.
There are clear signs, too,
That he's aiming to do some dreadful thing; his words
And his lamentations both somehow suggest it.
Friends—this was the thing I came to ask of you—
Won't you come in and comfort him, if you can?
He is noble, and may listen to his friends.   330

Chorus
Honored Tecmessa, what a fearful frenzy,
By your account, his griefs have moved him to!

> (*Ajax inside the tent gives a heavy groan, which rises*
> *slowly almost to a shriek.*)

Tecmessa
Worse may be coming. Didn't you hear his voice,
Ajax', distorted in that ghastly cry?

(*Ajax groans again miserably.*)

Chorus

Either he still is mad, or else can't bear
The company his madness made around him

Ajax (within)

Boy! Where is my child?

Tecmessa

Dear God! Eurysaces, it's you he's calling.   340
What can he want? Where are you? What shall I do?

Ajax (within)

Teucer! Where are you? Where is my brother Teucer?
Will that raid of his last forever? And I here perishing!

Chorus

No, he seems to be sane. Open the door.
Perhaps seeing someone, though it's only us,
May help him to compose himself.

*Tecmessa (opens the door, revealing Ajax sitting dejectedly in the
    middle of slaughtered bulls and sheep)*

There, now you see.
You can judge for yourself the state of his affairs,
And how the man is too.

Ajax

Ah!
Loved mariners, my only friends,
Still faithful in the old proved way,
Look at this swirling tide of grief   350
   And the storm of blood behind it,
   Coursing around and round me.

Chorus

Horrible!
Tecmessa, what you told us was too true—
Insanity stands here revealed indeed!

Ajax

　　Antistrophe

Ah!

Stout hearts and skilful seamen,

Strong hands to move the oar,

I see no friend but you,

No, none, to ease my pain. 360

For God's sake, help me die!

Chorus

Hush! Check those awful words!

Don't seek a worse cure for an ill disease,

And make your pain still heavier than it is.

Ajax

　　Strophe

Here I am, the bold, the valiant,

Unflinching in the shock of war,

A terrible threat to unsuspecting beasts.

Oh! what a mockery I have come to! What indignity!

Tecmessa

Ajax, my lord and master,

I beg you not to say such things.

Ajax

Go away! Take yourself out of my sight! 370

　　　　　　　　　　　　　　(He groans.)

Chorus

In God's name, be more gentle and more temperate.

Ajax

How could I be so cursed?

To let those precious villains out of my hand,

And fall on goats and cattle,

On crumpled horns and splendid flocks,

Shedding their dark blood!

Chorus

The thing is done. Why wail about it now?

You cannot make it undone.

Ajax

   Antistrophe

Ah, yes, son of Laertes
Spying everywhere, always 380
The tool of every mischief,
Filthiest scoundrel of all the army,
What a huge laugh you're laughing now, what gloating!

Chorus

It is God's giving if we laugh or weep.

Ajax

Ah, if I could just once catch sight of him!
Crushed as I am, I'd . . .

Chorus (interrupting)

My lord, no blustering words.
Your situation's desperate; can't you see?

Ajax

Zeus, father of my fathers,
How can I strike them down,
That devious, hateful rogue and the two joined kings, 390
And last find death myself?

Tecmessa

When you pray that prayer, why, pray for my death too;
Why should I live when once my lord is dead?

Ajax

   Strophe

O
Darkness that is my light,
Murk of the underworld, my only brightness,
Oh, take me to yourself to be your dweller,
Receive and keep me. I cannot look
To any of the race of gods for help,
Being no longer worthy,
Nor yet to humankind. 400
But the martial goddess, daughter of Zeus, cruelly works my ruin.

Where shall a man flee?
Where shall I turn for refuge?
All that I was has perished
With these poor creatures here,
And I abused by a fool's dream
Of stalk and capture. Friends, friends,
The massed army will take my life
With bloody insistent blows.

Tecmessa

What wretchedness, to hear a brave man speak   410
Such words as once he would not deign to use!

Ajax

   Antistrophe

O
Sounding straits of the sea
Caves by the sea's edge, meadows on the shore,
Long and long have you kept me here in Troyland;
But now I shall not revive again, never again—
A man of sense may know it.
Scamander, neighboring river, gentle to Greeks,   420
You shall no longer see this man,
Such a man (let me now speak my boast)
As Troy ne'er saw the like of, not in all
The warlike host that hither came from Greece.
But now in dishonor
I lie abject.

Chorus

I cannot bid you stifle such great griefs;
And yet it is agony to hear your grieving.

Ajax

Agony. Who would have thought my name and fortune   430
Could square so well together! My name is Ajax:
Agony is its meaning. And my fortunes
Are cause indeed for an agony of wailing,

Cause and enough twice over. How my father,
Fighting here under Ida long ago,
Won with his sword the loveliest prize of all
For valor, and sweet praise at his return;
But I, his son,
Coming in my turn with a force no less
To this same land of Troy, no less than he a champion,
Nor less deserving, yet am left an outcast,
Shamed by the Greeks, to perish as I do!   440
And yet I seem to know this simple truth:
If the bestowing of the famous armor
Had rested with Achilles while he lived,
To give them as a war-prize to the bravest,
No rival then would have filched them from my hands;
But now the sons of Atreus have contrived
That a man of most dishonest mind should have them,
Pushing my claims aside. And I say this,
That if my eyes and mind had not leapt whirling
Wide from my aim, those two would never again
Cheat anyone with their awards and ballots!
But, instead, the fierce-eyed, overpowering   450
Daughter of Zeus, just then as I was readying
My hand and plot against them, set me sprawling,
Distraught and frenzied, and I dipped my hands
In the blood of beasts like these. And now they are laughing
And triumph in their clear escape, which I
Never intended for them. But when God
Strikes harm, a worse man often foils his better.
And now, Ajax—what is to be done now?
I am hated by the gods, that's plain; the Greek camp hates me:
Troy and the ground I stand upon detest me.
Shall I go, then, from this place where the ships ride,   460
Desert the Atridae, and cross the Aegean to my home?
But when I'm there,
What countenance can I show my father Telamon?
How will he ever stand the sight of me

If I come before him naked, armed with no glory,
When he himself won chaplets of men's praise?
That won't bear thinking of. Well, then,
Shall I make a rush against the walls of Troy,
Join with them all in single combat, do
Some notable exploit, and find my death in it?
But that might give some comfort to the sons of Atreus.
No. I must find some better way entirely—   470
An enterprise which will prove to my old father
That the son of his loins is not by breed a weakling.
It's a contemptible thing to want to live forever
When a man's life gives him no relief from trouble.
What joy is there in a long file of days,
Edging you forward toward the goal of death,
Then back again a little? I wouldn't give much for a man
Who warms himself with the comfort of vain hopes.
Let a man nobly live or nobly die
If he *is* a nobleman: I have said what I had to say.   480

Chorus

Ajax, no one could ever call those words
Spurious or alien to you. They are your own heart's speech.
Pause, though, a moment; put aside these thoughts;
And give your friends a chance to win you over.

Tecmessa

Ajax, my master, life knows no harder thing
Than to be at the mercy of compelling fortune.
I, for example, was born of a free father;
If any man in Phrygia was lordly and prosperous, he was.
Now I'm a slave. Such, it seems, was the gods' will,
And the will of your strong hand. But since I've come   490
To share your bed with you, my thoughts are loyal
To you and yours. And I beg you
In the holy name of Zeus who guards your hearth-fire,
And by your bed, in which you have known peace with me,
Don't give me up to hear the harsh speech

Of your enemies and bow to it, their bondslave.
For this is certain: the day you die
And by your death desert me, that same day
Will see me outraged too, forcibly dragged
By the Greeks, together with your boy, to lead a slave's life.
And then some one of the lord class,   500
With a lashing word, will make his hateful comment:
"There she is, Ajax' woman;
He was the greatest man in the whole army.
How enviable her life was then, and now how slavish!"
Some speech in that style. And my ill fate
Will be driving me before it, but these words
Will be a reproach to you and all your race.
Ajax, revere your father; do not leave him
In the misery of his old age—and your mother,
Shareholder in many years, revere her too!
She prays the gods for your safe return, how often!
And last, dear lord, show pity to your child.   510
Robbed of his infant nurture, reft of you,
To live his life out under the rule of guardians
Not kind nor kindred—what a wretchedness
You by your death will deal to him and me!
And I no longer have anywhere to look for help,
If not to you. My country was destroyed
Utterly by your spear, and another fate
Brought down my mother and my father too,
To dwell in death with Hades. Then what fatherland
Shall I ever have but you? Or what prosperity?
You are my only safety. O my lord,
Remember even me. A man ought to remember   520
If he has experienced any gentle thing.
Kindness it is that brings forth kindness always.
But when a man forgets good done to him
And the recollection of it slips away,
How shall I any longer call him noble?

Chorus
    Ajax, I wish you could have pity in your heart
    As I do. For then you might approve her words.

Ajax
    Well, she can certainly count on my approval
    If only she sets her mind to do as I bid her.

Tecmessa
    Dearest Ajax, I will be all obedience.

Ajax
    Then bring me my child and let me see him.   530

Tecmessa
    It was only because of my fears that I removed him.

Ajax
    In all this terrible business? Or do I understand you?

Tecmessa
    For fear the poor little one might come in your way and be killed.

Ajax
    Yes, that would have been worthy of my evil genius.

Tecmessa
    At all events I took care that it shouldn't happen.

Ajax
    You did well and deserve credit for your foresight.

Tecmessa
    Is there anything, then, you want me to do for you?

Ajax
    Yes. Let me speak to my boy and see his face.

Tecmessa
    He's not far off. The servants are looking after him.

Ajax
    Why doesn't he come at once, then?   540

Tecmessa
    Eurysaces! Your father is calling for you.

(*To one of the servants inside.*)

You bring him! you have him by the hand.

Ajax

Is he coming? Doesn't he hear your words?

(*Enter, from the side door, a servant leading
Eurysaces by the hand.*)

Tecmessa

Here he is. See, the servant's bringing him.

Ajax

Lift him up, lift him to me. He won't be frightened,
Even by seeing this fresh-butchered gore,
Not if he really is my son. Break in
The colt straight off to his father's rugged ways;
Train him to have a nature like his sire.
My boy, have better luck than your father had,　　　　550
Be like him in all else; and you will not be base.
You know, even now I somewhat envy you:
You have no sense of all this misery.
Not knowing anything's the sweetest life—
Ignorance is an evil free from pain—
Till the time comes when you learn of joy and grief.
And when you come to that,
Then you must show your father's enemies
What sort of a man you are, and what man's son.
Till then feed on light breezes, basking
In the tenderness of your young life, giving your mother joy.
For rest assured, the Greeks will not offer you outrage　　　　560
Or hatefully insult you, even when we are parted.
I leave you a strong warden at the door,
Teucer. He will protect and rear you up
And stint you nothing, even though now he's far away,
Gone on a distant raid in enemy country.
—You, men at arms and seafarers, my followers,
I enjoin this act of kindness on you all:

Pass on my command to Teucer; bid him take
My boy here to my home, present him
To Telamon and my mother, Eriboea,
And let him tend and nourish their old age   570
With constancy, till at the last they find
Their dark apartments with the god below.
As for my arms—
I say no arbiter of the Greeks shall set them
As a prize of competition for the army;
Certainly my destroyer shall not. Rather
You, my boy, take from me this great weapon
From which you have your name, Eurysaces;
Hold and direct it by its stalwart strap,
This sevenfold-oxhide-thick unbreachable shield.
The rest of my armor shall be buried with me.
But there's enough. Come, take the child quickly;
Close up the house. And let there be no wailing
Here out of doors. Lord, what a plaintive creature   580
Womankind is! (*He goes inside.*) Make fast, and hurry!
No good physician quavers incantations
When the malady he's treating needs the knife.

Chorus
I'm terrified by your eager urgency,
And take no comfort in your whetted tongue.

Tecmessa
Ajax, my lord, what is your mind bent upon?

Ajax
Don't probe and question! It becomes you to submit.

Tecmessa
How my heart falters! Ajax, by your child
And by the gods I beg you, don't be our betrayer!

Ajax
You're growing tedious. Don't you know by now
That I owe the gods no service any more?   590

Tecmessa

What impious words!

Ajax

                  Reprove those who hear you.

Tecmessa

And will you not relent?

Ajax

                  You've said too much already.

Tecmessa

My lord, it is my fear that speaks!

Ajax (*to the servants*)

Shut the doors at once!

Tecmessa

In the gods' name, soften!

Ajax

                  You have a foolish thought
If you think at this late date to school my nature.

        (*The doors are shut; Tecmessa remains quietly crouching
          or kneeling beside them. A servant stands behind her,
                holding Eurysaces by the hand.*)

Chorus

  Strophe

O splendid Salamis, my heart recalls,
Blest island, where you lie
At peace in the surf's pounding,
Radiant in all men's sight and prized forever.
But Time has grown old since I   600
Have kept this wretched bivouac under Ida,
Losing count of the months' lapse,
Feeling the slow abrasion;
And dark is my thought's forecast:
Shall I win, shall I yet come, shall my coming be
To the somber and detested house of Death?

Antistrophe
And now wretchedly I must face
A new bout, for Ajax, ill to cure,   610
Sits by, and holy madness is his consort.
You sent him forth, fair island, in a time long past,
A warrior brilliant among warriors. Now
He keeps his thoughts' flock in loneliness
And grieves his friends.
And the works of war that once his strong hands did
Are fallen, fallen,
Undear, unfriended by the friendless kings.   620

Strophe
I think, too,
Of his mother, with the white of age upon her:
Surely when the news of his mind's ravage
Is brought to her (O lamentable! lamentable!)
Not like the poor lorn nightingale
In a low sob will she utter her heart's anguish,
But high, rending strains will break from her,   630
The breast be beaten, and the tresses torn.

Antistrophe
Better if he
Were hidden in Hades, now his mind is gone;
For though his proud lineage
Excelled his warlike peers,
He keeps no more the steady heart we knew,
But ranges in extravagant madness. Wretched father!   640
What a hard word you must hear! Calamity
Fallen upon your son, such as no other
Of all his race has borne, but only he.

(*Enter Ajax from the tent with a sword in his hand.*)

Ajax
Strangely the long and countless drift of time
Brings all things forth from darkness into light,
Then covers them once more. Nothing so marvelous

That man can say it surely will not be—
Strong oath and iron intent come crashing down.
My mood, which just before was strong and rigid,   650
No dipped sword more so, now has lost its edge—
My speech is womanish for this woman's sake;
And pity touches me for wife and child,
Widowed and lost among my enemies.
But now I'm going to the bathing place
And meadows by the sea, to cleanse my stains,
In hope the goddess' wrath may pass from me.
And when I've found a place that's quite deserted,
I'll dig in the ground, and hide this sword of mine,
Hatefulest of weapons, out of sight. May Darkness
And Hades, God of Death, hold it in their safe keeping.   660
For never, since I took it as a gift
Which Hector, my great enemy, gave to me,
Have I known any kindness from the Greeks.
I think the ancient proverb speaks the truth:
An enemy's gift is ruinous and no gift.
Well, then,
From now on this will be my rule: Give way
To Heaven, and bow before the sons of Atreus.
They are our rulers, they must be obeyed.
I must give way, as all dread strengths give way,
In turn and deference. Winter's hard-packed snow
Cedes to the fruitful summer; stubborn night   670
At last removes, for day's white steeds to shine.
The dread blast of the gale slackens and gives
Peace to the sounding sea; and Sleep, strong jailer,
In time yields up his captive. Shall not I
Learn place and wisdom? Have I not learned this,
Only so much to hate my enemy
As though he might again become my friend,
And so much good to wish to do my friend,   680
As knowing he may yet become my foe?
Most men have found friendship a treacherous harbor.

Enough: this will be well.
                        You, my wife, go in
And fervently and continually pray the gods
To grant fulfilment of my soul's desire.
And you, my friends, heed my instructions too,
And when he comes, deliver this to Teucer:
Let him take care for me and thought for you.
Now I am going where my way must go;   690
Do as I bid you, and you yet may hear
That I, though wretched now, have found my safety.

(*Ajax goes out through the wing; Tecmessa
and Eurysaces go into the tent.*)

Chorus
    Strophe
I shudder and thrill with joy,
I leap and take wings—Lord Pan!
Come to me over the sea
From your huge, snow-buffeted mountain,
From the long, harsh ridge of Cyllênê.
I would dance, I am bent upon dancing!
Teach me (you are the gods' teacher
And yourself you need no teacher)
Wild, high, excited dances, Mysian, Cnosian—   700
I would dance, I am bent upon dancing!
And over the open sea
Come to me in the clear light,
Apollo, Lord of Delos—
Be with me in kindness always.

    Antistrophe
The harsh god has taken
His siege of grief from our eyes.
(I exult with love and with joy!)
Once again, Zeus,
King of the bright air, your perfect daylight
May bathe our skimming seacraft in its whiteness.

Ajax forgets his pain, 710
And now, with holy rite and due observance,
Once more knows reverent thoughts.
Great Time makes all things dim,
And nothing seems beyond the verge of speech,
Since Ajax has resolved
(Amazing!) his heart's fierceness and his stern
Strife with the sons of Atreus.

(*Enter a Messenger.*)

Messenger

Friends, I would deliver this news first to you:
Teucer has just come back from rugged Mysia. 720
No sooner did he reach headquarters than
The whole Greek army gathered to abuse him.
They'd seen him coming quite a long way off
And, when he arrived, stood around him in a circle,
Jabbing at him with jeers from every side.
Called him the brother of a lunatic
And traitor to the army; threatened him
With stoning to a torn and bloody death.
So far they went that eager fingers then
Had plucked forth swords from scabbards, but the thing, 730
Just as it hurried toward its uttermost,
Grew quiet at the elders' peaceful words.
But where is Ajax? I must speak my charge,
And cannot do it but to my lord himself.

Chorus

He is not here. He went away just now;
His heart is changed, and bends to bear the yoke
Of a changed purpose.

Messenger

            May God help him then!
Perhaps the man that sent me was too slow
In sending, or I lingered on the way.

Chorus

What is so urgent? Why do you think you're late? 740

Messenger
 Teucer declared the man should not go out,
 But stay indoors, till he himself arrives.

Chorus
 He *has* gone out, though—seeking his truest good.
 He wants to be relieved of the gods' anger.

Messenger
 A very foolish and misguided thought,
 If Calchas can foresee events at all!

Chorus
 What are you saying? What can you know of it?

Messenger
 This much I know—I happened to be near:
 For Calchas rose and left the kingly circle   750
 And came to speak with Teucer privately
 Without the Atridae; gently he placed his hand
 In Teucer's own, and urged and pled with him
 To use all shifts to keep his brother safe
 Under his tent-roof, and confine him there
 Throughout the length of this now present day,
 If ever he wished to see him alive again.
 Only for this one day, the prophet said,
 Will the Goddess Athena vex him with her anger.
 "Wherever men forget their mere man's nature,
 Thinking a thought too high, they have no use
 Of their huge bulk and boldness, but they fall   760
 On most untoward disasters sent by Heaven.
 Ajax, even when he first set out from home,
 Proved himself foolish, when his father gave him
 His good advice at parting. 'Child,' he said,
 'Resolve to win, but always with God's help.'
 But Ajax answered with a senseless boast:
 'Father, with God's help even a worthless man
 Could triumph. I propose, without that help,
 To win my prize of fame.' In such a spirit

He boasted. And when once Athena stood   770
Beside him in the fight, urging him on
To strike the enemy with his deadly hand,
He answered then, that second time, with words
To shudder at, not speak: 'Goddess,' he said,
'Go stand beside the other Greeks; help them.
For where I bide, no enemy will break through.'
These were the graceless words which won for him
The goddess' wrath; they kept no human measure.
But if he lives this day out, then perhaps,
With God's help, we may be his saviors still."
This was the seer's message. Teucer rose   780
At once and sent me off, bearing you these
Instructions, with strict charge to keep them. But
If Ajax has deprived me of my hope,
His life is done. Else Calchas has no art.

Chorus

Tecmessa, I think you were born for every misery.
Come and attend to this man's fearful story.

(*As though to himself.*)

The razor grazes near, and I feel no comfort.

(*Enter Tecmessa, carrying Eurysaces.*)

Tecmessa

I have only just found respite from that other
Siege of calamities. What new alarm is this?

Chorus

Listen to the message this man has brought.
It concerns Ajax, and it sounds grim.   790

Tecmessa

Alas, what *is* your message? Not that we're ruined?

Messenger

As to your own case, I can't say. But if Ajax
Has left his tent, there is not much hope for him.

Tecmessa

But he *has* gone out. I tremble in suspense
To know your meaning.

Messenger

Teucer sends strict directions that Ajax
Must be kept under the cover of his tent
And not permitted to go out alone.

Tecmessa

But where *is* Teucer? And why does he say this?

Messenger

He has just returned. And he apprehends
That Ajax' going out will be his ruin.

Tecmessa

Heaven help us! Who was the man that told him this?   800

Messenger

Calchas the prophet. He warned us to be on our guard
All day, for it brings him either life or death.

Tecmessa

Alas, friends, stand between me and my doom!
Hurry, some of you, and bring Teucer quickly;
The rest divide—let one group search the eastward
And one the westward bendings of the shore,
To trace his dangerous path. I can see now
That I have been beguiled of his intent
And exiled from his kindness which I knew.
But oh! my child, what shall I do? Not stay,
But join the search as far as my strength supports me.   810
Come, let's be at the work! No time to linger,
If we aim to save a man that's bent on death.

Chorus

I am ready. More than my words shall show it.
You'll find me swift of foot and prompt in action.

*(Tecmessa leaves Eurysaces with the attendants and goes
hurriedly out. Meanwhile, the Chorus divides into
two equal semichoruses and exits through the
side entrances.)*

SCENE: *An empty place by the seashore. No scenery need be indicated
except some bushes, behind which Ajax' body will fall. His preparations, though, should be largely visible to the audience. Enter
Ajax.*

Ajax *(carefully fixes the sword in place, tamps down the ground, and feels
the edge of the blade)*

He's firm in the ground, my Slayer. And his cut
(If I have time even for this reflection)
Should now be deadliest. For, first, the sword
Was Hector's gift, a token of guest-friendship,
And he of all guest-friends my bitterest foe;
Here, too, it stands, lodged in this hostile ground
Of Troy, its edge made new with iron-devouring stone.   820
And, last, I've propped it, so, with careful handling,
To help me soon and kindly to my death.
This preparation I have made. And now,
Making my invocation, as is right,
I call first, Zeus, on you. Grant me a little thing:
Rouse up some messenger for me, to bear
The news of my disaster first to Teucer,
So that he first may gently lift me up
When I have fallen on this reeking sword.
I would not have some enemy spy me out
And cast me forth, a prize for birds and dogs.   830
Grant me, O Zeus, this one thing. And do you,
Hermes, Conductor to the Nether World,
Waft me with one swift unconvulsive leap
Upon this piercing blade. And you, Dread Furies—
You who are ever maidens and do watch
Above all fates and sufferings of men—

Come with long strides, my helpers; mark my end,
How Atreus' sons have brought me to my ruin,
And sweep upon them for their ruin too.
They see me falling now by my own hand;   840
So too by loved and kindred hand may they!
Go, swift and punishing Erinyes,
Taste the whole army's blood, and spare them nothing.
And you that drive your chariot up the steep
Of Heaven, Lord Helios—when you next shall see
My own dear country, check your golden reins,
And bring the tale of my distressful death
To my old father and to her that nursed me.
Poor mother! When she hears this wretched word,   850
How her grief's note will quaver through the town!
But I must leave this idle vein of weeping
And set about my business with some speed.
Strong God of Death, attend me now and come.
And yet I shall converse with you hereafter
And know you in the world below. But you,
Sweet gleam of daylight now before my eyes,
And Sun-God, splendid charioteer, I greet you
For this last time and never any more.
O radiance, O my home and hallowed ground
Of Salamis, and my father's hearth, farewell!   860
And glorious Athens, and my peers and kin
Nurtured with me, and here all springs and streams,
My nurses, you that wet the plains of Troy,
Farewell! This last word Ajax gives to you;
The rest he keeps, to speak among the dead.

(He falls on the sword and collapses behind the bushes.
Enter, from one wing, the first of the two divisions
of the Chorus.)

First Semichorus
Toil breeds toil upon toil,
Where, where have I not searched?

No place knows that I share its secret.
Listen! What noise was that? 870

(Enter, from the other wing, the other division
of the Chorus.)

Second Semichorus
  Only us, your shipmates.

First Semichorus
  What luck?

Second Semichorus
  From the ships to westward we've scanned all the ground.

First Semichorus
  And discovered . . . ?

Second Semichorus
  Labor enough; no trace of him we seek.

First Semichorus
  Nor yet on the path to eastward, facing the sunrise:
  No sign of him at all.

(The two halves of the Chorus unite.)

Chorus
  What struggling fisherman
  Of those that seek their haul
  With labor in the hours of sleep; 880
  What nymph of mountain side
  Or seaward-rolling river
  Might see the grim man
  Wandering somewhere and cry out to me?
  I wish one would! For surely
  It's a hard thing that I must range and plod,
  With never a fair course
  To bring me near my goal;
  But I cannot see the afflicted man's faint trace. 890

(Tecmessa has entered from the wing and reached the
place where Ajax has fallen. She is still invisible,
though, being masked by the bushes.)

« 252 »

Tecmessa
  Oh! No! No!

Chorus
  Whose is that harsh cry bursting from the copse?

Tecmessa
  Oh! Oh!

Chorus
  It is she, I see her now, the poor captive wife,
  Tecmessa. She is lost in lamentation.

Tecmessa
  Friends, I am ruined, overwhelmed, undone.

Chorus
  What is the matter?

Tecmessa
  Here at my feet lies Ajax, newly slain.
  His fallen body enfolds and hides the sword.

Chorus
  Oh, now I shall not win home!   900
  You have dealt me death, my lord,
  Your poor unhappy shipmate.
  —And I feel for her, poor wretched one, poor wife!

Tecmessa
  He is dead, dead. We can only weep for him.

Chorus
  Whose hand helped him to his fate?

Tecmessa
  His own hand and act. It's plain to see.
  This blade, packed in the ground,
  On which he fell, declares it.

Chorus
  How blind I was! And you bled alone, your friends not guarding!   910
  I was all deaf and stupid, totally heedless.

Let me see him,
Rugged and ill-starred Ajax, where he lies.

Tecmessa

You *must* not see him! I will cover him
With this enfolding garment from all sight.

(*She removes her own mantle, which should be ample
and rectangular, and covers him.*)

Surely no one who loved him could endure
To see the foam at his nostrils and the spout
Of darkening blood from the wound his own hand made.
Alas, what shall I do? Which of your friends   920
Will bear you up? Where's Teucer? Oh, may he come in time
To give fit tendance to his fallen brother!
Ajax! To be so great, and suffer this!
Even your enemies, I think, might weep for you.

Chorus

You were bound, hard spirit,
Bound in the end (it is clear now)
To work the term of your luckless
Life's share of affliction, that vast journey.
What could they mean but that,
The groans your fierce heart uttered
By night and in the sunlight,   930
Fraught with hate
For the sons of Atreus,
Fraught with a mind for harm?
That time was to be a great
Inaugural time of sorrows
When the strife was set for soldiership
Over the priceless armor.

Tecmessa

Oh! The pain of it!

Chorus

A noble grief, I know, goes to the heart.

Tecmessa
  Oh! Oh!

Chorus
  I don't wonder, lady,
  That you cry out, and again cry out, your grief,   940
  Deprived so recently of one so dear.

Tecmessa
  You may conjecture that;
  I know and feel it all too certainly.

Chorus
  That is true.

Tecmessa
  Poor little one! What a yoke of servitude
  We go to! What hard taskmasters!

Chorus
  They are ruthless indeed, the two sons of Atreus,
  If they do the unspeakable thing
  You have spoken in your distress:
  God forbid!

Tecmessa
  Even in what we suffer I see the gods' hand.   950

Chorus
  Yes, they have given an overload of grief.

Tecmessa
  I think Pallas, the dreadful goddess, has bred
  This pain, perhaps for her favorite, Odysseus.

Chorus
  That waiting, laboring man,
  How he insults in his black heart!
  He mocks our madding griefs
  With loud laughter, bitter to bear,
  And the twin kings hear and join him.   960

Tecmessa

Well, let them laugh their laughter and exult
In Ajax' downfall. They didn't want him living;
Perhaps, now he is dead, they will yearn for him,
When the fighting presses. Ignorant men
Don't know what good they hold in their hands until
They've flung it away. His death was a bitterer thing to me
Than sweet to them; but for himself a happiness.
For he won his great desire, the death he looked for.
Why should those others mock him any more?
His death concerns the gods, not them at all.   970
Let Odysseus think of this and make his empty insult.
For them there is no Ajax; mine is gone,
But not the grief and loss he leaves to me.

(Teucer is heard in the wing.)

Teucer

O God! God!

Chorus

Hush! For I think it's Teucer's voice I hear,
And his cry goes straight to the mark of this disaster.

(Teucer enters.)

Teucer

O my dear brother Ajax, have you come
To grief, as this strong rumor says you have?

Chorus

He is dead, Teucer. Know the simple truth.

Teucer

Then my ill-luck is bearing heavily down!   980

Chorus

It is true.

Teucer

      Miserable!

Chorus
  You may well groan.

Teucer

     Rash and calamitous!

Chorus
  Yes, Teucer.

Teucer

    The grief comes sharp. But where
Is the little one? Where in the whole width
Of Troyland shall I look for him?

Chorus

        He is alone

  By the tents.

Teucer (to Tecmessa)
  Go quickly, then,
  Quickly, and bring him here. Some enemy else
  May snatch him, as one would a lion-whelp
  Torn from its mother. Hurry and lose no time!
  When a man lies dead and cannot help himself,
  The world delights to mock and injure him.

              (Exit Tecmessa.)

Chorus
  Teucer, that was his last command to you,   990
  To take care for his child, as you are doing.

Teucer
  This sight of all sights that my eyes have seen
  To me is harshest, and no other road,
  Of all my feet have taken, so has grieved
  My soul as this, dear Ajax, which I took
  In haste to seek the truth and trace it home
  When first I heard the news of your disaster.
  It was sharp news, and sped through all the army
  As if some God had sent it: you were dead.
  And when I heard it, still a long way off,   1000

I groaned with inward misery; now I see;
It is true, and it destroys me.
Ah, me!
Come and uncover; let me see the worst.

(He uncovers the face of Ajax.)

Hard, bitter countenance, lines of fierce resolve,
How can I look at you? Oh, what a crop
Of anguish you have sown for me in death!
Where can I go? Who ever will receive me,
Now I have failed to help you in your need?
Old Telamon is your father, and mine too:
No doubt he'll welcome me and beam on me
When I come home without you. Very likely!   1010
He's not much given to smiling, even when things go well.
What will he not say? What reproach will he spare me?
Bastard and *gotten by the war-spear, coward,*
Nerveless deserter and *abandoner*—
Of you, dear Ajax! or perhaps suggest
I did it out of treachery, so that I
Might get your house and kingship by your death.
These will be that harsh old man's reproaches:
Age makes him morose and stirs him up
To causeless anger. In the end I'll be
Cast into exile and denied my country,
A slave in his account and not a freeman.   1020
At home those are my expectations; here in Troy
My enemies are numerous, my help small.
Such are the benefits your death has brought me.
What shall I do? How shall I disengage you,
Brother, from off this bitter, gleaming spike,
Your murderer, by whose cut you gasped your life out?
Do you see how in time Hector, though dead,
Was to destroy you? Only consider this
Amazing thing, the fortunes of two men:
The girdle Hector had as Ajax' gift
Was that which dragged him from the chariot rails,   1030

Clamping his flesh and grating him until
He swooned in death; this sword Hector gave Ajax,
Who perished on it with a death-fraught fall.
Did not a Fury beat this weapon out?
And was it not Aidoneus, that grim craftsman,
Who made that other one? In my opinion,
This was the gods' contrivance, like all other
Destinies of men, for the gods weave them all;
But if anyone should find my thought at fault,
Let him keep his opinion, and I mine.

Chorus

Cut short your speech, and quickly consider   1040
How best to hide him in some sort of grave,
And what you must say next. I see a man
Coming, our enemy, to laugh, I think,
Like one who means us harm, at our misfortunes.

Teucer

Which chief of the army is it that you see?

Chorus

Menelaus, the one we made this voyage to gratify.

Teucer

I see him now.
At closer range he's not hard to distinguish.

(Enter Menelaus, attended by two heralds.)

Menelaus

You, there! I tell you not to lift that corpse
Nor bury it, but leave it where it is.

Teucer

And why the expense of this somewhat grand announcement?

Menelaus

My pleasure, and the High Command's decree.   1050

Teucer

Perhaps you'd care to give some justification for it.

Menelaus

Listen, then.
When we brought Ajax here from Greece,
We thought he would be our ally and our friend:
On trial we've found him worse than any Trojan—
Plotting a murderous blow at the whole army,
A night attack, to nail us with his spear.
And unless some god had smothered that attempt,
We should have met the end that he has met,
Done to a helpless, miserable death,
And he be living still. But God changed   1060
His criminal heart to fall on sheep and cattle.
Therefore I say, no man exists on earth
Who shall have the power to give him burial,
But he shall be tossed forth
Somewhere on the pale sand, to feed the sea birds.
There it is, and I want no fire-breathing.
Maybe we couldn't rule him while he lived;
But now he is dead, we most assuredly will,
With a firm directing hand, whether you like it or not.
So long as he lived, he never would heed our words,   1070
Never. And yet it's a poor common soldier
That feels no duty to obey his betters.
Laws will never be rightly kept in a city
That knows no fear or reverence, and no army
Without its shield of fear can be well governed.
And even if a man rears a huge frame,
He had better know how small a cause can throw him.
When a man is moved by wholesome fear and shame,
You may know that combination makes for safety;   1080
But insubordination and the rule
Of do-as-you-like invariably, mark my words,
Sooner or later drive a city on
Before the gale into the sea's gulf.
Enact, I say, some salutary fear:
And let's not think we can do just what we please,

And then, when we grow vexatious, pay no fees.
There's turnabout in these things. A while ago
He was the hot aggressor; now it's I
Who entertain large ideas. And I give you notice,
Don't bury him. For you may find, if you do,
That you're apt to take a tombward fall yourself.   1090

Chorus

Menelaus, these are fine principles you've upreared;
Don't shame them now by outrage to the dead.

Teucer

Friends, I never shall be amazed again
To see a man of humble birth go wrong,
When those who claim the noblest birth of all
Utter such wrongful speech as you've just heard.
Come, tell me again: you say you brought this man
Here for the Greeks as an ally *you* enlisted?
Didn't he make the voyage here on his own,
As his own master? How, then, are you his general?   1100
What gives you title to command his people,
Who followed him from home? King of Sparta
You came, no general over us. You've no more claim
To marshal him than he has to drill you.
Why, you sailed here in a subordinate place,
Not lord of all, that you should ever claim
The right to captain Ajax! Rule your own;
Chastise their arrogant speech. But Ajax,
In spite of your prohibitions and your brother's,
I shall lay in his tomb, reverently and justly,
Regardless of your frowns. It wasn't at all   1110
For your wife's sake he made the expedition,
Like some poor, toiling subject; but for the oaths
Which he had sworn—no service due to you.
He took no stock of nobodies. Think this over,
And come then with more heralds at your back,

And maybe the general too. But I'll take no notice
Of your pother, so long as you're what you are.

Chorus

I can't approve such bold speech in misfortune;
Harsh words, however just they are, still rankle.

Menelaus

This bowman seems to think quite well of himself.   1120

Teucer

My archery is no contemptible science.

Menelaus

Think how he'd boast if he wore a warrior's armor!

Teucer

I'm a match light-armed for you in bronze, I think.

Menelaus

That tongue of yours! What a fierce heart it fosters!

Teucer

A man may have some boldness in the right.

Menelaus

So! It was right he should kill me and then prosper!

Teucer

Kill? Truly this *is* a miracle,
If you've been killed and still are living!

Menelaus

A god saved me; I was dead in *his* intention.

Teucer

Well, don't affront the gods, if the gods have saved you.

Menelaus

Could it be that I should fail to revere the gods' laws?   1130

Teucer

Yes, if you intervene
To interrupt the burial of the dead.

Menelaus

Of my own enemies! *They* must not be buried.

Teucer

   Ajax opposed you, then, on the field of battle?

Menelaus

   He hated me, as I did him. You knew that well.

Teucer

   There was some reason for it:
   You were found out procuring fraudulent votes.

Menelaus

   Charge his defeat to the judges, not to me.

Teucer

   You have a gift for suave and stealthy villainy.

Menelaus

   Someone is going to smart for that speech.

Teucer

   No worse, I judge, than the smart I shall inflict.

Menelaus

   I tell you just one thing. This man must not be buried.   1140

Teucer

   And this shall be your answer. He shall be
   Buried at once.

Menelaus

   I observed a man once of fast and saucy speech
   Who had pressed sailors to make a voyage in a storm;
   When the weather got really rough, you couldn't hear
   Him piping anywhere: he hid himself in his cloak,
   And anybody aboard could step on him at will.
   And very possibly you and your reckless speech—
   If a big whistling storm should suddenly come
   Out of a little cloud—your clamorous uproar
   Might be quenched in a very similar fashion.

Teucer

   And I once saw a man inflated with foolishness,   1150
   Who insulted the misfortunes of his neighbors.
   And another man, closely resembling me,

Quite like me in temperament, gave him a straight look
And said to him, "Man, don't outrage the dead.
You certainly shall regret it if you do."
That was the advice he gave that worthless man.
I see him now, and he is, it seems to me,
You, and nobody else. Am I speaking in riddles?

Menelaus

I'm leaving. I shall only look absurd
To stay and chide you, when I might use force.   1160

                                        (*Exit.*)

Teucer

Go, then. It does me little credit, either,
To listen to an empty man's loud talk.

Chorus

A great and wrathful contest is shaping.
Teucer, bestir yourself. Find him,
As quickly as you can, some hollow
Cavity in the earth, that shall become
His dank, capacious tomb, a signal
Reminder of him to men in after time.

Teucer

Here, just in time for that, his wife and child
Are coming, to perform with kindred touch
The service due his pitiable body.   1170

                        (*Enter Tecmessa with Eurysaces.*)
Come, little one, kneel down, as suppliants do,
Grasp your father, the creator of your life.
Hold in your hands this lock of mine

                        (*Cuts it, and puts it in the boy's hand.*)
                        and hers,

                                        (*Cuts it, etc.*)

And this, a third, your own

                        (*Puts his hand on the boy's head and separates the lock
                                in readiness to cut it.*)

—a suppliant's treasure.
Keep your station, and make your supplication.
And if anyone in the army tries to wrest you
Forcibly from this corpse, may his corpse be
Thrown out unburied from his land and home,
Wretchedly, as he is a wretch, cut off
At the root with all his race, even as I
Have cut this lock of hair.

(*Cuts it and gives it to Eurysaces.*)

Take it, dear child, and guard it, and let no one   1180
Remove you, but cling fast, inclining over him.

(*To the Chorus*)
And you, don't huddle near like a crowd of women,
Instead of the men you are, but rally round
And help, till I come back, having provided
A tomb for him, though all the world gainsay me.

(*Exit Teucer.*)

Chorus
   Strophe
Which year, I wonder, shall be my long toil's last,
And when shall the battered count of them all be full?
They bring upon me a ceaseless curse of spear-sped
Trouble over the length and breadth of Troy,   1190
A grief and a shame to all Greek men.

   Antistrophe
Whoever it was that first revealed to Hellas
Their common scourge, detested arms and war,
I curse him. Would the large air first had taken him
Or else the impartial house of Death. Generations
Of toil be made for us. Ah,
There indeed was a harrier of men!

   Strophe
It was he that denied my share
In the sweet companionship   1200

Of garland and deep cup;
And miserly he grudged me
The flute's soft lovely clamor
And a pleasant bed in the night,
And love, love he abridged and interdicted.
Ah, me! I languish, so. None cares
That my locks are damp with the thick continual dew
Which is all my thought of Troy.   1210

Antistrophe
And he, valorous Ajax,
Who was once my ward and cover
From every flying shaft
And dread in the hours of night,
Now is handed over to his harsh daemon.
What joy, then, is left to me?
Oh, if somehow I might find myself
Rounding a wood-topped bulwark of the sea,
Sunium's level tip where the surf washes,
And make my salutation   1220
To holy Athens!

> *(Enter Teucer hastily.)*

Teucer

I hurried back when I saw the commander-in-chief,
Agamemnon, approaching. And here he is;
I think he will give his hateful lips full freedom.

> *(Enter Agamemnon with retinue.)*

Agamemnon

You, there! Are you the one they tell me of,
Who has made bold to yawp these powerful speeches,
Unpunished, so far, against me? You,
The son of a captive slave-woman! What if your mother
Had been a princess? *Then* I think you'd strut,   1230
Then you'd talk big! Why, as it is, being
Nothing yourself, you have risen up to protect
That man who now is nothing, and have sworn
That I am not the general nor the admiral

Either of the Achaeans or of you,
Since Ajax, as you say, came under his own command!
These are quite some taunts to hear from a slave.
And what is the man on whose behalf you've bawled
These very ambitious claims? Where did he go,
Or stand in battle, where I did not too?
Was he the one real man in the whole Greek army?   1240
Ah! that contest for Achilles' armor!
We shall regret the day we published it
If every moment we must be defamed
And slandered by this Teucer, if you please!
Who can't accept the court's majority verdict,
Defeated as he is, or yield to it,
No! but you losers pelt us still with slanders,
And seek to wound us with your crafty plots.
Yet where such reckless courses have their head,
No law can stand unshaken, not when we
Must shove the lawful victors from their place,
And give precedence to the ranks behind.
This must be curbed. It's not a man's great frame   1250
Or breadth of shoulders makes his manhood count:
A man of sense has always the advantage.
A very little whip can serve to guide
A hulking ox straight forward on his road.
And I fancy something of that medicine
Is coming for you, unless you get some sense!
That man is dead, now—just a shadow;
And yet you seem to count on *him* to protect
Your sauciness! I say, learn moderation!
Think of your slave's birth; bring someone else,   1260
A freeman, here to plead your case before me.
I'm disinclined to hear more words from you,
Being not much versed in your barbarian speech.

Chorus
    I wish you both might learn a moderate mind!
    That is the best I have to say to you.

Teucer

   Alas! How fugitive is the gratitude
   Men owe the dead, how soon shown to deceive!
   This man has no trifling remembrance,
   Ajax, of you, though oftentimes for him
   You risked your life and bore the stress of war.
   All that is gone now, easily tossed away.
   You, who just now spoke that long, foolish speech,
   Can't you remember any more at all
   How you were penned once close behind your picket,
   And all but ruined in the rout of war   1270
   With flames licking the ships' quarter-decks
   Already, and Hector high in the air, leaping
   Over the fosse to board, but Ajax came,
   Alone, to save you? Who fended off *that* ruin?
   Wasn't it he, the very man you now   1280
   Declare fought nowhere but where you fought too?
   What do you say? Did he deal fairly then?
   And when that other time he closed alone
   In single fight with Hector, not conscripted,
   But chosen when each champion put his lot
   Into the crested helmet—Ajax then
   Put in no shirking lot among the rest,
   No clod of moist earth, no! but one to skip
   Lightly, first and victorious, from the helm.
   It was he that did those things, and I stood by him:
   The slave, yes! the barbarian mother's son!
   Wretched man, why do you light upon *that* taunt?   1290
   Aren't you aware that your own grandfather,
   Old Pelops, was a barbarous Phrygian? Or
   That Atreus, yes, your actual *father*, set
   Before his brother a most unholy dish
   Of his own sons' flesh? And you yourself
   Had a Cretan for your mother, in whose bed
   An interloping foreigner was discovered,
   And she consigned, and by her parent's order,

To drown among the fishes of the deep.
These are your origins. Can you censure mine?
Telamon was my father, and he won
My mother as his valorous prize of war. 1300
She was a princess by her birth, the child
Of King Laomedon, and Heracles
Distinguished her to be my father's gift.
Two royal races gave me to the world.
How shall I shame my kin if I defend them
In their adversity, when you with shameless words
Would fling them out unburied? Listen to this:
If you should venture to cast Ajax out,
You must cast out the three of us as well,
Together in one heap with him. I make my choice
To stand in public and to die for him, 1310
Rather than for your wife—or was it your brother's wife?
So! Think of your own case, and not merely mine;
For if you vex me, you may wish you had been
A coward, rather than too bold with me.

(*Enter Odysseus.*)

Chorus

You arrive, my lord Odysseus, just in time,
If you have come to make not strife but peace.

Odysseus

What is this, gentlemen? For quite some distance
I could hear the sons of Atreus raising their voices
Over this valiant corpse.

Agamemnon

Indeed we were.
Hadn't we just been hearing infamous language, 1320
My lord Odysseus, from this fellow here?

Odysseus

What language do you complain of? If he gave
Insult for insult, I could pardon him.

Agamemnon

I gave him ugly words:
It was an ugly wrong he offered me.

Odysseus

What did he do to injure you?

Agamemnon

He said
He would not leave that corpse unburied, but
Declared he'd bury it in spite of me.

Odysseus

Agamemnon, may a friend speak truth to you,
And still enjoy your friendship as before?

Agamemnon

Speak. I would be foolish to resent your words;   1330
You are my truest friend in the whole army.

Odysseus

Then listen. Don't cast out this brave man's body
Unburied; don't in the gods' name be so hard.
Vindictiveness should not so govern you
As to make you trample on the right. I too
Found this man hateful once, beyond the rest
Of all my fellow soldiers, since the time
I won Achilles' armor. Nevertheless,
In spite of his enmity, I cannot wish
To pay him with dishonor, or refuse
To recognize in him the bravest man   1340
Of all that came to Troy, except Achilles.
It would be wrong to do him injury;
In acting so, you'd not be injuring him—
Rather the gods' laws. It's a foul thing to hurt
A valiant man in death, though he *was* your enemy.

Agamemnon

Do you, Odysseus, take his part against me?

Odysseus
  I do.
  I hated him while it was fair to hate.

Agamemnon
  But now he is dead,
  Shouldn't you rightly trample on his corpse?

Odysseus
  Forbear, my lord, to seek unworthy triumphs.

Agamemnon
  Reverence doesn't come easily to a prince.   1350

Odysseus
  Regard for a friend's advice is not so difficult.

Agamemnon
  A good man should defer to his superiors.

Odysseus
  No more, now.
  You win the victory when you yield to friends.

Agamemnon
  Think what a man you're interceding for!

Odysseus
  My enemy, it's true. But he was noble.

Agamemnon
  Do you intend pity to a corpse you hate?

Odysseus
  His greatness weighs more than my hate with me.

Agamemnon
  Men who act so are changeable and unsteady.

Odysseus
  Men's minds are given to change in hate and friendship.

Agamemnon
  Do you, then, recommend such changeable friends?   1360

Odysseus
  I cannot recommend a rigid spirit.

Agamemnon
  You'll make me look a coward in this transaction.

Odysseus
  Generous, though, as all the Greeks will say.

Agamemnon
  You want me, then, to let this corpse be buried?

Odysseus
  Yes. For I too shall come to that necessity.

Agamemnon
  In everything, I see, men labor for themselves.

Odysseus
  For whom should I rather labor than myself?

Agamemnon
  Let this be called your doing, and not mine.

Odysseus
  However you do it, you will deserve praise.

Agamemnon
  Understand my position. I would do   1370
  This and much more at your request. But as for him,
  Whether on earth or in the underworld,
  I hate him. You may do whatever you wish.

                    (*Exit Agamemnon with his retinue.*)

Chorus
  Whoever fails to recognize your wisdom
  And value it, Odysseus, is a fool.

Odysseus
  And now I have a promise,
  Teucer, to make to you. From now on, I
  Shall be as much your friend as I was once
  Your enemy; and I should like to join

In the burial of your dead—doing with you
That labor, and omitting none of it,
Which men should give the noblest of their fellows.   1380

Teucer

Noble Odysseus, I can only praise you.
How greatly you deceived my expectations!
For though you hated him worst of the Argives,
You alone came to help, and did not wish,
Because you lived, to outrage him in death.
That wit-struck general did otherwise—
He and his noxious brother—and decreed
That Ajax' corpse should rot without a tomb.
Therefore, may Zeus who rules on high Olympus,
Remembering Furies, and avenging Justice   1390
Destroy them miserably, just as they
Sought to work outrage and abomination
On my dear brother's body. Son of Laertes,
I feel some hesitation at your offer
And fear I cannot let you touch the corpse:
That might offend the dead. But bear your part
In all the rest, and if you wish to bring
Any others of the army, they shall be welcome.
I'll see to all the rest. But you, Odysseus,
Are written in our hearts a nobleman.

Odysseus

I could have wished to help.   1400
But if your preference is otherwise,
I shall respect your wish and take my leave.

                                                        (*Exit Odysseus.*)

Teucer

Shoulder the work. Delay
Has grown too long already.
Some of you hurry and dig
The hollow trench; others
Set the tall cauldron

Amid the surrounding flames
To ready the holy bath;
And one troop bring from within the tent
His glorious suit of armor.

Now you, my boy,
Take hold with your little strength   1410
Upon your father's body,
And help in tenderness to lift him up;
For still the warm conduits
Spout forth his life's dark force.
Come now, come, everyone
That claims to be his friend,
Begin, proceed, and bear him up,
This man of perfect excellence—
No nobler one has ever been than he:
I speak of Ajax, while he lived.

(*The cortege forms.*)

Chorus
What men have seen they know;
But what shall come hereafter
No man before the event can see,
Nor what end waits for him.   1420

(*Exeunt, following the body.*)

THE WOMEN OF TRACHIS

Translated and with an Introduction by Michael Jameson

INTRODUCTION TO *THE WOMEN OF TRACHIS*

Heracles was rarely the subject of tragedy, although the most popular hero of Greek mythology. In the theater he was more commonly seen in satyr plays and comedy, and, indeed, this is an indication of his great appeal: he was both god and man, hero and buffoon. At times he appeared as a rescuer to conclude a play in which he was not the central character (in Aeschylus' lost *Prometheus Unbound*, in Euripides' *Alcestis*, in Sophocles' *Philoctetes*), but he is not tragic at such times or in the triumphant accomplishment of his labors but at the moment of his solitary defeat. Sophocles and Euripides (in his *Heracles*) each took for his plot one of his two defeats, while ignoring the other—his agony in the poisoned shirt and his homicidal madness against his wife and children. It may be that a single, terrible defeat is necessary to the career of one who is Everyman on a heroic scale and that the poisoned shirt and the madness are "doublets," coming from different versions of his life, concerning two different wives who are only later combined into a single account. Modern research suggests that at least two heroes have merged to form the classical Heracles—the one from Tiryns, the other from Thebes.

Our play contains the first sure reference to Heracles' decision to be burned alive on the pyre, although two divergent traditions about his end are as early as Homer and Hesiod: the one, that, great as he was, even the son of Zeus had to die like any other man; the other, that, after battling Death in various guises, he wins immortality among the gods on Olympus. In later times this latter is the dominant version, and the pyre which destroys his mortal body is the means of his ascent, as in Seneca's *Hercules Oetaeus*. The story of the pyre cannot be original with Sophocles, for we see it on Attic vases beginning in the early part of the century, and it seems always to have been connected with his becoming a god. Why, then, does

Sophocles avoid all reference to the final resolution of the hero's agony? For Heracles here expects death, and there is not the slightest hint of apotheosis, although it is explicit in the poet's *Philoctetes*. To find an answer, we must see the place of the last scene in the play, assuming that it is an integral part of the whole and not a conventional appendage dictated by mythology.

At the beginning Deianira tells us: "Now he wins through to the end of all his labors / and now I am more than ever afraid" (ll. 36–37), and soon after she reports a prophecy to her son Hyllus: "It said that either he would come to his life's end / or have by now, and for the rest of his time, / a happy life, once he had carried out this task" (ll. 79–81). So the play begins with his wife's anxiety over Heracles' last labors, which will mean the "end" (*telos*) for him and for her, in all its ambiguity; and it is the working-out of this end through a series of revelations constantly coming closer to the full truth that is the action of the play. When Heracles realizes that his end has come and has added further strokes to complete his fate, he closes the action with the order that he be carried out to the pyre to be burned alive: "The true / respite from suffering is this—my final end" (ll. 1255–56). It is this, the discovery of the end of Heracles, that gives the play its unity; for clearly, as the action is not centered on a single character, it does not have the obvious unity of an *Oedipus the King*, nor can it be made into such a play by ignoring either Heracles or Deianira and regarding the remaining character as the true hero. The title we have, avoiding both the principals, should be a warning. And once we allow that the subject of the play is larger than the tragedy of either character and inextricably involves both, we cannot stop short of the total action; to see the play, for instance, as an exposition of the destructive power of love makes a mere "afterpiece" of the last scene, where Heracles learns the truth and acts upon it. Rather, this is the play's climax as well as its conclusion.

The movement of the play as a series of revelations is expressed in action and imagery and is underscored in language through the prominent use in the Greek of the root of *phainein* ("reveal") and of its synonyms and opposites (there is a similar emphasis on *telos*, "end," and its derivatives). In imagery the contrast of the dark, secret, night-time, and deadly with the bright and clear, with sun, fire, and lightning, culminates in the black, dead enemies (the Hydra's poison, Nessus' gift) that defeat Heracles, and the fire with which in turn he will vanquish them and himself. In action, the expected appearance of Heracles, seemingly assured, is replaced by the silent mystery of Iole and the concealment of Lichas, which, when exposed, are followed by the secrecy of Deianira and of Nessus, revealed to Deianira by the sunlight on the tuft of wool, to the world by the altar fire at Cenaeum; the full revelation of his end to Heracles and of his further decision coincides with a new discovery— the revelation of Hyllus' character as a son worthy of his father.

There is also revelation of the divine agency behind the events: Lichas calls his false story of why Heracles has been absent so long "a tale where it is seen Zeus did the work" (l. 251, *praktōr phanei*); later, when the truth is out, "that silent / handmaiden, Cyprian Aphrodite / is revealed; this is her work" (ll. 859–61, *phanera . . . ephanē praktōr*); but in the end, when all is seen to agree with Zeus's oracles, "there is / nothing here which is not Zeus" (ll. 1277–78). Through the oracles mentioned at the beginning and near the end, we see that the events leading up to Heracles' defeat are part of the external, inevitable pattern against which the suffering and the actions of the characters must be seen. What happens when Heracles understands this pattern, being in accord with it and yet beyond it, may be the most important part of the play. As far as the characters, or we, can see, the Gods do not care. The meaning and worth of men's actions are what they make of them. We may remember now that "Sophocles claimed he depicted men as they ought to be, Euripides as they are" (Aristotle *Poetics* xxv. 11). If Euripides' characters were closer to reality, Sophocles' own were larger than life, on a heroic scale. How do his characters here fit his own description?

Deianira is easily the more sympathetic character for the modern reader, and many have been tempted to read the play as her tragedy. We see in the beginning her early fear of marriage and of lust, symbolized for her by the monstrous Acheloüs and then by Nessus; strictly outside the action, they are kept before us by her own and the chorus' reminiscence. For the end of Heracles' toils means her husband at rest at home and the end of violence and fear. No sooner has all this been realized, as it seems, than violence and lust burst into her own house and her own bed. Here we first see her stature in her kindness and her restraint after she knows who Iole is, in her refusal to hurt or even blame her husband or the girl. (Throughout there may well be a contrast intended with Aeschylus' Clytemnestra in the *Agamemnon*.) She resorts to a love charm with reluctance and misgivings, for they were unbecoming a great lady and notoriously dangerous. We feel that she was incredibly foolish to trust a gift from Nessus, and soon she thinks so too, and yet we may fail to appreciate how plausible is his magic: the blood of Nessus is to her vile and repulsive, no less so because of the vaguely apprehended effect of the Hydra's poison, but it is precisely from the vile and repulsive that the most potent magic comes. Furthermore, Nessus and the centaurs in general were an incarnation of the erotic (as his attempt on her confirms—the poet's taste seems to have suppressed a peculiarly appropriate ingredient of the charm found in the tradition, the centaur's semen). What better source for a love charm to turn back toward his wife the lust of Heracles, "all desire when the beast's / inducements, all dipped in persuasion, have melted him" (ll. 661–62)? When she is told of the deadly effect of the poison and is cursed by her son, she leaves without a word to justify herself and, re-enacting the central ritual of her life, she makes the bed of Heracles for the last time and kills herself upon it. "How could any woman bring her hands to this?" (l. 898) the Chorus asks, for this is not the hanging of Jocasta or Antigone but the more masculine self-destruction with the sword. A woman, ordinary in her devotion to her marriage and family, shows her extraordinary nobility and strength at the time of her utter disaster.

But, for the Greeks, Heracles has even more of the heroic properties. No man has done more or suffered more. This is not to say that he is likable or, in the sickness of his passion, admirable. Nonetheless, for Deianira and Hyllus, when they think of her losing such a husband, he is "the best of all men" (ll. 177, 811–12). There is no idea of his being punished for his immorality, nor is there any attempt to soften the impact of his enormous faults. Everything about him is larger than life. When his violent lust is revealed, it is not treated as showing him to be any less of a hero but as evidence of the superhuman power of the one foe that has overcome him. Love is seen as a sickness, and the poison, intended as a drug, a remedy, brings about another sickness that can be cured only by suicidal fire. "I ask you to be my healer, / the only physician who can cure my suffering," he begs his son (ll. 1208–9). But this last sickness, the working of the poison, is also conceived of as a beast, the last of all that he has faced (cf. ll. 987, 1009 f., 1028 ff., 1053 ff.), and in the poet's language the other beasts are linked together to form a composite enemy that gains its late revenge. In this play, Heracles is more the beast-slayer than the savior of mankind, and it is in this role that, before he knows the truth, he thinks to punish Deianira. There is no point in reproving him in his ignorance and his horrible pain for this desire. Is any other reaction conceivable for one who knows only what he knows, who is in his pain, and, most important, has led his life? ". . . alive / I punished the evil and I punish them in death" (ll. 1110–11). Nor need we reprove or gloss over his failure to forgive her when he knows she was innocent. The knowledge that the poison came from Nessus puts everything in a new light. Before, though he prayed for death, he had not, it would seem, admitted to himself that his end had come. Now he knows, and he turns to face it. His end is not to be avoided, but his agony remains, and he treats it as a sickness and as a beast. He had said that this "flowering of madness" was "inexorable" (akēlēton, l. 999, that is, "not to be charmed away"). "Is there any singer of spells, / any craftsman surgeon who can / exorcise this curse, but Zeus?" (ll. 1000–1002). Now, calmly, forcing his will on his son, he applies the measures he had called for in his delirium: the fire and the sword he had used in his purification, purging the earth of beasts (ll. 1013 ff.), he turns on himself, resuming the role he has played all his life.

One cannot doubt that the audience as a whole would have thought beyond to the apotheosis, but, by suppressing all mention of elevation to the Gods through fire and by not motivating the fire through an oracle, the poet focuses attention on the thing chosen—the fire itself as destroying and purifying—and on the act of choosing. Heracles suffers and acts not with the promise of immortality but with the firm expectation of death, and it is this which gives meaning to his choice. The hero who has wept and wailed, shamefully vanquished by a woman and his dead enemies, returns to the attack, even as Oedipus puts out his eyes, Ajax yields, only to choose suicide, and Antigone, buried alive, kills herself. Heracles tells his "tough soul," ". . . make an end / of this unwanted, welcome task" (ll. 1259 ff.). He makes his end his own.

Appropriately, it is Hyllus who closes the play, for it is through him that we have felt the emotional impact of the long last scene—Heracles, however stunning his actions, is hardly enough like us now for sympathy. When Hyllus accused his mother, we wanted to cry out, "She did not mean to . . ." and almost at once, with her death, his contrition acknowledges, as it were, that we were right. Now the new blows are felt through our sympathy with him. He must restrain his half-crazed father in his ghastly agony, he must brave a murderous anger to tell him the truth, and he must burn, or all but burn, his father alive and marry the woman he thinks of as his parents' murderer. The dramatic power of the scene needs no comment, but we should also see that thus he ends the chain of violent love by accepting a marriage that appalls him, assuming his father's mantle where alone his father had not triumphed through courage and endurance.

Finally, what of Zeus and the Gods who have shown so little compassion in "all that's happened; they / who are called our fathers, who begot us, / can look upon such suffering" (ll. 1266–69)? For Sophocles, in this play at least, the Gods are "the way things are"—the invincible power of love, the predicted and inevitable end; they form the immovable background to human suffering and heroism. The action of the play insists that this is so, that there is what we might call an "inhuman" design, but it is more concerned with what, this being so, Deianira, Heracles, and Hyllus do and suffer and with the way in which, whatever their weakness, they show how men ought to be.

The Date

The date of the play is not known. Internal evidence has led to widely different conclusions, but a comparison with certain features of Euripides' *Medea* (431 B.C.) and *Heracles* (420–419 B.C.?) seems to help in placing it in the twenties of the fifth century. The date is of interest primarily for the study of Sophocles' development and for possible relations with the work of Euripides. The play is utterly apolitical. It was, then, probably written after *Ajax* and *Antigone*, close to *Oedipus the King*, when the poet was past sixty, and with *Electra* (probably) and *Philoctetes* and *Oedipus at Colonus* certainly still to come.

A Note on the Text

For the most part I have translated the text of A. C. Pearson ("Oxford Classical Texts" [Oxford, 1923]); at a few points I have agreed with R. C. Jebb (*The Trachiniae*, Part V of *Sophocles, The Plays and Fragments* [Cambridge, 1892]) as against Pearson, especially in lines 207, 328, 526, 660, 837, 905, 1084, 1186, and 1191; more rarely I have departed from the interpretation of a word or phrase preferred by Jebb in his commentary, especially in lines 35, 101, 216, 231, 250, 309, 886, and 1010. In lines 100–102 the "sea-narrows" probably refer to the Bosphorus and Hellespont, the "twin continents" to Europe and Africa at the Pillars of Heracles (Gibraltar); this agrees with H. Lloyd-Jones, *Classical Quarterly*, XLVIII (1954), 91–92. Finally, with Wilamowitz, I add τέλος in line 528, and at line 857 I read Herwerden's ἅ τ'ὀλεθρίαν for τότε θοάν. I do not attempt any justification, since this is not the place and since, in any case, the choices have been much influenced by the exigencies of making a translation.

THE WOMEN OF TRACHIS

CHARACTERS

Deianira, *Wife of Heracles*

Nurse

Hyllus, *Son of Heracles and Deianira*

Chorus, *Women of Trachis, Friends of Deianira*

A *Messenger*

Lichas, *Herald of Heracles*

Captive *Women of Oechalia, Including the Young Iole (all silent parts)*

An *Old Man*

Heracles

Bearers *and Attendants of Heracles (silent parts)*

THE WOMEN OF TRACHIS

SCENE: *Trachis, before the house of Heracles and Deianira. Deianira and the Nurse enter from the house.*

Deianira

It was long ago that someone first said:
You cannot know a man's life before the man
has died, then only can you call it good or bad.
But I know mine before I've come to Death's house
and I can tell that mine is heavy and sorrowful.   5
While I still lived in Pleuron, with Oeneus my father,
I conceived an agonizing fear of marriage.
No other Aetolian woman ever felt such fear,
for my suitor was the river Acheloüs,
who used to come to ask my father for my hand,   10
taking three forms—first, clearly a bull, and then
a serpent with shimmering coils, then a man's body
but a bull's face, and from his clump of beard
whole torrents of water splashed like a fountain.
I had to think this suitor would be my husband   15
and in my unhappiness I constantly prayed for death
before I should ever come to *his* marriage bed.

But, after a time, to my joy there came
the famous Heracles, son of Alcmena and Zeus.
In close combat with Acheloüs, he won the contest   20
and set me free. I do not speak of the manner
of their struggles, for I do not know. Someone
who watched the spectacle unafraid could tell.
I sank down, overwhelmed with terror lest
my beauty should somehow bring me pain. Zeus of the contests   25
made the end good—if it has been good.

Chosen partner for the bed of Heracles,
I nurse fear after fear, always worrying
over him. I have a constant relay of troubles;
some each night dispels—each night brings others on.   30
We have had children now, whom he sees at times,
like a farmer working an outlying field,
who sees it only when he sows and when he reaps.
This has been his life, that only brings him home
to send him out again, to serve some man or other.   35

Now he wins through to the end of all his labors,
and now I find I am more than ever afraid.
Ever since he killed the mighty Iphitus,
we, his family, live here in Trachis, a stranger's guests,
forced to leave our home. But no one seems to know   40
where Heracles himself can be. I only know
he's gone and left with me a sharp pain for him.
I am almost sure that he is in some trouble.
It has not been a short time—first a year,
by now still more, and there has been no word of him.   45
Yes, this tablet he left behind makes me think
it must surely be some terrible trouble. Often
I pray the Gods I do not have it for my sorrow,

Nurse

Deianira, my mistress, many times before
I have watched as you wept and sobbed, bewailing   50
your absent Heracles, and I said nothing. But now
I wonder—if it is proper that the free should learn
from the thoughts of slaves and I give you advice—
how is it that your family abounds with sons, and yet
you send no one to inquire for your husband?   55
Hyllus, especially, it would be natural to send
if he is at all concerned for his father's safety.
See, here he is, running to the house,
so if what I have said seems of any value,
you can use the boy and follow my advice.   60

(Hyllus enters from the wings.)

Deianira

O my child, my son, even the low-born throw
a lucky cast when they speak well. This woman is
a slave, but what she says is worthy of the free.

Hyllus

What is it she said? Tell me, Mother, if you may.

Deianira

With your father abroad so long, it does not   65
look well that you have made no inquiry for him.

Hyllus

But I know where he is, if I can believe what I hear.

Deianira

My child, have you heard in what country he stays?

Hyllus

All this past year, in all its length of time
they say he was in service to a Lydian woman.   70

Deianira

If he could really endure that, then anything
might be said of him.

Hyllus

              He is free now, I hear.

Deianira

Then where is he now? Is he alive or dead?

Hyllus

They say he is in Euboea, where he campaigns against
the city of Eurytus, unless he is still preparing.   75

Deianira

Did you know, my child, that it was about
this very place he left me a true prophecy?

Hyllus

What prophecy, Mother? I knew nothing about this.

Deianira

It said that either he would come to his life's end
or have by now, and for the rest of his time,   80
a happy life, once he had carried out this task.
Child, his future lies in the balance. Surely, then,
you will go to help him, since we are only safe   83
if he can save himself. His ruin is ours.   85

Hyllus

I shall go, Mother, and had I known the contents
of this oracle before, I would have been there
long ago. As it was, my father's usual
good luck kept me from worrying and being too fearful.
Now that I know of it, I shall not stop until   90
I have learned the whole truth about his fate.

Deianira

Go now, my son. There is always some advantage
in learning good news, even if one learns it late.

(*Hyllus leaves by one of the side entrances; the Chorus
enters, speaking, by the other.*)

Chorus

Shimmering night as she lies despoiled brings you
to birth at dawn, lays you to bed ablaze—   95
O Sun, Sun! I beg you,
tell me of Alcmena's child.
Where, where is Heracles?
All afire with the brilliance of lightning, tell me!
—is he in the sea-narrows,   100
or does he rest against the twin
continents? Your sight is the strongest.

With longing in her heart for him, I learn
that Deianira, over whom men fought,
like some unhappy bird,   105
never lays to bed her longing,
her eyes tearless, but
nurses fear that well remembers her husband's

journey, worn upon her troubled
husbandless bed, miserable,   110
with expectation of misfortune.

As many waves under
the untiring south wind or north
may be seen on the wide
ocean coming on   115
and going by, so he, the descendant
of Cadmus is twisted, but on life's
next toilsome surge, as on the Cretan
deep, he will be elevated.
Some god always pulls him   120
safely back from the house of Death.

(*The Chorus turns toward Deianira.*)

Therefore, I reprove you,
respectfully, but still
dissenting. You should not let
all expectation of good   125
be worn away. Nothing painless
has the all-accomplishing King
dispensed for mortal men. But
grief and joy come circling
to all, like the turning paths   130
of the Bear among the stars.

The shimmering night does not stay
for men, nor does calamity,
nor wealth, but swiftly they are gone,
and to another man it comes
to know joy and its loss.   135
Therefore, I bid even you, O Queen, always
hold fast to this knowledge in your expectations.
When has Zeus been so careless of his children?   140

(*Deianira comes forward and speaks.*)

Deianira
    You are here, I suppose, because you have heard

of my suffering. May you never learn
by your own suffering how my heart is torn.
You do not know now. So the young thing
grows in her own places; the heat of the sun-god 145
does not confound her, nor does the rain, nor any wind.
Pleasurably she enjoys an untroubled life
until the time she is no longer called a maiden
but woman, and takes her share of worry in the night,
fearful for her husband or for her children. Then, 150
by looking at her own experience, she comes
to understand the troubles with which I am weighed down.

Many sufferings have made me weep before.
But I shall tell you of one unlike all the rest.
When King Heracles set off from home on his 155
last journey, he left an old tablet in the house,
on which some signs had been inscribed. Never before
could he bring himself to speak to me of this,
though he went out to many contests; he used to go
as if for some great achievement, not to die. 160
This once, as though he were no longer living, he told me
what property from our marriage I should take and how
he wished the portions of ancestral land divided
among the children, first fixing the time at three months
after he had been away from here one year: 165
then he would either die exactly at this time,
or, by getting past this time limit, he would
in the future live a life without grief.
He said that this was fated by the Gods to be
the final limit of the labors of Heracles, 170
as once at Dodona he heard the ancient oak
declare on the lips of the twin Doves, the priestesses.
The period of their prediction exactly coincides
with the present time, when all must come true;
so that I leap up from pleasant sleep in fright, 175
my friends, terrified to think that I may have to live
deprived of the one man who is the finest of all.

Chorus

    Peace—speak words of good omen. I see a man
    with laurel on his head who comes to speak to you.

             (A messenger enters from the side in a great hurry,
                        full of his important news.)

Messenger

    O Deianira, my mistress, I am the first messenger   180
    to free you from your uncertainty. You should know
    that Alcmena's son lives and is victorious
    and brings from battle first-fruits for the gods of the land.

Deianira

    What did you say, old man? What are you telling me?

Messenger

    Soon there shall come to your halls that most enviable man,   185
    your husband, appearing in his conquering might.

Deianira

    Who told you this? Some townsman or a stranger?

Messenger

    This is what Lichas, the herald, proclaims to many
    in the meadow where the cattle pasture. I heard him
    and rushed off, that, as the first to bring the news, I might   190
    profit from your gratitude and gain your favor.

Deianira

    Why is he not here himself if all is well?

Messenger

    He is not free to move as he would like, lady.
    Around him in a circle stand all the people of Malis
    and question him. He is not able to take a step.   195
    Everyone is curious and wants to know all
    and will not let him go until he's heard him to
    his heart's content. So though *he* does not want to, he stays
    with those who want him. You will see him soon in person.

Deianira

    O Zeus, master of the unharvested meadow of Oeta,   200
    though it has been long, you have given us joy.

Cry out, O you women who are within the house
and you who are without—now that the unhoped-for sunshine
of this news has risen high, we pluck its gladness.

Chorus

Let there be joyous shouting for this house and jubilation   205
around the hearth by girls whose wedding is to come; and let the
    clamor
of men among them go in chorus to honor Apollo,
who wears the fine quiver, our defender. Together
raise on high the paean, paean, O maidens,   210
and shout aloud the name of his sister,
Artemis Ortygia, deer-hunter, who holds the twin torches,
and of the nymphs our neighbors.   215
I take it up, I shall not
push the flute aside, you master of my heart.
See how it excites me—
Euoi!—
the ivy that lately set the bacchants whirling in rivalry.   220
Oh, Oh, Paean! See, see, dear lady,
you are face to face with it now,
it is clear to look upon.

                    (Enter Lichas, Heracles' envoy, followed by a group
                            of captive women, among them Iole.)

Deianira

I do see the group that comes to us, dear women.   225
The sight did not slip past my sentinel eyes.
I proclaim our welcome to the herald, here after
a long time—if the news he brings is welcome.

Lichas

Our coming is good, lady, and good, too, our message,
based on accomplished fact. When a man prospers,   230
his profit must be to earn an excellent report.

Deianira

O kindest of men, tell me first what I want first
to hear: Shall I have Heracles alive?

Lichas

    I can tell you that I left him not only alive
    but strong and flourishing and unburdened by disease.   235

Deianira

    Where? In a Greek or in a foreign land? Tell me.

Lichas

    On a shore of Euboea, where he marks out altars
    and tributes of the land's harvest for Cenaean Zeus.

Deianira

    Is he fulfilling a vow or obeying an oracle?

Lichas

    A vow he took while he tried with his spear to overthrow   240
    the country of these women whom you see before you.

Deianira

    And by the gods, who are they, and who is their master?
    They are pitiable, if their misfortune does not deceive me.

Lichas

    He selected them when he sacked the city of Eurytus
    as possessions for himself and a choice gift for the Gods.   245

Deianira

    Was it against this city, then, that he was gone
    an unforeseeable time, days beyond number?

Lichas

    No, most of this time he was kept in Lydia,
    and, as he himself declares, he was not free
    but a bought slave. (One should not hesitate, lady,   250
    to tell a tale where it is seen Zeus did the work.)
    He was sold to Omphale, the foreign queen,
    and served her a full year, as he says himself,
    and was so stung by this disgrace he had to bear
    that he set himself an oath and swore that he   255
    would live to see the author of his suffering,
    along with wife and child, all in slavery.

These were not empty words, but when he was pure again,
he raised an army of strangers and came against the city
of Eurytus, who alone of mortals was   260
responsible, he claimed, for what he had suffered.
Heracles had come to his house and to his hearth
as an old friend. But Eurytus thundered greatly against him
like the sea and spoke with great malice in his heart:
Let Heracles have in his hands, he said, inescapable arrows.   265
In the bow's test *his* sons left Heracles behind,
as for speech—Heracles was a free man's slave,
a broken thing! Then he got him drunk at the banquet
and threw him out of the house. It was this that galled;
and when one day Iphitus came to the hill of Tiryns,   270
searching for the tracks of horses that had strayed,
the moment his eyes looked one way, his mind on something else,
Heracles hurled him from the top of that flat bastion.
But the King was angry at this act of his,
he who is the father of all, Zeus Olympian,   275
and had him sold and sent out of the country and did not relent,
since this was the only man he had ever killed
by guile. If he had taken vengeance openly,
Zeus surely would have pardoned his rightful victory.
The Gods like foul play no better than do men.   280
They who were so arrogant with their vicious tongues,
they themselves all are inhabitants of Hell,
while their city is enslaved. The women you see
come to you, finding, in place of prosperity,
an unenviable existence. These were your husband's wishes   285
which he commanded and I, faithful to him, fulfil.
You may be sure that he himself will come as soon
as he has made the holy sacrifice to Zeus,
God of his fathers, for his conquest. Of much news
happily reported, this must be the sweetest to hear.   290

Chorus
O Queen, now your delight is clear, both for what
has come about already, and what you have heard promised.

Deianira

Yes, I should have every right to rejoice
when I hear the news of my husband's great success.
Surely my joy must keep pace with his good fortune.   295
Still, if one gives it much thought, one knows a feeling
of dread for the man who prospers so, lest he fall.
For a terrible sense of pity came over me,
my friends, when I saw these ill-fated women
wandering homeless, fatherless, in a foreign land.   300
Before they were, perhaps, the daughters of free men,
but now they shall have to pass their lives as slaves.

O Zeus, who turns the tide of battle, grant that I
may never see you come like this against *my* children,
and if you will come, at least not while I am alive.   305
This is the fear I feel when I look at them.

                       (Deianira comes close to Iole.)
O unfortunate girl, tell me who you are.
Are you married? Are you a mother? To judge by your looks,
you have never known treatment like this, but you
are someone noble. Lichas, whose daughter is this girl?   310
Who was her mother, and who was the father that begat her?
Speak out, for on seeing her I pitied her most
among these women, since only she knows how to feel.

Lichas

What do *I* know? Why do you question me? Perhaps
in birth she is not among the humblest of that land.   315

Deianira

Not of royal birth? Had Eurytus a daughter?

Lichas

I do not know. I made no long interrogation.

Deianira

Did you not learn her name from one of her companions?

Lichas

No, I did not. I performed my task in silence.

Deianira

Then do tell us yourself, my poor child, for it   320
would be a great shame not to know who *you* are.

Lichas

It will be quite unlike her manner up to now
if she begins to speak, I can assure you, since
she has not said a single thing, not one word yet.
She suffers constantly the weight of her misfortune   325
like pangs of labor, weeping and miserable, from the time
she left her wind-blown fatherland. Truly, it is her
bad luck that she cannot speak, but pardon her.

Deianira

Then let her be, and let her go into the house
however she please. She should not have further grief   330
on my account to add to her present unhappiness.
What she has already is enough. Let us all
enter the house so you may hasten wherever you wish
to go and I may see to the preparations within.

> (*Deianira turns to lead Lichas and the captive women into the*
> *house; the Messenger, who had stayed to one side while*
> *Lichas spoke with Deianira, approaches and*
> *detains her while the others pass indoors.*)

Messenger

Wait! Stay a moment here that you may learn,   335
without these others, who they are that you lead inside,
and, since you have heard nothing at all, you may discover
what you must. For of all this I have knowledge.

Deianira

What do you want? Why have you stopped me from going in?

Messenger

Stay and hear me. The earlier message you had from me   340
was no waste of time, nor, I think, will this be.

Deianira

Should we call the others back, or do you wish
to speak only to me and to my friends here?

Messenger

    To you and your friends I may speak—leave the others.

Deianira

    They are gone now, so please give me an explanation.   345

Messenger

    Nothing that man has just been telling you was spoken
    in strict honesty. Either he is a liar now,
    or he was no honest messenger before.

Deianira

    What are you saying? Tell me clearly everything
    you know. I cannot understand what you have said.   350

Messenger

    I myself heard this man say—and many men
    were present who can bear me out—that for the sake
    of this girl Heracles destroyed Eurytus
    and his high-towered Oechalia; and, of the Gods, it was
    Love alone who bewitched him into this violence—   355
    not his laborious service in Lydia for Omphale,
    nor the fact that Iphitus was hurled to his death—
    it was Love, whom he brushes aside in this new version.
    But the truth is that when he could not persuade the father
    to give the child to him for his secret bed,   360
    he fabricated a petty complaint, an excuse
    to campaign against the girl's country, and sacked   362/364
    the city. And now, as you see, he is coming home   365
    and has sent her here, not without a reason, lady,
    and not to be a slave. You must not expect that!
    It would not be likely if he is inflamed with desire.
    So I thought it best to reveal the whole affair
    to you, my mistress, just as I happened to hear it from him,   370
    and there were many others listening to this same story
    in the public gathering of the men of Trachis who can
    refute him as well as I. If what I say is unkind,
    I am sorry, but still I have told the strict truth.

Deianira

    Oh! Oh! What has happened to me? I have   375
    welcomed a secret enemy under my roof.
    Oh, I am miserable, miserable! How truly nameless
    is she, as the man who brought her swore to me—
    a girl so brilliant in her looks and in her birth!

Messenger

    Yes, she had Eurytus for her father and was called   380
    Iole, but of course *he* could tell you nothing
    of her origin since he had never asked!

Chorus

    Damn all scoundrels, but damn him most of all
    who practices a secret, degrading villainy.

Deianira

    What shall I do? I must ask you, for the story   385
    which has now come out leaves me utterly stunned.

Chorus

    Go and talk to Lichas. Perhaps he would speak out
    if you insisted on knowing, whether he liked it or not.

Deianira

    I shall go. Your advice is not unreasonable.

Messenger

    Shall I wait meanwhile? What do you wish me to do?   390

Deianira

    Stay, for I see the man has started from the house
    of his own accord, without my summoning him.

                      (Lichas enters from the house.)

Lichas

    Lady, what should I say when I come to Heracles?
    Give me instructions, for, as you see, I am on my way.

Deianira

    How quickly you are rushing off when you were   395
    so long in coming, before we have even talked again.

Lichas
If there is anything you wish to ask me, I am at your service.

Deianira
Will I be able to trust in the truth of what you say?

Lichas
Yes—great Zeus be my witness!—as far as my knowledge goes.

Deianira
Tell me, then, who is the woman you brought with you?   400

Lichas
A Euboean. But I do not know her parents.

Messenger
You there! Look here! To whom do you think you are talking?

Lichas
And you—what do you mean asking such a question?

Messenger
You would be well advised to try to answer me.

Lichas
I speak to her who commands, Deianira, daughter   405
of Oeneus and the consort of Heracles, if my eyes
do not deceive me—it is my *mistress* that I address.

Messenger
There it is, the very thing I wanted to hear.
You say she is your mistress?

Lichas
                    It is the honest truth.

Messenger
Well, then, what do you think should be your punishment   410
if you are discovered to have been dishonest with her?

Lichas
What do you mean "dishonest"? What are these tricky riddles?

Messenger
No riddles at all! You are the one who is being tricky.

Lichas

I am leaving. I have been a fool to listen so long.

Messenger

Not yet, not before you answer a few questions.   415

Lichas

Say what you want. You'll not be at a loss for words.

Messenger

That captive girl whom you brought to the house, you know
whom I mean?

Lichas

I do, but why do you ask about her?

Messenger

You look at her with no sign of recognition,
but did you not say she was Iole, the daughter of Eurytus?   420

Lichas

Where on earth did I say so? Who is going to come
and testify that he was there and heard me talk?

Messenger

You spoke before many of the townspeople. A large crowd
in the public place of Trachis heard you say this.

Lichas

Oh, yes—
They may have said they heard me. But to repeat an impression   425
is not the same as giving an accurate account.

Messenger

Impression, indeed! Did you not state under oath that you
were bringing this girl as a consort for Heracles?

Lichas

I said that? By the Gods, explain to me,
dear mistress—this stranger here, who on earth is he?   430

Messenger

A man who was there and heard you say her city was

completely crushed through desire for her; no woman
of Lydia destroyed it, but his clear love for her.

Lichas

Please have this fellow leave. No sensible person,
mistress, wastes his time exchanging words with a madman.   435

Deianira

By Zeus who flashes lightning over the topmost glen
of Oeta, do not cheat me of the truth! Speak,
and you will find that I am not a spiteful woman
nor one who does not know how it is with man—
we cannot always enjoy a constant happiness.   440
How foolish one would be to climb into the ring
with Love and try to trade blows with him, like a boxer.
For he rules even the Gods as he pleases, and
he rules me—why not another woman like me?
You see that I would be altogether mad   445
to blame my husband, because he suffers from this sickness,
or that woman. She has been guilty of nothing shameful,
and she has done no harm to me. No, it is
inconceivable. If you have learned to lie from him,
then you are not learning honest lessons. If you school   450
yourself in this fashion, you succeed only
in seeming dishonest when you are trying to be decent.
Tell me the whole truth. To gain the reputation
of a liar is utter dishonor for a free man.
You cannot think that I will not hear. There are   455
many men to whom you have spoken, and they will tell me.

                    (*Deianira pauses, but Lichas remains silent.*)
Are you afraid of hurting me? You are wrong.
The only thing that could hurt would be not to know.
Where is the danger in knowing? One man and many women—
Heracles has had other women before.   460
Never yet has one of them earned insults
from me, or spiteful talk, nor will *she*, even
if she is utterly absorbed in her passion,

for I pitied her deeply when I saw her because
her own beauty has destroyed her life, and, against her will,　465
this unfortunate girl has sacked and enslaved the land
of her fathers. Now let all this flow away
on the wind. To you I have this to say: You may
be dishonest with others, but never lie to me.

Chorus

Obey her. What she says is good. You will have　470
no cause to complain later, and you will gain our thanks.

Lichas

Well, dear mistress, I realize that you are not
unreasonable. You see things as we mortals must.
So I shall tell you the whole truth. I shall not hide it.
It is just as this man said. A terrible longing　475
ran through Heracles—and it *was* for this girl.
Because of her, Oechalia, the land of her fathers,
was overthrown by his spear with great destruction.
None of this did he tell me to hide, I must say
in fairness to him; none of this did he ever deny.　480
I myself, O my mistress, was fearful lest I
should cause pain in your breast by these words of mine.
It was I who erred, if you would call this error.
But since, as it turns out, you know the whole story,
for your own sake as much as for his, be kind　485
to the woman and show that the words you spoke to her
before you knew were said in all sincerity.
Against all else he has won by sheer strength; but by
this love for her he has been completely vanquished.

Deianira

Those are my feelings too, and so too shall I act.　490
You may be sure I shall not choose to add to my
afflictions hopeless resistance to the Gods. Now let us
go into the house. I have messages for you
to carry, and there are gifts to match the gifts you brought—
these too you must take. It would not be right to leave　495
empty-handed when you came so well provided.

(Deianira and Lichas and perhaps the Messenger,
who must be rewarded, enter the house.)

Chorus

Strong is the victory the Cyprian Goddess always wins.
I pass by
the Gods; I would not tell how Zeus was tricked by her;   500
nor Hades, who lives in the night;
nor Poseidon, the shaker of the earth.
But for our lady's hand
who were the two valiant contenders in courtship?
Who were they who came out to struggle in bouts that were   505
all blows and all dust?

One was a strong river with the looks of a high-horned
four-footed bull,
Acheloüs from Oeniadae; the other   510
came from the Thebes of Bacchus,
shaking his back-sprung bow, his spears and club
—the son of Zeus. They came
together then in the middle, desiring
her bed. Alone, in the middle with them, their referee,   515
Cypris, goddess of love's bed.

Then there was thudding of fists and clang of bows
and confusion of bulls' horns;
and there was contorted grappling,   520
and there were deadly blows from butting heads
and groaning on both sides.
But the tender girl with the lovely
eyes sat far from them on a hillside,
waiting for the one who would be her husband.   525
So the struggle raged, as I have told it;
but the bride over whom they fought
awaited the end pitiably.
And then she was gone from her mother,
like a calf that is lost.   530

(*Deianira comes out from the house.*)

Deianira

    Dear friends, while our visitor is in the house
talking to the captured girls before he leaves,
I have come out to you, unobserved. I want
to tell you the work my hands have done, but also to have
your sympathy as I cry out for all I suffer.   535
For here I have taken on a girl—no,
I can think that no longer—a married woman, as
a ship's master takes on cargo, goods that outrage my heart.
So now the two of us lie under the one sheet
waiting for his embrace. This is the gift my brave   540
and faithful Heracles sends home to his dear wife
to compensate for his long absence! And yet, when he
is sick as he so often is with this same sickness,
I am incapable of anger. But to live
in the same house with her, to share the same marriage,   545
that is something else. What woman could stand that?
For I see her youth is coming to full bloom
while mine is fading. The eyes of men love to pluck
the blossoms; from the faded flowers they turn away.
And this is why I am afraid that he may   550
be called my husband but be the younger woman's man.
But no sensible woman, as I've said before,
should let herself give way to rage. I shall tell you,
dear friends, the solution I have to bring myself relief.

    I have had hidden in a copper urn   555
for many years the gift of a centaur, long ago.
While I was still a child, I took it from the wounds
of the hairy-chested Nessus as he was dying.
He used to ferry people, for a fee, across
the deep flood of the Evenus, in his arms   560
with no oars to drive him over nor ships' sails.
I too was carried on his shoulders when my father
sent me to follow Heracles for the first time

as his wife. When I was halfway across
his hands touched me lustfully. I cried out and at once   565
the son of Zeus turned around, raised his hands,
and shot a feathered arrow through his chest; into
his lungs it hissed. The beast spoke his last words to me
as he died: "Daughter of old Oeneus,
if you listen to me, you shall have great profit   570
from my ferrying, since you are the last I have brought across.
If you take in your hands this blood, clotted in
my wounds, wherever it is black with the bile
of the Hydra, the monstrous serpent of Lerna, in which
he dipped his arrows, you will have a charm over   575
the heart of Heracles, so he will never look
at another woman and love her more than you."
I have thought of this, my friends, for since his death
I have kept it in the house, tightly closed.
I followed all instructions he gave me while he still lived   580
and dipped this robe in the charm. Now it is all done.

I am not a woman who tries to be—and may
I never learn to be—bad and bold. I hate
women who are. But if somehow by these charms,
these spells I lay on Heracles, I can defeat   585
the girl—well, the move is made, unless you think
I am acting rashly. If so, I shall stop.

Chorus
  If there is reason for confidence in these measures,
  you do not seem to us to have acted badly.

Deianira
  I have this much confidence only: there seem to be   590
  good prospects, but I have never brought them to the test.

Chorus
  One can only tell from action. Whatever you think,
  you have no way of judging before you try it out.

Deianira

> Well, we shall know soon. I see the messenger
> coming out of doors, and he will be going shortly. 595
> Only be discreet. In darkness one may be
> ashamed of what one does, without the shame of disgrace.

> *(Lichas comes out from the house.)*

Lichas

> What would you wish me to do? Command me, O daughter of
> Oeneus.
> I have already stayed too long, and now I am late.

Deianira

> Lichas, this is the very thing I have looked after 600
> while you were talking to the foreign women inside.
> Here is a gift made by my own hands for you
> to take to my husband—this long, fine-woven robe.
> When you give it to him, you must tell him that it
> should touch the skin of no man before it touches his, 605
> nor should he let the light of the sun look upon it,
> nor any holy inclosure, nor the gleam from a hearth,
> until he himself stands, conspicuous before all,
> and shows it to the Gods on a day of bull-slaughtering.
> For this was my vow: if I should ever see or hear 610
> that he was coming safe to his home, in all piety
> I would dress him in this robe to appear before
> the Gods to make new sacrifice in new clothing.
> And you shall carry a token of this vow which he
> will understand from the familiar encircled print 615
> of my seal.
> 　　　　Go now, and as a messenger
> be sure to keep the rule not to exceed your orders.
> In this way, with thanks both from my husband and
> from me, you will earn our double gratitude.

Lichas

> If I, the messenger, practice this art of Hermes 620
> soundly, I shall never fail in serving you.

I shall present this chest exactly as it is,
and in explanation I shall repeat your words.

Deianira

Then you should be going now. You understand
completely how everything is here in this house.   625

Lichas

I understand, and I shall report that all is well.

Deianira

And, of course, since you saw it, you know the girl's
reception—you know I received her as a friend.

Lichas

Yes, I do, and I am astonished and delighted.

Deianira

What else is there to tell him? For I am afraid   630
you would be talking too soon of my longing for him
before I know if *he* feels longing for me.

(*Exit Lichas through a side entrance; Deianira enters the house.*)

Chorus

Safe harbors, hot-springs among
the rocks, the high cliffs of Oeta—
all you who live by these and by the inmost reaches   635
of the sea in Malis,
the coast of the Maid who shoots the golden shaft,
and there at the Gates,
the famous gatherings of the Greeks—

Soon again the lovely cries   640
of the flute will rise among you;
now it will not ring in disagreeable clamor
but like the lyre, music
for the gods. The son of Zeus and Alcmena
hurries to his home   645
bearing the prizes of all valor.

Gone from the city completely,
we missed him, waiting a long twelve months, while he
was on the sea, but we knew
nothing, and his loving wife   650
all lamentation always, sadly, most
sadly, broke her heart.
But now Ares, God of War,
stung to madness, dispels her day of troubles.

Oh let him come, let him come,   655
and his ship of many oars; let it
not stop before he ends his journey
at this city, leaving the island
hearth where, they say, he makes sacrifice.
Let him come from there   660
all desire when the beast's
inducements, all dipped in persuasion, have melted him.

                    (Deianira comes out from the house.)

Deianira
  O my friends, I am afraid! Can it be
  I have gone too far in all I have just done?

Chorus
  What is the matter, Deianira, child of Oeneus?   665

Deianira
  I don't know. I have a foreboding that I'll be shown
  to have done great harm when I hoped to do good.

Chorus
  Surely you do not mean your gift to Heracles?

Deianira
  Yes, yes. Now I see that one should never
  plunge eagerly into anything obscure.   670

Chorus
  Explain the cause of your fear, if it can be explained.

Deianira

Something has happened which, if I tell you, my friends,
will seem a marvel such as you never thought to hear.
Just now, when I anointed the robe I sent to be
my husband's vestment, I used a tuft of fleecy white wool.   675
This piece has disappeared, devoured by nothing in
the house but destroyed by itself, eaten away
and crumbled completely to dust. I want to tell you this
in detail, so you may know the whole story.

I neglected none of the instructions that beast   680
the centaur explained to me, lying in agony
with the sharp arrowhead in his side. I kept them
like an inscription on bronze that cannot be washed away.
And I only did what I was told to do—
I must keep this drug away from fire and always   685
deep in the house where no warm ray of light may touch it
until I should want to apply it freshly smeared.
And this is what I did. Now, when it had to do its work,
at home, inside the house, secretly I smeared it on
some wool, a scrap I pulled from one of the household sheep,   690
and then I folded my gift and put it in a chest
before the sun could shine on it, as you saw.

But when I go in again, I see something
unspeakable, incomprehensible to human reason.
Somehow I had happened to throw the ball of wool,   695
which I had used to smear the robe, into the full heat
of the sun's rays, and, as it became warm,
it all ran together, a confused mass, and crumbled
to bits on the ground, looking most like the dust one sees
eaten away in the cutting of a piece of wood.   700
Like this it lies where it fell. But from the earth
on which it rests, clotted foam boils up
like the rich liquid of the blue-green fruit
from the vines of Dionysus, poured on the earth.

And now I do not know what to think. I see   705
myself as someone who has done a terrible thing.
From what possible motive, in return for what,
could the dying beast have shown me kindness, when he
was dying because of me? No, he beguiled me,
only to destroy the man who shot him. But I   710
have come to understand now when it is too late.
I alone, unless my fears are fanciful,
I, his unhappy wife, shall destroy him.
I know that arrow which struck Nessus injured even
Chiron, who was a god, and all animals,   715
whatever it touches, it kills. This same poison which seeped,
black and bloody, from the wounds of Nessus, how can
it fail to kill Heracles too? At least, this is
my fear. And yet I have made a decision: if he goes down,
under the same blow I will die with him.   720
I could not bear to live and hear myself called evil
when my only wish is to be truly good.

Chorus
  Terrible results are appalling, but one
  should not expect the worst before anything has happened.

Deianira
  When the plans themselves are bad, there can be   725
  no expectations that leave any place for courage.

Chorus
  But whenever we trip up unwillingly,
  the anger felt is tempered, and so it should be with you.

Deianira
  You may talk like this, since you have no share
  in the wrong; you have no burden all your own.   730

Chorus
  Better to be silent now—say nothing more,
  if you do not want to tell it to your son.
  The one who went away to search for his father is here.

(*Hyllus enters from the side.*)

Hyllus

    Mother! I wish I could have found you not as you are

    but no longer alive, or safe but someone else's   735

    mother, or somehow changed and with a better heart

    than now. Three ways—Oh, for any one of them!

Deianira

    My son, what has happened that I should be so hateful?

Hyllus

    What has happened? Your husband, my father—

    do you hear me?—you have killed him.   740

Deianira

    No, no, my child! What have you blurted out?

Hyllus

    Only what cannot fail to be. Once a thing

    is seen, who can cause it never to have been?

Deianira

    How could you say it? Who on earth told you

    that I did this awful crime you charge me with?   745

Hyllus

    I saw my father's heavy fall with my own eyes

    myself; I did not hear of it from anyone.

Deianira

    Where did you come upon him? Were you at his side?

Hyllus

    If you must hear, then I must talk and tell you all.

    When he sacked the famous city of Eurytus,   750

    he marched away with the trophies and the first-fruits of victory.

    On a wave-beaten shore of Euboea there is

    a point called Cenaeum, where he marked out altars

    and a whole precinct for Zeus, god of our fathers.

    There I first saw him, glad after my longing.   755

    He was about to make great slaughter for sacrifice

when his own herald Lichas arrived from our home,
bringing with him that gift of yours, the deadly robe.
He clothed himself in it just as you had instructed
and killed first his bulls, twelve perfect victims,   760
the pick of the booty; then he brought the number to
one hundred, driving a mixed herd to the altar.
And at first the poor wretch, his mind at ease,
rejoicing in his handsome dress, prayed to the Gods.
But as the flame from the juicy pine-wood fire   765
blazed high and bloody from the solemn rites,
the sweat broke out on his skin; the robe enfolded him
around his limbs, joined tightly to his sides
like the work of a sculptor. Spasms of pain
bit into his bones. Then like the vicious, murderous   770
viper's poison, it began to consume him.

Now he shouted for that unfortunate Lichas, who was
in no way guilty of your crime, demanding
to know the plot behind his bringing him this robe.
Unlucky man, he knew nothing and said it was   775
a gift from you alone, just as you had sent it.
And at that moment, as Heracles listened to his answer,
a piercing, tearing pain clutched at his lungs; he caught
Lichas by the foot where the ankle turns
and threw him against a wave-beaten rock that juts from the sea.   780
It pressed the pale brains out through his hair,
and, split full on, skull and blood mixed and spread.
All the people there cried out in horror for
the one man in his suffering, the other dead.
No one had the courage to come to Heracles.   785
He would be wrenched now to the ground, now in the air,
crying, shrieking. All around the rocks echoed,
the mountain headlands of Locris, the high cliffs of Euboea.
When he gave up at last, after throwing himself
miserably again and again to the earth, crying   790

and groaning again and again, damning the mismating
in your wretched bed, the whole marriage that he
had won from Oeneus, only to befoul his life,
he raised his eyes, distorted, from the dark smoke
that hung around him and saw me in the great crowd,   795
tears pouring down my face, and, looking at me, called:
"My son, come to me! Do not run from me
in my pain, even if you must die with me.
Take me away! Above all else I ask you to put me
in a place where no man can look at me.   800
If you have pity, at least carry me out of this land
as soon as you can, that I may not die here."
These were his orders; we placed him in the middle of
a boat and with difficulty landed him here,
howling in spasms of pain. You shall be seeing him   805
at once, still alive or dead only now.

Mother, this is what you have planned and done to my father,
and you are caught. For this, Justice who punishes
and the Fury will requite you. If it is right
for a son, I curse you, and it *is* right, since you   810
have given me the right by killing the best of all men
on earth, such as you shall never see again.

(Deianira moves away and leaves by the side.)

Chorus (*to Deianira*)
    Why do you go off in silence? Surely you see
    that by silence you join your accuser and accuse yourself?

Hyllus
    Let her go, and I hope a fair wind blows   815
    to carry her far out of my sight. For why should she
    maintain the pointless dignity of the name
    of mother when she acts in no way like a mother?
    No, let her go—goodbye to her. And the delight
    she gave my father, may she find the same herself.   820

(Hyllus enters the house.)

Chorus

See, maidens, how, suddenly, it has closed
with us, the prophetic word spoken
with foreknowledge long ago, that said
when the year of the twelfth plowing came to an end,
then it would bring an end for the true-born son of Zeus   825
to his relay of toils. And now, surely,
at the right time, it all comes home.
How can he who no longer sees
still have, still, toilsome
servitude, when he is dead?   830

If there clings to him in a murderous cloud
the centaur's treacherous, sure trap
and his sides are soaked with venom
that Death begat and the shimmering serpent bred,
how shall he see another sun after today's   835
when the Hydra, horrible and monstrous, has
soaked in? From the black-maned beast's
treacherous words there comes to torture him
a murderous confusion,
sharp points brought to burning heat.   840

She, poor woman, knew nothing of this
but, seeing great injury for her home
from a new marriage swiftly approaching,
applied her remedy;   845
but what came from another's will, a fatal meeting,
truly, lost, she laments,
truly, she weeps a pale,
foaming flood of tears. Doom
as it advances makes clear before
it comes a great disaster from treachery.   850

A spring of tears burst open.
Such sickness, alas, has poured upon him, suffering
to pity as never yet came upon the hero

from his enemies. 855
Woe for the dark head of the front-fighting spear
that won in battle this
fatal bride from steep
Oechalia. But that silent
handmaiden, Cyprian Aphrodite, 860
is revealed; it is her work.

(*Wailing is heard inside the house.*)

Chorus (*the women speak separately throughout this scene*)
Can I be mistaken? Do I hear something,
a cry of grief surging now through the house?

What can I say? 865
The sound is all too clear. They are shrieking for
misfortune inside. The house suffers a new blow.

(*The Nurse comes out of the house.*)

And see
this old woman who is coming toward us, to tell us
something, see how sad she is and how she frowns. 870

Nurse
O maidens, that gift she sent to Heracles,
truly it was the beginning of great sorrow for us.

Chorus
What new calamity have you to tell us, old woman?

Nurse
Deianira, motionless, has moved away
to start upon the very last of all her journeys. 875

Chorus
No, you cannot mean she is dead?

Nurse
You know all.

Chorus
Then she is dead, the poor woman?

Nurse
I tell you again, she is.

Chorus

Gone, poor thing! Can you tell us how she died?

Nurse

Horrible, the way it happened!

Chorus

                     Tell us, woman,
the fate she met   880

Nurse

She destroyed herself.

Chorus

Was her mind in a passion or sick?

Nurse

The weapon's cruel point
killed her.

Chorus

              How could she think of
death on top of death   885
and end her life all alone?

Nurse

The grim steel cut her.

Chorus

And helpless did you see her awful act?

Nurse

Yes, I saw it. For I was standing near her there.

Chorus

Oh, what was it? How? Tell us.   890

Nurse

She herself by herself set her hand to it.

Chorus

What are you saying?

Nurse

                  The clear truth.

Chorus
  That bride, newly come,
  has borne, has borne a mighty
  Fury for this house.   895

Nurse
  Yes, and if you had been near and had seen
  what Deianira did, still more would you pity.

Chorus
  How could any woman bring her hands to this?

Nurse
  Yes, it was terrible. You will learn everything
  and bear me witness. When she went into the house, alone,   900
  and saw her son in the courtyard, arranging a cushioned bed
  to take with him as he went back to meet his father,
  she hid herself where no one might look at her and groaned,
  falling against the altars, that now they would be
  deserted; and whenever she touched some household thing   905
  she used to use before, the poor creature would weep.
  Here and there, from room to room, she kept turning,
  and if she saw some servant of the household who was
  dear to her, she would look at her sadly and weep,
  and she would call out loud to her fate and to   910
  her house that would have no children any more.

  Then she stops all this, and suddenly I see her
  rushing into the bedchamber of Heracles,
  and secretly, from the shadows, I keep watch
  over her. I see the woman casting sheets   915
  and spreading them upon the bed of Heracles.
  Then, as soon as she had finished, she leapt up
  and sat there in the middle of her marriage bed,
  and, bursting into torrents of hot tears, she said:
  "O my bed, O my bridal chamber, farewell   920
  now forever, for never again will you take me
  to lie as a wife between these sheets of yours."

She says nothing more, but with a violent sweep
of her arm unfastens her gown where a pin
of beaten gold lies above her breast. She had   925
uncovered her whole side and her left arm.
And I go running off with all the strength I have
and tell her son what his mother is planning to do.
But in the time I have been rushing there and back
we see that she has cut her side to the liver   930
and the seat of life with a double-bladed sword.
Her son shrieked, for he realized, poor boy,
that in his anger he had forced her to this act.
He had just learned from people in the house that she
had done unwittingly the will of the beast.   935

Then the miserable boy abandoned himself utterly
to sobs and mourning for his mother; he threw himself
upon her lips and there, pressing his side to hers,
he lay and groaned over and over that he
had struck her thoughtlessly with a cruel accusation,   940
weeping because at one moment he was doubly
orphaned for all his life, losing his father and her.

(*The Nurse throws open the doors of the house, revealing
Hyllus and the body of Deianira,
lying on a couch.*)

This is the way things are within. If anyone
counts upon one day ahead or even more,
he does not think. For there can be no tomorrow   945
until we have safely passed the day that is with us still.

(*The Nurse enters the house.*)

Chorus
    Which shall I lament first?
    Which is the more final disaster?
    In my distress I cannot tell.
    The one we can see in the house,   950

the other besets us in our thoughts—
to have and to await are the same.

Oh for a strong blast
of fair wind coming to my hearth
to carry me away from this place   955
that I may not die of fright
when I no more than look
at Zeus's valiant son.
They say he is coming to the house
in unassuageable pain,   960
a wonder beyond telling.

(Men enter from the side, carrying Heracles in a litter,
accompanied by an old man; Hyllus enters from
the house, closing the doors after him.)

Near, then, not distant
is he for whom I cried, like the shrill
nightingale. Here strangers are approaching.   965
How are they carrying him? As though
mourning for a friend,
their steps are slow, soundless.
Ah! He is carried without a word.
Am I to think that he
is dead or only asleep?   970

Hyllus

O my father!
O my sorrow! What is left
for me? How can I help?

Old Man

Be silent, child, do not excite
the wild pain that makes him savage.   975
He still lives, though fallen. You must
bite your lips.

Hyllus

       What? Alive?

Old Man

    Do not wake him, held fast in sleep.
    Do not excite, do not set stirring
    that awful returning   980
    sickness.

Hyllus

        But it drives me mad,
    so helpless under an immense weight!

Heracles

    O Zeus,
    what land have I come to? Among what men
    do I lie worn out by these   985
    unceasing pains? O my agony!
    The filthy thing eats me again.

Old Man

    Now do you see how much better it was
    to hide your sorrow in silence, nor shatter
    sleep from his head   990
    and eyes?

Hyllus

        No, I cannot stand it
    when I see him in this suffering.

Heracles

    O altar steps of Cenaeum, is this
    all the thanks you win me for all
    the sacrifice I made on you?   995
    O Zeus! Torture, torture is all
    you give me! I wish I had never seen you
    with these poor eyes that must face now
    this inexorable flowering of madness.
    Is there any singer of spells,   1000
    any craftsman surgeon who can
    exorcise this curse, but Zeus?
    Even to see him would be a wonder!

(The bearers set the litter down.)

Oh! Let me be. Let
me sleep in my misery,   1005
let me sleep my last sleep.

Where are you touching me? Where are you laying me?
You are killing me, killing me.
You have prodded awake what slumbered.

It has caught me. Oh! It comes on again.   1010
O most ungrateful of the Greeks, where are all you
for whom I destroyed myself purging so many beasts
from all the seas and woods? Now when *I* am sick,
will no one turn the beneficial fire, the sword on me?

Oh! Why will no one   1015
come and cut away
my head from my abominable body.

(The Old Man tries to restrain and support Heracles.)

Old Man

Come, you are the man's son. The task is more
than my strength can manage. You must help. Your strength
can easily do more for him than I.

Hyllus

                                    I touch him,   1020
but to make him unconscious of pain, that is beyond
my power or any man's. Such is the will of Zeus.

Heracles

My son, my son! where are you? Help me, here,
here, lift me up. Oh! Oh! My fate!   1025

It lunges, lunges again, the vile thing
is destroying me—
savage, unapproachable sickness.   1030

O Pallas! It is torturing me again. O my son,
pity me who begot you, draw the sword—no one   1035

will blame you—strike me in the breast, heal the pain
with which your godless mother has made me rage. Oh
to see her fallen, felled by this death she deals me!   1040

Sweet Hades, kinsman, brother of Zeus, lull me to sleep,
to sleep; with quick death end my agony.

Chorus

My friends, I hear and shudder at the king's misfortunes—
so great a man, hounded by such suffering.   1045

Heracles

Many are the toils for these hands, this back,
that I have had, hot and painful even to tell of.
But neither the wife of Zeus nor hateful Eurystheus
has ever condemned me to such agony as this
that the false-faced daughter of Oeneus has fastened   1050
upon my shoulders, a woven, encircling net
of the Furies, by which I am utterly destroyed.
It clings to my sides, it has eaten away
my inmost flesh; it lives with me and empties the channels
of my lungs, and already it has drunk up   1055
my fresh blood, and my whole body is
completely killed, conquered by these unspeakable fetters.
Neither the spear of battle, nor the army of
the earth-born Giants, nor the violence of beasts,
nor Greece, nor any place of barbarous tongue, not all   1060
the lands I came to purify could ever do this.
A woman, a female, in no way like a man,
she alone without even a sword has brought me down.

O my son, now truly be my true-born son
and do not pay more respect to the name of mother.   1065
Bring her from the house with your own hands and put
her in my hands, that woman who bore you, that I may know
clearly whether it pains you more to see *my* body
mutilated or *hers* when it is justly tortured.
Come, my child, dare to do this. Pity me,   1070

for I seem pitiful to many others, crying
and sobbing like a girl, and no one could ever say
that he had seen this man act like that before.
Always without a groan I followed my painful course.
Now in my misery I am discovered a woman.   1075

Come close to me now, stand by your father and
look well at my misfortune, see what I suffer.
I shall take off the coverings and show you. Look,
all of you, do you behold this poor body?
Can you see how miserable, how pitiful I am?   1080

Oh, oh, the pain!
That malignant tearing scorches me again,
it shoots through my sides, it *will* have me struggle,
it will not let me be—miserable, devouring sickness.
O King Hades, receive me!   1085
O flash of Zeus, strike!
Drive against me, O King, hurl down the bolt
of lightning, Father. Now it feeds on me again,
it has sprung out, it blooms. O my hands, my hands,
O my back, my chest, O my poor arms, see   1090
what has become of you from what you once were.
The lion that prowled the land of Nemea, that scourge of herds-
     men,
that unapproachable, intractable creature,
with your strength once you overpowered it,
and the serpent of Lerna and that galloping army   1095
of double-bodied, hostile beasts, violent, lawless,
supremely strong, and the boar of Erymanthus,
and under the earth the hell hound with three heads,
irresistible monster, the awful Echidna's whelp,
and guarding the golden apples the dragon at the end of the
     earth—   1100
and I have had my taste of ten thousand other toils,
but these hands let no one set his trophies over me.

Now look at me, torn to shreds, my limbs unhinged,
a miserable ruin sacked by invisible disaster, I
who am called the son of the most noble mother,   1105
I who claim to be begotten of Zeus in the heavens.
But I tell you this, even if I am nothing,
nothing that can even crawl, even so—
only let her come who has done this to me—
these hands will teach her, and she can tell the world: alive   1110
I punished the evil, and I punish them in death.

Chorus

O unhappy Greece, I can see how great
a mourning you shall have if you lose this man.

Hyllus

Father, since you let me speak to you now,
let me have silence while I speak, though you are sick.   1115
I ask only for what is right. Give me yourself
without this grim anger which stings you to such fury.
Otherwise you cannot know how mistaken
is the pleasure your fury craves, the pain it feels.

Heracles

Say what you want and be done with it. I am too sick—   1120
I can make no sense at all of your riddles.

Hyllus

It is about my mother that I come to speak,
about her present state and her unwilling error.

Heracles

Damn you! How dare you speak of her again, the mother
Who is a father's murderer—and in my hearing?   1125

Hyllus

Her state is such that one should not keep silent.

Heracles

No, no silence for the crime she has committed!

Hyllus

Nor for what she has done today, you will admit.

Heracles
Speak, but beware. Do not disgrace yourself.

Hyllus
I shall speak. She is dead. She has just been killed.   1130

Heracles
By whom? I cannot believe it. It is too bitter news.

Hyllus
She is dead by her own hand and by no other.

Heracles
Ah! She's dead too soon. She should have died by mine.

Hyllus
Even your fury would turn aside if you knew all.

Heracles
A strange beginning, but go on—what do you mean?   1135

Hyllus
In all that she did wrong she had intended good.

Heracles
Good? Does she do good when she kills your father?

Hyllus
It was a charm for love she wanted to put on you
that failed—when she saw that marriage in her house.

Heracles
Who in Trachis knows such deadly drugs as this?   1140

Hyllus
Nessus the centaur long ago persuaded her
to excite your desire with this fatal charm.

Heracles
Woe, woe is me! This is my miserable end.
Lost! I am lost! I see the light no longer.
Ah! Now I know the doom that is upon me.   1145
Come, my child. You no longer have a father.
Call together all my children, your brothers,

and call the unhappy Alcmena who was the bride of Zeus
to her cost. You shall learn from me with my
last words all the prophecies I know.   1150

Hyllus

But your mother is not here. It happens that
she is living now at Tiryns on the sea,
and of your children she has taken some with her
to care for, and others, I must tell you, are living in Thebes.
But all of us who are here—if there is anything,   1155
Father, we must do, we shall listen and serve you.

Heracles

Then hear your task. You have come to that point
where you must show the sort of man you are that you
are called my son. Long ago my father revealed
to me that I should die by nothing that draws breath   1160
but by someone dead, an inhabitant of Hell.
This was that beast, the centaur, who has in death killed me
alive, even as it had been divinely revealed.
Now I shall show you how more recent prophecies
agree with this exactly and give support to the old.   1165
I went to the grove of the mountain-dwelling Selli who sleep
upon the ground and I copied down the words
from my father's oak that speaks with many tongues,
which told me that, at this present, living time,
release from all the toils imposed on me would be   1170
complete. And I thought that then I would be happy.
But it only meant that I would die then.
For the dead there are no more toils. My son,
since all this is coming true so clearly, you must
be ready to stand by my side in the fight, and you must not   1175
hesitate till I am forced to use sharp words.
On your own, agree to act with me; discover
yourself the finest rule—obedience to your father.

Hyllus
> Father, I am alarmed to see where your words lead,
> but I shall obey you in whatever you decide.   1180

Heracles
> You must give me your right hand first of all.

Hyllus
> Will you tell me why you must have this strong pledge?

Heracles
> Quickly, give me your hand. Do not disobey me.

Hyllus
> Here, I reach my hand. I shall deny you nothing.

Heracles
> Swear now by the head of Zeus who begot me.   1185

Hyllus
> Swear to do what? Will you tell me that?

Heracles
> Swear to fulfil completely the task I give to you.

Hyllus
> I do swear, and I take my oath on Zeus.

Heracles
> And pray for punishment if you break your oath.

Hyllus
> I pray, though I shall keep my oath and not be punished.   1190

Heracles
> You know that high crag of Zeus on Mount Oeta?

Hyllus
> Yes. I have often stood there to sacrifice.

Heracles
> Then you must take my body up there, with your
> own hands and with the help of any friends you wish,
> and you must fell a great forest of deep-rooted oak,   1195
> and many trees of the lusty wild olive

you must cut down as well, and put my body on them,
and then take the flaming brand of a pine torch
and burn. Let me have no tears, no mourning. Do
your job without lamentation, without tears,   1200
if you are your father's son, or even below
I shall wait for you, a crushing curse forever.

Hyllus

Oh! What are you saying? What have you forced me to do?

Heracles

What must be done. If you do not do it, then be
another man's son—do not call yourself mine.   1205

Hyllus

Father, Father, how can you? You are asking me
to be your murderer, polluted with your blood.

Heracles

No, I am not. I ask you to be my healer,
the only physician who can cure my suffering.

Hyllus

How would I cure your body by setting it on fire?   1210

Heracles

If that frightens you, do the rest at least.

Hyllus

I shall carry you there—that I could not begrudge you.

Heracles

And you will complete the pyre as I told you?

Hyllus

So long as I do not touch it with my own hands.
Everything else I shall do. You can be sure of me.   1215

Heracles

Even that much is enough. Now after your other
great kindness, do me this one small favor.

Hyllus

No matter how great a favor it is, it shall be done.

Heracles
You know, of course, the girl who is the daughter of Eurytus?

Hyllus
It is Iole you mean, I suppose.   1220

Heracles
I see you know her. This, then, is what I tell you to do,
my son. When I die, if you wish to be pious
and remember the oaths you have sworn to your father,
you must take this girl as your wife, and do not
disobey me. No other man but you must ever   1225
have her who has lain with me at my side. You,
my son, must engage yourself to her bed.
Obey. Although you listen to me in greater matters,
disobedience in lesser things wipes out the favor.

Hyllus
Ah! It is wrong to argue with a sick man,   1230
yet how can one stand to see him with such thoughts as these?

Heracles
You speak as if you would do none of the things I ask.

Hyllus
How could anyone when she alone shares
the blame for my mother's death and your condition?
How could anyone choose to do that, unless   1235
avenging fiends had made his mind sick? Better
for me, too, to die than live with my worst enemy.

Heracles
I see the man will not give me my due, though I
am dying; but I tell you, if you disobey
my commands, the curse of the Gods will be waiting for you.   1240

Hyllus
Oh! Soon, I can see, you will show how sick you are.

Heracles
You! You rouse my agony from its sleep.

Hyllus

So wretched, so helpless am I, no matter where I turn.

Heracles

Because you do not choose to listen to your father.

Hyllus

But shall I listen, Father, and learn impiety? 1245

Heracles

It is no impiety if you give my heart pleasure.

Hyllus

Do you command me and make it right for me to do this?

Heracles

I do command you, and I call the Gods to witness.

Hyllus

I shall do it then, and I shall not forswear
since you have shown the Gods it is your will. No one 1250
could think me wrong in obeying you, Father.

Heracles

In the end you act well. Now make your mercy
follow swift upon your words. Put me on
the pyre before another tearing, stinging blow
can strike. Come, hurry. Lift me up. The true 1255
respite from suffering is this—my final end.

Hyllus

Nothing can prevent its full accomplishment
for you, since you command and compel me, Father.

Heracles

Come then, O my tough soul,
before this sickness is stirred again, 1260
set a steel bit in my mouth,
hold back the shriek, and make an end
of this unwanted, welcome task.

> (*The bearers raise the litter and leave by the side,
> followed by Hyllus and the Chorus.*)

Hyllus

Raise him, my helpers. From you let me have
much compassion now for what I do.   1265
You see how little compassion the Gods
have shown in all that's happened; they
who are called our fathers, who begot us,
can look upon such suffering.
No one can foresee what is to come.   1270
What is here now is pitiful for us
and shameful for the Gods;
but of all men it is hardest for him
who is the victim of this disaster.

                (Hyllus turns to the leader of the Chorus.)
Maiden, come from the house with us.   1275
You have seen a terrible death
and agonies, many and strange, and there is
nothing here which is not Zeus.

                        (Exeunt.)

ELECTRA

Translated and with an Introduction by David Grene

INTRODUCTION TO THE
ELECTRA

IT IS often said by classical scholars that, of the three dramatic treatments of the Orestes legend which we possess in the Greek tragedies, that of Sophocles stands closest to the Homeric account. Homer introduces the story of Orestes several times in the *Odyssey* and always for its exemplary effect. The return of Orestes and the punishment of Aegisthus, and only incidentally Clytemnestra, is mentioned as a warning of what will happen to the suitors when Odysseus comes home. Homer shows no awareness of the brutality of the murder of the mother by her son or of any of the consequences, religious or sociological, which interest both Aeschylus and Euripides later. The whole is a saga of successful revenge. It is worth noticing, of course, that Homer introduces the incident as an *example* of what may happen when Odysseus comes home. He is not giving us his speculations on matricide. Still, even at that, it is perhaps curious that the revenge taken, including the killing of Clytemnestra, can be treated with such clarity of moral judgment in favor of the killers.

In outline Sophocles appears to handle the story as Homer does, as a revenge theme, with no divine or other sanctions invoked against the murderers. But it is difficult to believe that Sophocles' interpretation should be taken on so simple a level. Almost forty-five years before the Sophoclean play, Aeschylus had written the *Oresteia*, which treated the legend with exactly the questions in mind that Homer had omitted. The *Oresteia* was a great popular success. It is extremely unlikely that Sophocles later could have reverted to the older and simpler explanation of the story without submitting a new interpretation of his own. The latter is, in fact, what he did.

He certainly did write with the Homeric outline in mind. For instance, in Aeschylus the responsibility for goading Orestes to kill both Aegisthus and Clytemnestra is Apollo's, and consequently the purification, with all its attendant complications and conflict, belongs to Apollo. Sophocles minimized Apollo's role, mentioning him only a few times in the play as the author of indefinitely favorable oracles. The question of the purification or of Orestes' madness after the killing of his mother does not arise. But Sophocles has used the very flatness of the Homeric version to emphasize the unspoken questions which are in the mind of his fifth-century audience. If this is simply a story of murder and the settlement of a family feud, including the killing of a mother by her son, we are given a special Sophoclean portrait of the figures involved—mother, daughter, son, and Aegisthus, but especially Electra, the elder daughter.

For the play is rightly called after Electra. All the other people are included, principally, so that we should know more about her when we see her dealing with them—the savage, yet frightened, mother; the cautious and rather colorless Orestes; the timid, sensible, and unattractive sister; and the vulgar and bullying Aegisthus. Everyone acts as the foil of Electra. Everyone brings out another shade in the character previously missing. Electra makes no soliloquies to reveal herself as she does in Euripides. She is herself, in relation to others. She seems hardly to exist as a person except as a combination of reactions to others' deeds and words. Her father's death, her mother's enmity, her sister's passiveness, her brother's delay, Aegisthus' tyranny—these are her life. She says again and again that they are the causes for her being what she is.

Furthermore, Sophocles shows us Electra in reaction to happenings that in fact never took place. The disguised Paedagogus gives a vivid account of a chariot race in which Orestes is killed, the whole story being false. Orestes arrives, disguised, accompanied by the urn which supposedly contains his own ashes. Both of these are remarkable incidents as we have them in the play. The chariot race which occupies nearly 200 lines, or almost one-seventh of the entire piece, is based partly on that described in the *Iliad*, Book xxiii. It may also be based partly on some famous contemporary chariot race in which the audience would be interested and of which we know nothing. But the more exciting the account, the more it engaged the audience's attention, the greater, surely, must have been the jolt when it was realized that the description corresponded to no dramatic reality.

The terrible grief felt by Electra when she saw the urn believed to contain her brother's ashes must have awakened a jarring emotion in the audience, who knew that he was not dead, and some resentment at Orestes for standing by his sister and not telling her. These things are too gross to be explained away by any contrast between the Athenian audience's expectation and those of the theater of our own time. I think we are meant to see Electra not as a real person in her own right but as a mass of responses to other persons and their deeds and words, whether true or false. It is hard to imagine her loving someone understandingly, as Tecmessa and Deianeira did. Husbandless, childless, as she describes herself, cut off from father and mother and sister, she moves in an atmosphere of hate and hysteria provoked by facts and lies indiscriminately.

If we still think that Electra is justified by Sophocles, let us notice that she directs Aegisthus' body to be thrown to the dogs. This is, as all Greek students know, an outrage on religion and human decency, as the fifth century understood it, and is described as such by Sophocles himself in the *Ajax* and the *Antigone*. It happened at times, it is true, during the Peloponnesian War, and it is always regarded as barbaric.

No, this is no justification of Electra. Sophocles is often concerned with the power of hate—in the *Ajax*, the *Trachiniae*, the *Philoctetes*, and the *Oedipus at Colonus*. The *Electra* is a play about the power of hate and misery bred in a particular personality which finally seems to lose the natural power to create. The girl cannot live spontaneously. Her life is a series of responses—of hate for ill treatment, of love and hope for the fulfilment of revenge. The events of the years gone by shape everything else, to the elimination of any sense of the immediate present, except as the continuation of the past. The *Electra* is perhaps the best-constructed and most unpleasant play that Sophocles wrote. The tightness and cogency of the plot go together with the absence of nobility and magnitude in the chief character in a way which never occurred again in the extant plays. For sheer clarity and power, its author probably never improved on it.

ELECTRA

CHARACTERS

Paedagogus, the Old Servant Who Looked after Orestes when a Boy

Orestes, Son of Agamemnon, Murdered King of Mycenae

Electra, Daughter of Agamemnon

Chorus of Women of Mycenae

Chrysothemis, Sister of Electra

Clytemnestra, Widow of Agamemnon and Wife of Aegisthus

Aegisthus, Usurping King of Mycenae

ELECTRA

SCENE: *Before the royal palace in Mycenae.*

Paedagogus

Son of Agamemnon, once general at Troy,
now you are here, now you can see it all,
all that your heart has always longed for.
This is old Argos of your yearning, the grove
of Inachus' gadfly-haunted daughter.
And here, Orestes, is the Lycean market place
of the wolf-killing God. Here on the left
the famous temple of Hera. Where we have come now,
believe your eyes, see golden Mycenae,
and here the death-heavy house of the Pelopidae.   10

Once on a time, your father's murder fresh,
I took you from this house, received you from the hand
of your sister, whose blood and father were yours.
I saved you then. I have raised you from that day
to this moment of your manhood to be the avenger
of that father done to death. Orestes, now,
and you, Pylades, dearest friend, take counsel
quickly on what to do. Already the sunlight,
brightening, stirs dawning bird song into clearness,
and the black, kindly night of stars is gone.
Before a man leaves his house, sets foot on the path,   20
let us hold our parley. We are where
we must not shrink. It is high time for action.

Orestes

Dearest of servants:
very plain are the signs you show of your nobility
toward me. It is so with a horse of breeding.
Even in old age, hard conditions
do not break his spirit. His ears are still erect.

So it is with you. You urge me, and yourself
follow among the first. Therefore, I will make plain
all my determinations. Give keen ear   30
to what I say, and where I miss the mark
of what I should, correct me.

When I came to Pytho's place of prophecy
to learn to win revenge
for my father's murder on those that did that murder,
Phoebus spoke to me the words I tell you now:
"Take not spear nor shield nor host;
go yourself, and craft of hand
be yours to kill, with justice but with stealth."
Now we have heard the oracle together.
Go you into this house when occasion calls you.
Know all that is done there, and, knowing, report   40
clear news to us. You are old. It's a long time.
They will never know you. They will not suspect you
with your gray silver hair. Here is your story.
You are a stranger coming from Phanoteus,
their Phocian friend, the greatest of their allies.
Tell them a sudden accident befell
Orestes, and he's dead. Swear it on oath.
Say in the Pythian games he was rolled
out of his chariot at high speed.
That is your story now.   50

We shall go first to my father's grave
and crown it, as he bade us, with libations
and with cuttings from my thick, luxuriant hair.
And then we shall come here again
and in our hands a carved bronze-sided urn,
the urn that you know I hid here in the bushes.
By these means we shall bring the pleasant news
with our tale of lies, that here is my body,
quite gone to ashes, charred and burned, before them.

For why should it irk me if I die in word
but in deed come through alive and win my glory?   60
To my thinking, no word is base when spoken with profit.
Before now I have seen wise men often
dying empty deaths as far as words reported them,
and then, when they have come to their homes again,
they have been honored more, even to the skies.
So in my case I venture to predict
that I who die according to this rumor
shall, like a blazing star, glare on my foes again.

Land of my father, Gods of my country,
welcome me, grant me success in my coming,
and you, too, house of my father;
as your purifier I have come,
in justice sent by the Gods.   70
Do not send me dishonored out of this country,
but rich from of old time, restorer of my house.
This is all that I have to say. Old man,
let it be yours to go and mind your task.
We two must go away. It is seasonable,
and seasonableness is greatest master of every act.

Electra (from inside the house cries out)
    Ah! Ah!

Paedagogus
    Inside the house some one of the servants,
    I think, is crying.

Orestes
    Might it not be   80
    unfortunate Electra? Do you want us
    to stay here and to listen to her cries?

Paedagogus
    No. Nothing must come before we try
    to carry out what Loxias has bidden us.
    From there we must make our beginning,

pouring the lustral offerings for your father.
For that, I think, will bring us victory,
and mastery in our enterprise.

(*Orestes and his friends withdraw; Electra emerges.*)

Electra

O Holy Light
and air, copartner with light in earth's possession,
how many keening dirges,
how many plangent strokes
laid on the breast till the breast was bloody,   90
have you heard from me
when the darkling night withdrew?
And again in the house of my misery
my bed is witness to my all-night sorrowing
dirges for my unhappy father.
Him in the land of the foreigner
no murderous god of battles entertained.
But my mother and the man who shared her bed,
Aegisthus, split his head with a murderous ax,
like woodsmen with an oak tree.
For all this no pity was given him,   100
by any but me, no pity for your death,
father, so pitiful, so cruel.
But, for my part, I
will never cease my dirges and sorrowful laments,
as long as I have eyes to see
the twinkling light of the stars and this daylight.
So long, like a nightingale, robbed of her young,
here before the doors of what was my father's house
I shall cry out my sorrow for all the world to hear.

House of the Death God, house of Persephone,   110
Hermes of the Underworld, holy Curse,
Furies the Dread Ones, children of the Gods,
all ye who look upon those who die unjustly,
all ye who look upon the theft of a wife's love,

come all and help take vengeance for my father,
for my father's murder!
And send me my brother to my aid.
For alone to bear the burden I am no longer strong enough,   120
the burden of the grief that weighs against me.

Chorus

Electra, child of the wretchedest of mothers,
why with ceaseless lament do you waste away
sorrowing for one long dead,
Agamemnon, godlessly trapped
by deceits of your treacherous mother,
betrayed by her evil hand?
May evil be the end
of him that contrived the deed,
if I may lawfully say it!

Electra

True-hearted girls,
you have come to console me in my troubles.   130
I know, I understand what you say,
nothing of it escapes me.
But, all the same, I will not
leave my mourning for my poor father.
You whose love responds to mine in all ways,
suffer me my madness,
I entreat you.

Chorus

But from the all-receptive lake
of Death you shall not raise him,
groan and pray as you will.
If past the bounds of sense you dwell in grief   140
that is cureless, with sorrow unending,
you will only destroy yourself,
in a matter where the evil knows no deliverance.
It is only your discomfort.
Why do you seek it?

Electra

Simple indeed is the one
that forgets parents pitifully dead.
Suited rather to my heart
the bird of mourning
that "Itys, Itys" ever does lament,
the bird of crazy sorrow, Zeus's messenger.
And Niobe, that suffered all, you, too,   150
I count God
who weeps perpetually
in her rocky grave.

Chorus

Not alone to you, my child,
this burden of grief has come.
You exceed in your feeling far
those of your kin and blood.
See the life of Chrysothemis
and Iphianassa,
and that one whose manhood grows in secret,
sorrowing, a prince,   160
whom one day this famed land of noble Mycenae
shall welcome back, if God will bless his coming,
Orestes.

Electra

I have awaited him always
sadly, unweariedly,
till I'm past childbearing,
till I am past marriage,
always to my own ruin.
Wet with tears, I endure
an unending doom of misfortune.
But he has forgotten
what he has suffered, what he has known.
What message comes from him to me
that is not again belied?   170

Yes, he is always longing to come,
but he does not choose to come, for all his longing.

Chorus

Take heart, take heart, my child.
Still great above is Zeus,
who oversees all things in sovereign power.
Confide to him your overbitter wrath.
Chafe not overmuch against
the foes you hate, nor yet forget them quite,
for Time is a kindly God.
For neither he that lives
by Crisa's cattle-grazing shore,   180
the son of Agamemnon, will be heedless,
nor the God that rules by Acheron's waters.

Electra

But for me already the most of my life
has gone by without hope.
And I have no strength any more.
I am one wasted in childlessness,
with no loving husband for champion.
Like some dishonored foreigner,
I tenant my father's house in these ugly rags   190
and stand at a scanty table.

Chorus

Pitiful was the cry at the homecoming,
and pitiful, when on your father on his couch
the sharp biting stroke of the brazen ax
was driven home.
Craft was the contriver, passion the killer,
dreadfully begetting between them a Shape,
dreadful, whether divine or human,
was he that did this.   200

Electra

That day of all days that have ever been
most deeply my enemy.

O night, horrible burden
of that unspeakable banquet.
Shameful death that my father saw
dealt him by the hands of the two,
hands that took my own life captive,
betrayed, destroyed me utterly.
For these deeds may God in his greatness,
the Olympian one, grant punishment to match them.   210
And may they have no profit of their glory
who brought these actions to accomplishment.

Chorus

Take heed you do not speak too far.
Do you not see from what
acts of yours you suffer as you do?
To destruction self-inflicted
you fall so shamefully.
You have won for yourself
superfluity of misfortune,
breeding wars in your sullen soul
evermore. You cannot fight
such conflicts hand to hand, with mighty princes.   220

Electra

Terrors compelled me,
to terrors I was driven.
I know it, I know my own spirit.
With terrors around me, I will not hold back
these mad cries of misery, so long as I live.
For who, dear girls, who that thought right
would believe there were suitable comforting
words for me?
Forbear, forbear, my comforters.
These ills of mine shall be called cureless   230
and never shall I give over my sorrow,
and the number of my dirges none shall tell.

Chorus

But only in good will to you I speak
like some loyal mother, entreating
not to breed sorrow from sorrow.

Electra

What is the natural measure of my sorrow?
Come, how when the dead are in question,
can it be honorable to forget?
In what human being is this instinctive?
Never may I have honor of such,
nor, if I dwell with any good thing,   240
may I live at ease, by restraining
the wings of shrill lament to my father's dishonor.
For if he that is dead
is earth and nothing,
poorly lying,
and they shall never in their turn
pay death for death in justice,
then shall all shame be dead
and all men's piety.   250

Chorus

My child, it was with both our interests at heart
I came, both yours and mine. If what I say
is wrong, have your own way. We will obey you.

Electra

Women, I am ashamed if I appear
to you too much the mourner with constant dirges.
What I do, I must do. Pardon me. I ask you
how else would any well-bred girl behave
that saw her father's wrongs, as I have seen these,
by day and night, always, on the increase
and never a check?   260
First there's my mother, yes, my mother, now become
all hatred. Then in the house I live with those
who murdered my father. I am their subject, and

whether I eat or go without depends
on them.
      What sort of days do you imagine
I spend, watching Aegisthus sitting
on my father's throne, watching him wear
my father's self-same robes, watching him
at the hearth where he killed him, pouring libations? 270
Watching the ultimate act of insult,
my father's murderer in my father's bed
with my wretched mother—if mother I should call her,
this woman that sleeps with him.
She is so daring that she paramours
this foul, polluted creature and fears no Fury.
No, as though laughing at what was done,
she has found out the day on which she killed
my father in her treachery, and on that day
has set a dancing festival and sacrifices 280
sheep, in monthly ritual, "to the Gods that saved her."
So within that house I see, to my wretchedness,
the accursed feast named in his honor.
I see it, moan, and waste away, lament—
but only to myself. I may not even cry
as much as my heart would have me.
For this woman, all nobility in words,
abuses me: "You hateful thing, God-hated,
are you the only one whose father is dead?
Is there no one else of human kind in mourning? 290
My curse upon you! May the Gods below
grant you from your present sorrows no release!"
Such is the tone of her insults, unless she hears
from someone of Orestes' coming. Then
she grows really wild and stands beside me shrieking:
"Are you too not responsible for this?
Is not this your doing, you who stole
Orestes from these hands of mine, conveying him
away? But you may be sure you will pay for it

and pay enough." She howls so, and nearby her
is her distinguished bridegroom, saying the same,   300
that utter dastard, mischief complete,
who makes his wars with women.
But I am waiting for Orestes' coming,
waiting forever for the one who will stop
all our wrongs. I wait and wait and die.
For his eternal going-to-do-something
destroys my hopes, possible and impossible.

In such a state, my friends, one cannot
be moderate and restrained nor pious either.
Evil is all around me, evil
is what I am compelled to practice.

Chorus
    Tell me, as you talk like this, is Aegisthus here,   310
    or is he gone from home?

Electra
    Certainly, he's gone.
    Do not imagine, if he were near, that I
    would wander outside. Now he is on his estate.

Chorus
    If so, I can talk with you with better heart.

Electra
    For the present, he is away. What do you want?

Chorus
    Tell me: what of your brother? Is he really coming
    or hesitating? That is what I want to know.

Electra
    He says he is—but does nothing of what he says.

Chorus
    A man often hesitates when he does a big thing.   320

Electra
    I did not hesitate when rescuing him.

Chorus

Be easy.
He's a true gentleman and will help his friends.

Electra

I believe in him, or else had not lived so long.

Chorus

Say no more now. I see your sister,
blood of your blood, of the same father and mother,
Chrysothemis, in her hands burial offerings,
the usual sacrifice to the Gods below.

(*Enter Chrysothemis, Electra's sister.*)

Chrysothemis

What have you come to say out of doors,
sister? Will you never learn, in all this time,   330
not to give way to your empty anger?
Yet this much I know, and know my own heart, too,
that I am sick at what I see, so that
if I had strength, I would let them know how I feel.
But under pain of punishment, I think,
I must make my voyage with lowered sails,
that I may not seem to do something and then prove
ineffectual. But justice, justice,
is not on my side but on yours. If I am
to live and not as a prisoner, I must
in all things listen to my lords.   340

Electra

It is strange indeed that you who were born
of our father should forget him
and heed your mother. All these warnings
of me you have learned from her. Nothing is your own.
Now you must make your choice, one way or the other,
either to be a fool
or sensible—and to forget your friends.
Here you are saying: "If I had the strength,

I would show my hatred of them!" You who, when I
did everything to take vengeance for my father,
never did a thing to help—yes, discouraged the doer.   350
Is not this cowardice on top of baseness?
Tell me, or let me tell you, what benefit
I would achieve by giving up my mourning?
Do I not live? Yes, I know, badly, but
for me enough. And I hurt them
and so give honor to the dead, if there is, there
in that other world, anything that brings pleasure.
But you who hate, you tell me, hate in word only
but in fact live with our father's murderers.

I tell you: never, not though they brought me your gifts
in which you now feel pride, would I yield to them.   360
Have your rich table and your abundant life.
All the food I need is the quiet of my conscience.
I do not want to win your honor.
nor would you if you were sound of mind. Now, when you could
be called the daughter of the best of fathers,
be called your mother's. Thus to most people prove base,
traitor to your dead father and your friends.

Chorus
    No anger, I entreat you. In the words of both
    there is value for both, if you, Electra, can   370
    follow her advice and she take yours.

Chrysothemis
    O ladies, I am used to her and her words.
    I never would have mentioned this, had not
    I learned of the greatest of misfortunes coming
    her way to put a stop to her long mourning.

Electra
    Tell me of your terror. If you can speak to me
    of something worse than this condition of mine,
    I'll not refuse it still.

Chrysothemis

Well, I shall tell you.
From what I learned—and if you don't give over
your present mourning—they will send you where
never a gleam of sun shall visit you.
You shall live out your life in an underground cave
and there bewail sorrows of the world outside.
With this in mind, reflect. And do not blame me
later when you are suffering.
Now is a good time to take thought.

Electra

So this is what they have decided to do with me.

Chrysothemis

Yes, this exactly, when Aegisthus comes home.

Electra

As far as this goes, let him come home soon.

Chrysothemis

Why such a prayer for evil, my poor darling?

Electra

That he may come—if he will do what you say.

Chrysothemis

Hoping that *what* may happen you? Are you crazy?

Electra

That I may get away from you all, as far as I can.

Chrysothemis

Have you no care of this, your present life?

Electra

Mine is indeed a fine life, to be envied.

Chrysothemis

It might be, if you could learn common sense.

Electra

Do not teach me falseness to those I love.

Chrysothemis
  That, that is not what I teach, but to yield to authority.

Electra
  Practice your flattery. This is not my way.

Chrysothemis
  It is a good thing, though, not to fall through stupidity.

Electra
  I shall fall, if I must, revenging my father.

Chrysothemis
  My father will have pardon for me, I know.   400

Electra
  These are words that the base may praise.

Chrysothemis
  You will not heed me then? You will not agree?

Electra
  No, certainly.
  May I not yet be so empty-witted.

Chrysothemis
  Then I must go on the errand I was bid.

Electra
  Where are you going? To whom
  bringing burnt offering?

Chrysothemis
  My mother sent me with offerings for father's grave.

Electra
  What are you saying? To her greatest enemy?

Chrysothemis
  "Whom she has killed"—you would add.

Electra
  Which of her friends persuaded her? Who thought of this?

Chrysothemis

I think it was night terrors drove her to it.   410

Electra

Gods of my father, now or never stand my friends!

Chrysothemis

Why do "night terrors" make you confident?

Electra

I'll tell you that when you tell me the dream.

Chrysothemis

I cannot tell you much, only a little.

Electra

Tell me it, all the same. Often this little
has made or ruined men.

Chrysothemis

There is a story that she saw my father,
the father that was yours and mine, again
coming to life, once more to live with her.
He took and at the hearth planted the scepter   420
which once he bore and now Aegisthus bears,
and up from out the scepter foliage sprang
luxuriantly, and shaded all the land
of this Mycenae. This is what I heard
from someone present when she told the Sun
the nature of her dreams.

                                But beyond this
I know no more, only that she sends me
because of her fear. And, by the Gods, I pray you,
the Gods that live in this country, listen to me
and do not fall out of stupidity.
For if you should reject me, she will come
again to harry you with punishment.   430

Electra

My dear one, not a morsel that you hold
allow to touch that grave, no, nothing.

It would not be God's law nor pious that you
should offer to my father sacrifices
and lustral offerings from that enemy woman.
Throw them to the winds! Or hide them in deep hollowed
earth, somewhere where no particle of them
may ever reach my father where he lies.
But let them be stored up for her as treasures
below, against the day when *she* shall die.
I tell you, if she were not the most brazen   440
of all of womankind, would she have dared
to pour these enemy libations
over the body of the man she killed?
Consider if you think that the dead man,
as he lies in his grave, will welcome kindly
these offerings from her by whom he was robbed
of life and honor? By whom, mutilated?
And for her purification she wiped
the blood stains on his head? Can you believe
that these will prove for her a quittance offering?
No, no. You let them be. You cut a lock
out of your own hair, from the fringe and mine,
mine, too, his wretched daughter's. Such a small offering   450
yet all I have! Give it to him, this lustrous
lock of hair, and here, my girdle, unadorned.
Kneel then and pray that from that nether world
he may come, a friendly spirit, to our help
against his enemies. Pray that the boy Orestes
may live to fight and win against his enemies,
may live to set his foot upon them.
                    And so
in days to come we shall be able to dress
this grave with richer hands than we can now.
I think, oh yes, I think that it was he
that thought to send this evil-boding dream   460
to her.
      Yet, sister, do yourself this service

and help me, too, and help the dearest of all,
our common father, that lies dead in the underworld.

Chorus

The girl speaks well. And you, my dear,
if you are wise, will follow her advice.

Chrysothemis

I will do it. It is not reasonable for us two
to squabble about what is just. We must haste to do something.
But, my friends, if I attempt this, I must have your silence.
If my mother hears of this, I am sure I shall rue   470
indeed the attempt I shall make.

Chorus

If I am not a distracted prophet
and lacking in skill of judgment,
Justice foreshadowing the event
shall come, in her hands a just victory.
Yes, she will come, my child, in vengeance
and soon.
Of that I was confident
when I lately heard,   480
of this dream of sweet savor.
Your father, the king of the Greeks,
has never forgotten,
nor the ax of old,
bronze-shod, double-toothed,
which did him to death
in shame and baseness.

There shall come many-footed, many-handed,
hidden in dreadful ambush,   490
the bronze-shod Fury.
Wicked indeed were they who were seized
with a passion for a forbidden bed,
for a marriage accursed, stained with murder.
In the light of this, I am very sure

that never, never shall we see
such a portent draw near without hurt
to doers and partners in crime.
There are no prophecies for mortal men
in dreadful dreams and soothsayings
if this night vision come not,   500
well and truly to fulfilment.

Horsemanship of Pelops of old,
loaded with disaster,
how deadly you have proved
to this land!
For since the day that Myrtilus
fell asleep, sunk in the sea,
wrecked utterly with the unhappy
wreck of his golden carriage,   510
for never a moment since
has destruction and ruin
ever left this house.

(*Queen Clytemnestra enters from the palace.*)

Clytemnestra
It seems you are loose again, wandering about.
Aegisthus isn't here, who always restrains you
from going abroad and disgracing your family.
But now that he is away you pay no heed
to me, although there's many a one you have told   520
at length how brutally and how unjustly
I lord it over you, insulting
you and yours.
                 There is no insolence in myself,
but being abused by you so constantly
I give abuse again.
                 Your father, yes,
always your father. Nothing else is your pretext—
the death he got from me. From me. I know it,
well. There is no denial in me. Justice,

Justice it was that took him, not I alone.
You would have served the cause of Justice if
you had been right-minded.
For this your father whom you always mourn,   530
alone of all the Greeks, had the brutality
to sacrifice your sister to the Gods,
although he had not toiled for her as I did,
the mother that bore her, he the begetter only.
Tell me, now, why he sacrificed her. Was it
for the sake of the Greeks?

They had no share in my daughter to let them kill her.
Was it for Menelaus' sake, his brother,
that he killed my child? And shall he not then pay for it?
Had not this Menelaus two children who
ought to have died rather than mine? It was their parents   540
for whose sake all the Greeks set sail for Troy.
Or had the God of Death some longing to feast
on my children rather than hers? Or had
that accursed father lost the love of mine
and felt it still for Menelaus' children?
This was the act of a father thoughtless
or with bad thoughts. That is how I see it
even if you differ with me.
                         The dead girl,
if she could speak, would bear me out.
I am not dismayed by all that has happened.
If you think me wicked, keep your righteous judgment   550
and blame your neighbors.

Electra

This is one time you will not be able to say
that the abuse I receive from you was provoked
by something painful on my side.
                         But if
you will allow me I will speak truthfully
on behalf of the dead man and my dead sister.

Clytemnestra

Of course, I allow you. If you had always begun
our conversations so, you would not have been
so painful to listen to.

Electra

I will tell you, then.
You say you killed my father. What claim more shameful
than that, whether with justice or without it?   560
But I'll maintain that it was not with justice
you killed him, but the seduction of that bad man,
with whom you now are living, drew you to it.
Ask Artemis the Huntress what made her hold
the many winds in check at Aulis. Or
I'll tell you this. *You* dare not learn from her.

My father, as I hear, when at his sport,
started from his feet a horned dappled stag
within the Goddess' sanctuary. He
let fly and hit the deer and uttered some boast
about his killing of it. The daughter of Leto   570
was angry at this and therefore stayed the Greeks
in order that my father, to compensate
for the beast killed, might sacrifice his daughter.

Thus was her sacrifice—no other deliverance
for the army either homeward or toward Ilium.
He struggled and fought against it. Finally,
constrained, he killed her—not for Menelaus.
But if—I will plead in your own words—he had done so
for his brother's sake, is that any reason
why he should die at your hands? By what law?
If this is the law you lay down for men, take heed   580
you do not lay down for yourself ruin and repentance.
If we shall kill one in another's requital,
you would be the first to die, if you met with justice.

No. Think if the whole is not a mere excuse.
Please tell me for what cause you now commit
the ugliest of acts—in sleeping with him,
the murderer with whom you first conspired
to kill my father, and breed children to him, and
your former honorable children born   590
of honorable wedlock you drive out.
What grounds for praise shall I find in this? Will you say
that this, too, is retribution for your daughter?
If you say it, still your act is scandalous.
It isn't decent to marry with your enemies
even for a daughter's sake.
                      But I may not
even rebuke you! What you always say
is that it is my mother I am reviling.
Mother! I do not count you mother of mine,
but rather a mistress. My life is wretched
because I live with multitudes of sufferings,
inflicted by yourself and your bedfellow.   600
But the other, he is away, he has escaped
your hand, though barely. Sad Orestes now
wears out his life in misery and exile.
Many a time you have accused me
of rearing him to be your murderer.
I would have done it if I could. Know that.
As far as that goes, you may publicly
proclaim me what you like—traitor, reviler,
a creature full of shamelessness.
                      If I am
naturally skilled as such, I do no shame
to the nature of the mother that brought me forth.

Chorus

    I see she is angry, but whether it is in justice,   610
    I no longer see how I shall think of that.

Clytemnestra
> What need have *I* of thought in her regard
> who so insults her mother, when a grown woman?
> Don't you think she will go to any lengths, so shameless
> as she is?

Electra
> You may be sure I am ashamed,
> although you do not think it. I know why
> I act so wrongly, so unlike myself.
> The hate you feel for me and what you do
> compel me against my will to act as I do.   620
> For ugly deeds are taught by ugly deeds.

Clytemnestra
> O vile and shameless, I and my words and deeds
> give you too much talk.

Electra
> It is you who talk, not I. It is your deeds,
> and it is deeds invent the words.

Clytemnestra
> Now by the Lady Artemis you shall not escape
> the results of your behavior, when Aegisthus comes.

Electra
> You see? You let me say what I please, and then
> you are outraged. You do not know how to listen.

Clytemnestra
> Hold your peace at least. Allow me sacrifice,   630
> since I have permitted you to say all you will.

Electra
> I allow you, yes, I bid you, sacrifice.
> Do not blame my lips; for I will say no more.

Clytemnestra (to the maid)
> Come, do you lift them up, the offerings

of all the fruits of earth, that to this King here
I may offer my prayers for freedom from my fears.

(She speaks to the image of Apollo.)

Phoebus Protector, hear me, as I am,
although the word I speak is muted. Not among friends
is it spoken, nor may I unfold the whole
to the light while this girl stands beside me,   640
lest with her chattering tongue, wagging in malice,
she sow in all the city bad reports.
Yet hear me as I speak. So I will put it:
the dreams of double meaning I have seen
within this night, for them, Lycaean King,
grant what is good in them prosperous issue
but what is ill, turn it again upon
those that do us ill.
If there are some that from my present wealth
plot to expel me with their stratagems,
do not permit them. Let me live out my life,   650
just as my life is now, to the end uninjured,
controlling the house of Atreus and the throne,
living with those I love as I do now,
the good days on our side, and with such children
as do not hate me nor cause bitter pain.
These are my prayers, Lycaean Apollo, hear them
graciously. Grant to all of us what we ask.
For all the rest, although I am silent,
I know you are a God and know it all.
It is natural that the children of Zeus see all.

(Enter Paedagogus.)

Paedagogus

Foreign ladies, how may I know for certain,   660
is this the palace of the King Aegisthus?

Chorus

This is it, sir. Your own guess is correct.

Paedagogus
> Would I then be right in thinking this lady
> his wife? She has indeed a royal look.

Chorus
> Quite right. Here she is for you, herself.

Paedagogus
> Greetings, your Majesty. I come with news,
> pleasant news for you and Aegisthus and your friends.

Clytemnestra
> I welcome what you have said. I would like first
> to know who sent you here.

Paedagogus
> The Phocian,
> Phanoteus, charging me with a grave business.   670

Clytemnestra
> What is it, sir? Please tell me. I know well
> you come from a friend and will speak friendly words.

Paedagogus
> Orestes is dead. There it is, in one short word.

Electra
> O God, O God! This is the day I die.

Clytemnestra
> What is this you say, sir, what? Don't listen to her.

Paedagogus
> What I said and say now is "Orestes is dead."

Electra
> God help me, I am dead—I cannot live now.

Clytemnestra
> Leave her to herself. Sir, will you tell me the truth,
> in what way did he meet his death?

Paedagogus
> This
> I was sent to tell, and I will tell you it all.   680

He went to the glorious gathering that Greece holds
in honor of the Delphic Games, and when
he heard the herald's shrill proclamation
for the first contest—it was a running race—
he entered glorious, all men's eyes upon him.
His running was as good as his appearance.
He won the race and came out covered with honor.
There is much I could tell you, but I must tell it briefly.   690
I do not know a man of such achievement
or prowess. Know this one thing. In all the contests
the marshals announced, he won the prize, was cheered,
proclaimed the victor as "Argive by birth,
by name Orestes, son of the general
Agamemnon who once gathered the great Greek host."
So much for that. But when a God sends mischief,
not even the strong man may escape.
                                        Orestes,
when, the next day, at sunset, there was a race
for chariot teams, entered with many contestants.   700
There was one Achaean, one from Sparta, two
Libyans, masters in driving racing teams.
Orestes was the fifth among them. He
had as his team Thessalian mares. The sixth
was an Aetolian with young sorrel horses.
The seventh was a Magnesian, and the eighth
an Aenean, by race, with a white team.
The ninth competitor came from God-built Athens,
and then a Boeotian, ten chariots in all.
They stood in their allotted stations where   710
the appointed judges placed them. At the signal,
a brazen trumpet, they were off. The drivers
cheered their horses on, their hands vibrating the reins,
all together. All the course was filled
with the noise of rattling chariots. Clouds of dust
rose up. The mass of drivers, huddled together,
did not spare the goad as each one struggled

to put the nave of his wheel or the snorting mouths
of his horses past his rival, wheels and backs
of the foremost drivers all beslobbered with foam,   720
as the breath of the teams behind beat on them.
So far all chariots were uninjured. Then
the Aenean's hard-mouthed colts got out of hand
and bolted as they finished the sixth lap
and turned into the seventh. There they crashed
head on with the Barcaean. After that,
from this one accident, team crashed team
and overset each other. All the plain
of Crisa was full of wrecks. But the man from Athens,   730
a clever driver, saw what was happening, pulled
his horses out of the way and held them in check,
letting past the disordered mass of teams in the middle.
Orestes had been driving last and holding
his horses back, putting his trust in the finish.
But when he saw the Athenian left alone,
he sent a shrill cry through his good horses' ears
and set to catch him. The two drove level,
the poles were even. First one, now the other,
would push his horses' heads in front.   740
Orestes always drove tight at the corners
barely grazing the edge of the post with his wheel,
loosing his hold of the trace horse on his right
while he checked the near horse. In his other laps
the poor young man and his horses had come through safe.
But this time he let go of the left rein
as the horse was turning. Unaware, he struck the edge
of the pillar and broke his axle in the center.
He was himself thrown from the rails of the chariot
and tangled in the reins. As he fell, the horses
bolted wildly to the middle of the course.
When the crowd saw him fallen from his car,
they shuddered. "How young he was," "How gallant his deeds,"   750
and "How sadly he has ended," as they saw him

thrown earthward now, and then, tossing his legs
to the sky—until at last the grooms
with difficulty stopped the runaway team
and freed him, but so covered with blood that no one
of his friends could recognize the unhappy corpse.
They burned him on the pyre. Then men of Phocis
chosen for the task have brought here in a small urn
the lamentable ashes—all that is left
of this great frame, that he may have his grave   760
here in his father's country.
                         That is my story,
bitter as stories go, but for us who saw it,
greatest of all ill luck these eyes beheld.

Chorus

  Woe, woe. The ancient family
  of our lords has perished, it seems, root and branch.

Clytemnestra

  Zeus, what shall I say? Shall I say "good luck"
  or "terrible, but for the best"? Indeed,
  my state is terrible if I must save
  my life by the misfortunes of myself.

Paedagogus

  My lady, why does this story make you dejected?

Clytemnestra

  Mother and child! It is a strange relation.   770
  A mother cannot hate the child she bore
  even when injured by it.

Paedagogus

  Our coming here, it seems, then is to no purpose.

Clytemnestra

  Not to no purpose. How can you say "no purpose"?—
  if you have come with certain proofs of death
  of one who from my soul was sprung,
  but severed himself from my breast, from my nurture, who

became an exile and a foreigner;
who when he quitted this land, never saw me again;
who charged me with his father's murder, threatened
terrors against me. Neither night nor day   780
could I find solace in sleep. Time, supervisor,
conducted me to inevitable death.
But now, with this one day I am freed from fear
of her and him. She was the greater evil;
she lived with me, constantly draining
the very blood of life—now perhaps I'll have peace
from her threats. The light of day will come again.

Electra
My God! My God! Now must I mourn indeed
your death, Orestes, when your mother here
pours insults on you, dead. Can this be right?   790

Clytemnestra
Not right for you. But he is right as he is.

Electra
Hear, Nemesis, of the man that lately died!

Clytemnestra
She has heard those she should and done all well.

Electra
Insult us now. For now the luck is yours.

Clytemnestra
Will you not stop this, you and Orestes both?

Electra
We are stopped indeed. We cannot make you stop.

Clytemnestra (to the messenger)
Your coming will be worth much, sir, if you
have stopped my daughter's never ceasing clamor.

Paedagogus (with a feint at departure)
Well, I will go now, if all this is settled.

Clytemnestra

O no! I should do wrong to myself and to   800
the friend who sent you if I let you go.
Please go inside. Leave her out here to wail
the misfortunes of herself and those she loves.

      (Clytemnestra and the assumed messenger go into the house.)

Electra

There's an unhappy mother for you! See
how agonized, how bitter, were the tears,
how terribly she sorrowed for her son
that met the death you heard of! No, I tell you,
she parted from us laughing. O my God!
Orestes darling, your death is my death.
By your passing you have torn away from my heart
whatever solitary hope still lingered   810
that you would live and come some day to avenge
your father and my miserable self.
But now where should I turn? I am alone,
having lost both you and my father. Back again
to be a slave among those I hate most
of all the world, my father's murderers!
Is this what is right for me?
                  No, this I will not—
live with them any more. Here, at the gate
I will abandon myself to waste away
this life of mine, unloved. If they're displeased,
let someone kill me, someone that lives within.   820
Death is a favor to me, life an agony.
I have no wish for life.

Chorus

Where are Zeus's thunderbolts?
Where is the glowing sun?
If they see this and hide it
and hold their peace?

Electra (*cries out*)
   Oh!

Chorus
   Why do you cry, child?

Electra (*cries again*)
   Oh!

Chorus
   Speak no great word.   830

Electra
   You will destroy me.

Chorus
   How?

Electra
   If you suggest a hope
   when all is plain, when they are all gone
   to the house of Death, and when I waste
   my life away, you tread me further down.

Chorus
   King Amphiaraus, as I know,
   was caught in woman's golden snares
   and now beneath the earth
   reigns over all the spirits there.

Electra
   Oh! Oh!   840

Chorus
   Alas indeed, for pitiably

Electra
                              he died.

Chorus
   Yes.

Electra
   I know, I know. For him in sorrow
   there came a deliverer.

None such for me. For one there was,
but he is gone, ravished by death.

Chorus

Unhappy girl, unhappiness is yours!

Electra

I bear you witness with full knowledge.   850
Knowledge too full, bred of a life,
the crowded months surging with horrors
many and dreadful!

Chorus

We know what you mean.

Electra

So do not then, I pray you,
divert my thoughts to where . . .

Chorus

What do you mean?

Electra

. . . there is no hope, no kinsfolk,
and none among the nobles that will help.

Chorus

Death is the common lot of death-born men.   860

Electra

Yes, but to meet it so,
as he did, poor darling,
tangled in the leather reins,
among the wild competing hoofs.

Chorus

None can guess whence death will come.

Electra

True indeed. He is now a stranger
that was hidden in earth, by no hand of mine,
knew no grave I gave him,
knew no keening from me.   870

(*Enter Chrysothemis.*)

Chrysothemis
My darling,
I am so glad, I have run here in haste,
regardless of propriety. I bring you
happiness and a relief from all
the troubles you have had and sorrowed for.

Electra
Where could you find a cure—and who are you
to find it—for my troubles which know no cure?

Chrysothemis
We have Orestes here among us—that is
my news for you—as plain as you see myself.

Electra
Are you mad, poor girl, or can it be you laugh
at what are your own troubles as well as mine?   880

Chrysothemis
I swear by our father's hearth. It is not in mockery
I speak. He is here in person with us.

Electra
                              Ah!
Wretched girl! Who told you this that you believed him,
too credulous?

Chrysothemis
                    My own eyes were the evidence
for what I saw, and no one else.

Electra
                              Poor thing!
Poor thing! What proof was there to see? What did you
see that has set your heart incurably
afire?

Chrysothemis
          I pray you, hear me by the Gods,
and having heard me, call me sane or foolish.   890

Electra
>Tell me, then, if the story gives you pleasure.

Chrysothemis
>Yes, I will tell you all I saw.
>When I came to our father's ancient grave,
>I saw that from the very top of the mound
>newly spilled rills of milk were flowing. Round
>the coffin was a wreath of all the flowers
>that grow. I saw in wonder, looked about
>for someone who would be near me. When I saw
>that all was quiet, I approached the grave.   900
>At the top of the pyre there was a lock of hair;
>as soon as I saw that, something jumped within me
>at the familiar sight. I know I saw
>the token of my dearest, loved Orestes.
>I took it in my hands, never saying a word
>for fear of saying what would be ill-omened,
>but with my joy my eyes were filled with tears.
>Both then and now I know with certainty
>this offering could come from him alone.
>Whom else could this concern, save you and me?
>I did not do it, I know, and neither did you.   910
>How could you? For you cannot leave this house,
>even to pray, but they will punish you for it.
>Nor can it be our mother. She is not inclined
>to do such things, nor, doing them, to be secret.
>These offerings at the grave must be Orestes'.
>Darling, take heart. It is not always the same
>Genius that stands by the same people. Till now
>he was hateful to us. But now perhaps
>this day will seal the promise of much good.

Electra
>Oh, how I have been pitying you for your folly!

Chrysothemis
>What is this? Do I not say what is to your liking?   920

Electra

You do not know where you are, nor where your thoughts are.

Chrysothemis

Why should I not have knowledge of what I saw?

Electra

He is dead, my dear. Your rescue at his hands
is dead along with him. Look to him no more.

Chrysothemis

Alas! From whom on earth did you hear this?

Electra

From one that was near to him, when he was dying.

Chrysothemis

Where is he then? I am lost in wonderment.

Electra

In the house. He is our mother's welcome guest.

Chrysothemis

Alas again! But who then would have placed   930
these many offerings on our father's tomb?

Electra

I think perhaps that someone put them there
as a remembrance of the dead Orestes.

Chrysothemis

Unlucky I! I was so happy coming,
hurrying to bring my news to you, not knowing
what misery we were plunged in. Now when I've come,
I find both our old sorrow and the new.

Electra

That is how you see it. But now listen to me,
and you can relieve the suffering that weighs on us.

Chrysothemis

How can I bring the dead to life again?   940

Electra

This is not what I mean. I am no such fool.

Chrysothemis
> What do you bid me do, of which I am capable?

Electra
> To have the courage to follow my counsel.

Chrysothemis
> If I can help at all, I will not refuse.

Electra
> Look: there is no success without hardship.

Chrysothemis
> I see. As far as my strength goes, I will help.

Electra
> Hear me tell you, then, the plans that I have laid.
> Friends to stand by and help us we have none—
> nowhere—you know that quite as well as I.
> Death has taken them and robbed us. We alone,   950
> the two of us, are left.
> While I still heard my brother flourished,
> alive, I had my hopes he would still come,
> some day, to avenge the murder of his father.
> But now that he's no more, I look to you,
> that you should not draw back from helping me,
> your true-born sister, kill our father's murderer
> that killed him with his own hand—Aegisthus.
> There is nothing I should now conceal from you.
> What are you waiting for, that you are hesitant?
> What hope do you look to, that is still standing?
> Now you must sorrow for the loss of fortune   960
> that was our father's. Now you must grieve
> that you have already so many years
> without a marriage and a husband. Do not
> hope you will get them now. For Aegisthus
> is not such a fool to suffer to grow up
> children of you and me, clearly to harm him.
> But if you follow my plans,

first, you will win from that dead father, gone
to the underworld, and from our brother with him,
the recognition of your piety.
And, secondly, as you were born to freedom,   970
so in the days to come you will be called free
and find a marriage worthy of you; for all
love to look to the noble.
Do you not see how great a reputation
you will win yourself and me by doing this?
For who of citizens and foreigners
that sees us will not welcome us with praise:
"These are two sisters, friends. Look on them well.
They saved their father's house when their foes
were riding high, stood champions against murder,
sparing not to risk their lives upon the venture.   980
Therefore, we all should love them, all revere them,
and all at feasts and public ceremonies
honor these two girls for their bravery."

This is what everyone will say of us,
in life and death, to our undying fame.
My dear one, hear me. Take sides with your father
and with your brother. Give me deliverance
from what I suffer. Deliver yourself, knowing this:
life on base terms, for the nobly born, is base.

Chorus

In such concerns forethought is an ally   990
to the one that gives, and her that gets advice.

Chrysothemis

Ladies, before she spoke, if she had good sense,
she would have held to prudence, as she has not.

(To Electra.)

To what can you look to give you confidence
to arm yourself and call on me to help?
Can you not see? You are a woman—no man.

Your physical strength is less than is your enemies'!
Their Genius, day by day, grows luckier
while ours declines and comes to nothingness. 1000
Who is there, plotting to kill such a man
as this Aegisthus, would come off unhurt?
We two are now in trouble. Look to it that
we do not get ourselves trouble still worse
if someone hears what you have said.
There is no gain for us, not the slightest help,
to win a noble reputation if
the way to it lies by dishonorable death.
For death is not the worst but when one wants
to die and cannot even have that death.
I beg of you, before you utterly
destroy us and exterminate our family, 1010
check your temper. All that you have said to me
shall be, for my part, unspoken, unfulfilled.
Be sensible, you, and, at long last, being weaker,
learn to give in to those that have the strength.

Chorus

Give heed to her. No greater gain for man
than the possession of a sensible mind!

Electra

You have said nothing unexpected. Well
I knew you would reject what I proposed.
The deed must then be done by my own hand
alone. For I will not leave it unfulfilled. 1020

Chrysothemis

Ah!
I would you had felt so when our father died.
You would have carried all before you.

Electra

I was the same in nature, weaker in judgment.

Chrysothemis

Practice to keep that judgment through your life.

Electra
That is advice which means you will not help me.

Chrysothemis
Yes—for the effort itself implies disaster.

Electra
I envy you your "judgment," hate your cowardice.

Chrysothemis
I will be equally patient when you praise me.

Electra
That you will never experience from me.

Chrysothemis
There's a long future to determine that.   1030

Electra
Begone; for there's no help in you for me.

Chrysothemis
There is, but there's no learning it in you.

Electra
Go and tell all this story to your mother.

Chrysothemis
On my side there is no such hatred as that.

Electra
Understand, at least, how you dishonor me.

Chrysothemis
There is no dishonor, only forethought for you.

Electra
Must I then follow *your* conception of justice?

Chrysothemis
You will think it *ours*, when you come to your senses.

Electra
It is terrible to speak well and be wrong.

Chrysothemis
A very proper description of yourself.   1040

Electra
> What! Do you not think that I say what I do with justice?

Chrysothemis
> There are times when even justice brings harm with it.

Electra
> These are laws by which I would not wish to live.

Chrysothemis
> If you made your attempt, you would find that I was right.

Electra
> Yes, I will make it. You will not frighten me.

Chrysothemis
> Are you sure now? You will not think again?

Electra
> No enemy is worse than bad advice.

Chrysothemis
> You cannot agree with any of what I say?

Electra
> I have made my mind up—and not of yesterday.

Chrysothemis
> I will go away then. You cannot bring yourself   1050
> to find my words right, nor I your disposition.

Electra
> Go then. I will never call you back,
> not though you long for it. It would be utter
> folly to make so hopeless an attempt.

Chrysothemis
> Well, if you think that you are right, go on
> thinking so. When you are deep in trouble, then
> you may agree with what I said.

Chorus
> We see above our heads the birds,
> true in their wisdom,

caring for the livelihood   1060
of those that gave them life and sustenance.
Why do we not pay our debts so?
By Zeus of the Lightning Bolt,
by Themis, Dweller in Heaven,
not long shall they go unpunished.
O Voice that goes to the dead below,
carry piteous accents,
to the Atridae in the underworld,
and tell of wrongs untouched
by joy of the dance.

Tell them that now their house is sick,   1070
tell them that their two children
fight and struggle, that they cannot
any more live in harmony together.
Electra, betrayed, alone,
is down in the waves of sorrow,
constantly bewailing her father's fate,
like the nightingale lamenting.
She takes no thought of death;
she is ready to leave the light
if only she can kill
the two Furies of her house.
Was there ever one so noble   1080
born of a noble house?

None of the good will choose to live
basely, if so living
they cloud their renown and die nameless.
O my child, my child, even so you
have chosen the common lot of mourning,
have rejected dishonor,
to win at once two reputations
as wise and best of daughters.

I pray that your life may be lifted high   1090

over your foes,
in wealth and power as much as now
you lie beneath their hand.
For I have found you in distress
but winning the highest prize
by piety toward Zeus
for observance of nature's greatest laws.

Orestes (disguised as a Phocian countryman)
I wonder, ladies, if we were directed right
and have come to the destination that we sought?

Chorus
What do you seek? And what do you want here?   1100

Orestes
I have asked all the way here where Aegisthus lives.

Chorus
You have arrived and need not blame your guides.

Orestes
Would some one of you be so kind to tell
the household we have come, a welcome company?

Chorus
This lady, nearest you, will bear the message.

Orestes
Then, lady, will you signify within
that certain men of Phocis seek Aegisthus.

Electra
O God, O God, are these the certain proofs
you bring of rumors we had before you came?

Orestes
I do not know about rumor. Old Strophius sent me   1110
here to bring news about Orestes.

Electra
What is it, sir? How fear steals over me!

Orestes

We have the small remains of him in this urn,
this little urn you see us carrying.

Electra

Alas, Alas! This is it indeed, all clear.
Here is my sorrow visible, before me.

Orestes

If you are one that sorrows for Orestes
and his troubles, know this urn contains his body.

Electra

Sir, give it to me, by the Gods. If he
is hidden in this urn—give it into my hands,   1120
that I may keen and cry lament together
for myself and all my race with these ashes here.

Orestes (speaking to his men)

Bring it and give it to her, whoever she is.
It is not in enmity she asks for it.
One of his friends perhaps, or of his blood.

Electra (speaking to the urn)

Oh, all there is for memory of my love,
my most loved in the world, all that is left
of live Orestes, oh, how differently
from how I sent you forth, how differently
from what I hoped, do I receive you home.
Now all I hold is nothingness,
but you were brilliant when I sent you forth.   1130
Would that you had left life before I sent you
abroad to a foreign country, when I stole you
with these two hands, saved you from being murdered.
Then on that very day you would have died,
have lain there and have found your share,
your common portion, of your father's grave.
Now far from home, an exile, on alien soil

without your sister near, you died unhappily.
I did not, to my sorrow, wash you with
the hands that loved you, did not lift you up,
as was my right, a weight of misery, 1140
to the fierce blaze of the pyre. The hands of strangers
gave you due rites, and so you come again,
a tiny weight inclosed in tiny vessel.
Alas for all my nursing of old days,
so constant—all for nothing—which I gave you;
my joy was in the trouble of it. For never
were you your mother's love as much as mine.
None was your nurse but I within that household.
You called me always "sister." Now in one day
all that is gone—for you are dead. All, all
you have snatched with you in your going, like 1150
a hurricane. Our father is dead and gone.
I am dead in you; and you are dead yourself.
Our enemies laugh. Frantic with joy, she grows,
mother, no mother, whom you promised me,
in secret messages so often, you
would come to punish. This, all this, the Genius,
the unlucky Genius of yourself and me,
has stolen away and sent you back to me,
instead of the form I loved, only your dust
and idle shade. Alas! Alas!

     (*She takes up an attitude of formalized mourning by the urn.*)
O body pitiable! Alas! 1160
O saddest journey that you went, my love,
and so have ended me! Alas!
O brother, loved one, you have ended me.
Therefore, receive me to your habitation,
nothing to nothing, that with you below
I may dwell from now on. When you were on earth,
I shared all with you equally. Now I claim
in death no less to share a grave with you.
The dead, I see, no longer suffer pain. 1170

Chorus

Think, Electra, your father was mortal,
and mortal was Orestes. Do not sorrow too much.
This is a debt that all of us must pay.

Orestes

Ah!
What shall I say? What words can I use, perplexed?
I am no longer master of my tongue.

Electra

What ails you? What is the meaning of your words?

Orestes

Is this the distinguished beauty, Electra?

Electra

Yes.
A miserable enough Electra, truly.

Orestes

Alas for this most lamentable event!

Electra

Is it for me, sir, you are sorrowing?   1180

Orestes

Form cruelly and godlessly abused!

Electra

None other than myself must be the subject
of your ill-omened words, sir.

Orestes

O, alas!
For your life without husband or happiness!

Electra

Why do you look at me so, sir? Why lament?

Orestes

How little then I knew of my own sorrows!

Electra

In what of all that was said did you find this out?

Orestes

So great, so sore, I see your sufferings.

Electra

It's little of my suffering that you see.

Orestes

How can there be things worse than those I see?

Electra

Because I live with those that murdered him.   1190

Orestes

Murderers? And whose? Where is the guilt you hint at?

Electra

My father's murderers. I am their slave perforce.

Orestes

Who is it that forces you to such subjection?

Electra

She is called my mother—but like a mother in nothing.

Orestes

How does she force you? Hardship or violence?

Electra

With violence and hardship and all ills.

Orestes

You have none to help you or to hinder her?

Electra

No. There was one. You have shown me his dust.

Orestes

Poor girl! When I look at you, how I pity you.

Electra

Then you are the only one that ever pitied me.   1200

Orestes

Yes. I alone came here and felt your pain.

Electra

You haven't come as, in some way, our kinsman?

Orestes

I will tell—if (*pointing to the Chorus*) I may speak here among
friends.

Electra

Yes, friends indeed. You may speak quite freely.

Orestes

Give up this urn then, and you shall know all.

Electra

Don't take it from me, stranger—by the Gods!

Orestes

Do what I bid you. You will not be wrong.

Electra

By your beard! Do not rob me of what I love most!

Orestes

I will not let you have it.

Electra

O Orestes!

Alas, if I may not even give you burial!   1210

Orestes

No words of ill omen! You have no right to mourn.

Electra

Have I no right to mourn for my dead brother?

Orestes

You have no right to call him by that name.

Electra

Am I then so dishonored in his sight?

Orestes

No one dishonors you. Mourning is not for you.

Electra

It is—if I hold Orestes' body here.

Orestes

No body of Orestes—except in fiction.

Electra

Where is the poor boy buried then?

Orestes

                              Nowhere.

There is no grave for living men.

Electra

                            How, boy,

What do you mean?

Orestes

                   Nothing that is untrue.   1220

Electra

Is he alive then?

Orestes

                Yes, if I am living.

Electra

And are you he?

Orestes

                Look at this signet ring

that was our father's, and know if I speak true.

Electra

O happiest light!

Orestes

                Happiest I say, too.

Electra

Voice, have you come?

Orestes

                    Hear it from no other voice.

Electra

Do my arms hold you?

Orestes

                  Never again to part.

Electra (to the Chorus)
　　Dearest of women, fellow citizens,
　　here is Orestes, that was dead in craft,
　　and now by craft restored to life again.

Chorus
　　　　We see, my child, and at your happy fortune　　　　　　　　1230
　　　　a tear of gladness trickles from our eyes.

Electra
　　Child of the body that I loved the best,
　　at last you have come,
　　you have come, you have found, you have known those you
　　　　yearned for.

Orestes
　　Yes, I have come.
　　But bide your time in silence.

Electra
　　Why?

Orestes
　　Silence is better, that none inside may hear.

Electra
　　No, by Artemis, ever virgin.
　　That I will never stoop to fear—
　　the women inside there,　　　　　　　　　　　　　　　　　　1240
　　always a vain burden on the earth.

Orestes
　　Yes, but consider that in women too
　　there lives a warlike spirit. You have proof of it.

Electra
　　Alas, indeed.
　　You have awakened my sorrow no cloud can dim,
　　no expiation wash away,
　　no forgetfulness overcome,
　　no measure can fit,
　　in all its frightfulness.

　　　　　　　　　　　　　　　　　1250

Orestes

> I know that too. But when you may speak freely,
> then is the time to remember what was done.

Electra

> Every moment, every moment of all time
> would fit justly for my complaints.
> For hardly now are my lips free of restraint.

Orestes

> And I agree. Therefore, hold fast your freedom.

Electra

> By doing what?

Orestes

> Where there is no occasion,
> do not choose to talk too much.

Electra

> Who could find a fit bargain   1260
> of words for that silence,
> now you have appeared?
> Past hope, past calculation,
> I see you.

Orestes

> You see me when the Gods moved me to come.

Electra

> You tell me then of a grace surpassing
> what I knew before, if in very truth
> the Gods have given you to this house.
> This I count an action divine.   1270

Orestes

> Indeed, I hesitate to check your joy;
> only I fear your pleasure may be too great.

Electra

> Orestes, you have come at last,
> have made the journey worth all the world to me,

have come before me at last.
Now that I see you
after so much sorrow,
do not, I beg you—

Orestes

What should I not do?

Electra

                  Do not deprive me
of the joy of seeing your face.

Orestes

I would be angry if I saw another
trying to take me from you.

Electra

                You agree?

Orestes

                     Yes.   1280

Electra

My dear one, I have heard you speaking,
the voice I never hoped to hear.
Till now I have held my rage speechless;
I did not cry out when I heard bad news.
But now I have you. You have come,
your darling face before me
that even in suffering I never forgot.

Orestes

Spare me all superfluity of speech.
Tell me not how my mother is villainous,
nor how Aegisthus drains my father's wealth   1290
by luxury or waste. Words about this
will shorten time and opportunity.
But tell me what we need for the present moment,
how openly or hidden we may make
this coming of ours a check for mocking foes.
Take care, you, that our mother may not discover you
by your radiant face, when we two go inside.

Groan as for my destruction, emptily
described in words. For when we have reached success,
then you may freely show your joy, and laugh.   1300

Electra

Brother, your pleasure shall be mine. These joys
I have from you. They are not mine to own.
To grieve you, though it were ever so little,
I would not buy a great good for myself.
If I did so, I would not properly
be servant to the Genius who attends us.
You know the situation. You have heard
Aegisthus is not at home, our mother is.
Do not be afraid that she will see my face
radiant with smiles. Our hatred is too old.   1310
I am too steeped in it. And since I have seen you,
my tears of joy will still run readily.
How can they cease when on the selfsame day
I have seen you dead and then again alive?
For me your coming is a miracle,
so that if my father should come back to life
I would think it no wonder but believe
I saw him. Since your coming is such for me,
lead as you will. Had I been all alone,
I would not have failed to win one of two things,   1320
a good deliverance or a good death for me.

Orestes

Hush, hush! I hear one of the people within
coming out.

Electra (still loudly to the servants of Orestes)
                    In with you, friends and guests,
more so, since what you are carrying in is that
which no one will reject there—nor be glad,
once he has got it.

Paedagogus (coming from inside)
                    Fools and madmen! No
concern for your own lives at all! No sense

to realize that you are not merely near
the deadliest danger, but in its very midst.   1330
If I had not, this while past, stood sentry here
at the door, your plans would now be in the house
before your bodies. I and I only
took the precautions. Have done once and for all
with your long speeches, your insatiate
cries of delight! And in with you at once.
As we are now, delay is ruinous.
It is high time to have done with our task.

Orestes
How shall I find everything inside?

Paedagogus
Well. There is no chance of your recognition.   1340

Orestes
You have announced my death, I understand.

Paedagogus
You are dead and gone—for all your being here.

Orestes
Were they glad of it? Or what did they say?

Paedagogus
I will tell you at the end. As things are now,
all on their side is well—even what is not so.

Electra
Brother, who is this man? I beg you, tell me.

Orestes
Do you not know him?

Electra
                              I cannot even guess.

Orestes
Do you not know him to whose hands you gave me?

Electra
What, this man?

Orestes

> By his hands and by your forethought
> I was conveyed away to Phocian country.   1350

Electra

> Is this the man, alone among so many,
> whom I found loyal when my father was murdered?

Orestes

> This is he. There is no need for further questions.

Electra

> O light most loved! O only rescuer
> of Agamemnon's house, in what a shape
> you come again! Are you indeed that other
> who saved me and Orestes from many sorrows?
> O most loved hands, service of feet most kind!
> To think you have stood beside me for so long,
> I not to know you, you to give no sign!
> You killed me with your words while you had for me
> most sweet reality. Bless you, my father,   1360
> for in you I think I see my father. Bless you!
> Within the selfsame day, of all mankind
> I have most hated and loved you most.

Paedagogus

> Enough, I think. As for the story
> of the happenings in between, there are many days
> and nights, as time comes round, to tell you all
> clearly, Electra. But as you two stand here
> I say to you: now is your chance to act.
> Clytemnestra is alone. No man is there.
> If you stop now, you will have others to fight   1370
> more clever and more numerous than these.

Orestes

> Pylades, we have time no longer for lengthy speeches.
> We must get inside as quick as ever we can,
> only first worshiping the ancestral Gods
> whose statues stand beside the forecourt here.

(*Exit Orestes.*)

Electra (*praying to the statue of Apollo*)
 Apollo, Lord, give gracious ear to them
 and to me, too, that often made you offerings,
 out of such store as I had, with hand enriching.
 Lycean One, Apollo, now I pray,
 adore, entreat you on my knees, with all   1380
 the resources that I have, be kind to us,
 help us in the fulfilment of our plans
 and prove to all mankind the punishment
 the Gods exact for wickedness.

Chorus
 See how the War God approaches,
 breathing bloody vengeance, invincible.
 They have gone under the rooftree now,
 the pursuers of villainy,
 the hounds that none may escape.
 So that the dream that hung hauntingly   1390
 in my mind shall not lack fulfilment.
 Stealthy, stealthy, into the house,
 he goes, the champion of dead men,
 to his father's palace, rich from of old,
 with his hands on the tool of blood, new-whetted.
 Hermes, the child of Maia, conducts
 the crafty deed to its end, and delays not.

Electra
 Dear ladies, now is the moment that the men
 are finishing their work. Wait in silence.

Chorus
 What do you mean? What are they doing?

Electra
           She is preparing   1400
 the urn for burial, and they stand beside her.

Chorus
 Why have you hurried out here?

Electra

                          To watch
That Aegisthus does not come on them unawares.

Clytemnestra (cries from within the house)
    House, O house
    deserted by friends, full of killers!

Electra
    Someone cries out, inside. Do you hear?

Chorus
        What I hear is a terror to the ear.
        I shudder at it.

Clytemnestra (cries again)
    Oh! Oh!
    Aegisthus, where are you?

Electra
    Again, that cry!

Clytemnestra
    My son, my son,   1410
    pity your mother!

Electra
    You had none for him,
    nor for his father that begot him.

Chorus
                          City,
    and miserable generation, now
    the day-to-day pursuing fate is dying.

Clytemnestra
    Oh! I am struck!

Electra
                If you have strength—again!

Clytemnestra
    Once more! Oh!

Electra
                Would Aegisthus were with you!

Chorus

> The courses are being fulfilled;
> those under the earth are alive;
> men long dead draw from their killers
> blood to answer blood.   1420

> And here they come. The red hand reeks
> with War God's sacrifice. I cannot blame them.

Electra

> Orestes, how have you fared?

Orestes

>   In the house, all
> is well, if well Apollo prophesied.

Electra

> Is the wretch dead?

Orestes

>   You need fear no more
> that your proud mother will dishonor you.

Chorus

> Stop! I can see Aegisthus clearly
> coming this way.

Electra

> Boys, back to the house!   1430

Orestes

> He is in our power!

Electra

> He walks from the suburb full of joy.

Chorus

> Back to the vestibule, quick as you can.
> You have done one part well. Here is the other.

Orestes

> Do not be concerned, we will do it.

Electra

Go

where you will, then.

Orestes

See, I am gone (*hiding himself*).

Electra

Leave what is here to me.

Chorus

A few words spoken softly in his ear
would be good, that unawares
he may rush to his fight where Justice   1440
will be his adversary.

Aegisthus

Which of you knows where the Phocians are?
I am told they are come here with news for me
that Orestes met his end in a chariot wreck.
You there, yes, I mean you, you, you—
you have been bold enough before, and I should think
it is you these news concern most and therefore
you will know best to tell me.

Electra

I know. Of course. Were it not so, I would
be outcast from what concerns my best beloved.

Aegisthus

Where are the strangers then? Tell me that.   1450

Electra

Inside. They have found their hostess very kind.

Aegisthus

And do they genuinely report his death?

Electra

Better than that. They have brought himself, not news.

Aegisthus

Can I then see the body in plain sight?

Electra

You can indeed. It is an ugly sight.

Aegisthus

What you say delights me—an unusual thing!

Electra

You may delight, if you can find it here.

Aegisthus

Silence now! (*to the servants*) I command you, open the doors
for Mycenaeans, Argives all, to see
that if there be a man whom empty hope   1460
has still puffed up, he may look on the dead
and so accept my bitting, so may shun
a forcible encounter with myself
and punishment to make him grow some sense.

Electra

I have done everything on my side. At long last
I have learned some sense, agreement with the stronger.

Aegisthus (*looking at the shrouded corpse*)

O Zeus, I see an image of what happened
not without envy of Gods. If that is something
I should not say, because of Nemesis,
I take it back. Draw all the covers from
his face that kinship at least may have due mourning.

Orestes

Touch it yourself. This body is not mine,   1470
it is only yours—to see and greet with love.

Aegisthus

True. I accept that. Will you call out
Clytemnestra if she is at home?

Orestes

               She is near you.
You need not look elsewhere.

Aegisthus (as the face of Clytemnestra confronts him)
What do I see?

Orestes
Something you fear? Do you not know the face?

Aegisthus
Who are you that have driven us into the net
in which this victim fell?

Orestes
Did you take so long
to find that your names are all astray
and those you call the dead are living?

Aegisthus
Ah!
I understand. And you who speak to me   1480
can only be Orestes.

Orestes
Were you, so good a prophet, so long misled?

Aegisthus
This is my end then. Let me say one word.

Electra
Not one, not one word more,
I beg you, brother. Do not draw out the talking.
When men are in the middle of trouble, when one
is on the point of death, how can time matter?
Kill him as quickly as you can. And killing
throw him out to find such burial as suit him
out of our sights. This is the only thing
that can bring me redemption from
all my past sufferings.   1490

Orestes (to Aegisthus)
In with you, then. It is not words that now
are the issue, but your life.

Aegisthus
> Why to the house?
> Why do you need the dark if what you do
> is fair? Why is your hand not ready to kill me?

Orestes
> You are not to give orders. In where you killed him,
> my father, so you may die in the same place!

Aegisthus
> Must this house, by absolute necessity,
> see the evils of the Pelopidae, now and to come?

Orestes
> Yours it shall see, at least.
> At least yours. There I am an excellent prophet.

Aegisthus
> Your father did not have the skill you boast of.   1500

Orestes
> Too many words! You are slow to take your road.
> Go now.

Aegisthus
> You lead the way.

Orestes
> No, you go first.

Aegisthus
> Afraid that I'll escape you?

Orestes
> No, but you shall not
> die as you choose. I must take care that death
> is bitter for you. Justice shall be taken
> directly on all who act above the law—
> justice by killing. So we would have less villains.

Chorus
> O race of Atreus, how many sufferings
> were yours before you came at last so hardly
> to freedom, perfected by this day's deed.   1510

PHILOCTETES

Translated and with an Introduction by David Grene

INTRODUCTION TO
PHILOCTETES

THE *Philoctetes* is the second-last play that Sophocles wrote. It probably came out in 409 B.C., and the last play, the *Oedipus at Colonus*, in 404, the year of Sophocles' death. Aristotle in the *Poetics* criticizes the *Philoctetes* for its happy ending, and many commentators since have been annoyed, or puzzled, or both by the solution of the play, which involves the God from the machine. Latterly, however, it has been more appreciated. There have been performances on the radio, and a surprising amount has been written about it, including a very interesting essay by Edmund Wilson in the *Wound and the Bow*. It is perhaps the most modern in feeling of all Sophocles' tragedies, and Sophocles is the most modern, the nearest to us, of the three Greek tragedians.

We may see the play simply as a duel between Philoctetes and Odysseus, with Neoptolemus as a pawn in the contest. But this play has a theme and a pattern which become deeper and more complicated, if we realize that in many of its aspects the story is the same as that of the *Oedipus at Colonus*. Each play, seen in the light of the other, makes more comprehensible Sophocles' tragic vision. Out of what personal suffering or vicarious experience he wrote this story twice in his last years, we shall never know. It is not only a preoccupation with the end of his life. With certain important differences the *Ajax*, written more than thirty years earlier than the *Philoctetes*, shows him thinking in the same way. Of course, each of these plays is individual in tone and character. What I mean is that, in both, the story is of a man offensive to his own society and banished by it, who, at last, must be reinstated and who becomes again miraculously potent, both alive and dead. And this story is the same in both plays in all its significant aspects.

Philoctetes is afflicted by some divine power without having committed a crime or being guilty of anything which the words "conscious guilt" mean, either to the fifth-century Greek or to ourselves.

He had unconsciously stumbled into a precinct or shrine of a God. Such shrines must not be thought of in the light of the Christian associations with the word. This was probably an unmarked and unfenced place, similar to the grove of the Eumenides in the *Oedipus at Colonus*. A snake—very often in Greece a symbol of a God's power —bit him in the foot and left him crippled. It is worth noting that Philoctetes' offense against the Gods is left at this. We are not allowed by the dramatist to speculate on any symbolic significance of his act of guilt or to construe it in any way as peculiar to Philoctetes. It is, in fact, an accident. He thus becomes burdened with the mark of God's resentment without any explanation for it humanly cogent either for himself or for others. The smell of his wound and his cries of agony render him so offensive to his comrades that he is marooned on a desert island for ten years, at the end of which time the Gods intervene to rescue him as mysteriously as they had injured him at the first. A glance at the Oedipus figure later and that of the Ajax in the earlier play shows a similar emphasis on the hero's innocence. It is true that Ajax is driven mad in the commission of an attempted murder against his generals, but Sophocles never tries to emphasize the matter of the murder afterward; it is only the performance of his act of frustration and misery by Ajax that we are likely to concern ourselves with.

Philoctetes is now an outcast from human sympathy but also the future conqueror of Troy. In both destruction and triumph, his lot does not make sense for ordinary men. This troubles them very little. They discarded him out of disgust at his affliction, when it looked as though God's hatred of him made that a safe course as well as a convenient one for themselves. Now that, with similar incomprehensibility, the divine purpose insists on the value of his bow and himself for the capture of Troy, they are prepared to restore him again to their society, particularly as the God has also arranged for his healing. In the *Philoctetes* Sophocles expresses what it feels like to be a man so isolated, so impersonally, so instrumentally used by his fellows.

The moment chosen is when the restoration to potency is near. Characteristically, Odysseus, who had marooned him originally and had taken advantage of Philoctetes when off his guard, plans to recapture him by similar strategic means. Neither time is he concerned to establish any human contact with the strange magical monster, so tormented and so honored by the non-human forces of the world. In this, Odysseus is blood-brother of Creon, who, in the *Oedipus at Colonus*, plays a similar role with the terrifying old beggar, Oedipus. In neither play does this cynical inhumanity have success. But neither are Philoctetes' brooding hatred and resentment allowed to have their way entirely. Here is where the role of Neoptolemus is important.

By trying to obey Odysseus, this boy comes to realize what cruelty is being inflicted on Philoctetes. So he undoes his offense and gives back the bow. However, when the deception is over and when the opportunity of healing and renown are offered Philoctetes again, by Neoptolemus this time, and as equal to equal, Philoctetes still refuses. The issue is clearly joined. Philoctetes' final refusal is the refusal of a man so wounded as to be unwilling to resume normal life itself because, with that life, will come new and unpredictable suffering. Better the old known pain, with the old known remedies, than the new hurt as unforeseeable as the future itself:

> It is not the sting of wrongs past,
> but what I must look for in wrongs to come.

This is all understandable, and, more than understandable, it claims our sympathy. But it is also irreconcilable with the vital principle which in anyone's life involves change and risk. It is easy for young Neoptolemus to face the future confidently. He has not yet been hurt enough to know what it feels like. Philoctetes' refusal is a great tragic human truth.

So Heracles is invoked not as an ordinary God from the machine but as the influence of a hero and old comrade, similarly injured, similarly restored, whose example must force Philoctetes to a step which will bring him healing and renown—but also more suffering. It is not that, as Aeschylus says, "out of suffering comes learning," but that only at the cost of suffering does life itself exist. As Philoctetes' final refusal is the mark of the play's truth to humanity, so is his final acquiescence in Heracles' order the mark of a truth to a universal principle, more imperative than humanity. But it is not the Philoctetes of the island, whom we have come to know so well, who goes to Troy with Odysseus and Neoptolemus. The significant part of that Philoctetes died, persisting to the end not to surrender his resentment and to risk new wrongs. This tragedy ends with his renewed refusal of Neoptolemus. What follows is what might well happen in the world as in the theater—the surrender of the individual life to the universal demands of life itself. As Hamlet must die and Fortinbras succeed, the new Philoctetes succeeds the old; but with the other Philoctetes of the island are buried all the years of wrong and of suffering and also the meaning that they had rendered to his agony.

CHARACTERS

Odysseus

Chorus of Sailors under the Command of Neoptolemus

The Spy Disguised as a Trader

Neoptolemus, Prince of Scyrus and Son of Achilles

Philoctetes

Heracles

PHILOCTETES

SCENE: *A lonely spot on the island of Lemnos. Enter Odysseus and Neoptolemus.*

Odysseus
This is it; this Lemnos and its beach
down to the sea that quite surrounds it; desolate,
no one sets foot on it; there are no houses.
This is where I marooned him long ago,
the son of Poias, the Melian, his foot
diseased and eaten away with running ulcers.

Son of our greatest hero,
son of Achilles, Neoptolemus,
I tell you I had orders for what I did:
my masters, the princes, bade me do it.

We had no peace with him: at the holy festivals,
we dared not touch the wine and meat; he screamed
and groaned so, and those terrible cries of his
brought ill luck on our celebrations; all
the camp was haunted by him.   10

Now is no time to talk to you of this,
now is no time for long speeches.
I am afraid that he may hear of my coming
and ruin all my plans to take him.

It is you who must help me with the rest. Look about
and see where there might be a cave with two mouths.
There are two niches to rest in, one in the sun
when it is cold, the other a tunneled passage
through which the breezes blow in summertime.

A man can sleep there and be cool. To the left, 20
a little, you may see a spring to drink at—
if it is still unchoked—go this way quietly,
see if he's there or somewhere else and signal.
Then I can tell you the rest. Listen:
I shall tell you. We will both do this thing.

Neoptolemus
What you speak of is near at hand, Odysseus.
I think I see such a cave.

Odysseus
Above or below? I cannot see it myself.

Neoptolemus
Above here, and no trace of a footpath.

Odysseus
See if he is housed within, asleep. 30

Neoptolemus
I see an empty hut, with no one there.

Odysseus
And nothing to keep house with?

Neoptolemus
A pallet bed, stuffed with leaves, to sleep on, for someone.

Odysseus
And nothing else? Nothing inside the house?

Neoptolemus
A cup, made of a single block, a poor
workman's contrivance. And some kindling, too.

Odysseus
It is his treasure house that you describe.

Neoptolemus
And look, some rags are drying in the sun
full of the oozing matter from a sore.

Odysseus
　　Yes, certainly he lives here, even now　　　　　　　40
　　is somewhere not far off. He cannot go far,
　　sick as he is, lame cripple for so long.
　　It's likely he has gone to search for food
　　or somewhere that he knows there is a herb
　　to ease his pain. Send your man here to watch,
　　that he may not come upon me without warning.
　　For he would rather take me than all the Greeks.

Neoptolemus
　　Very well, then, the path will be watched.
　　Go on with your story; tell me what you want.

Odysseus
　　Son of Achilles,　　　　　　　　　　　　　　50
　　our coming here has a purpose; to it be loyal
　　with more than with your body. If you should hear
　　some strange new thing, unlike what you have heard
　　before, still serve us; it was to serve you came here.

Neoptolemus
　　What would you have me do?

Odysseus
　　　　　　　　　　　　Ensnare
　　the soul of Philoctetes with your words.
　　When he asks who you are and whence you came,
　　say you are Achilles' son; you need not lie.
　　Say you are sailing home, leaving the Greeks
　　and all their fleet, in bitter hatred. Say
　　that they had prayed you, urged you from your home,　　60
　　and swore that only with your help
　　could Troy be taken. Yet when you came and asked,
　　as by your right, to have your father's arms,
　　Achilles' arms, they did not think you worthy
　　but gave them to Odysseus. Say what you will
　　against me; do not spare me anything.

Nothing of this will hurt me; if you will not
do this, you will bring sorrow on all the Greeks.
If this man's bow shall not be taken by us,
you cannot sack the town of Troy.

Perhaps you wonder why you can safely meet him,   70
why he would trust you and not me. Let me explain.
You have come here unforced, unpledged by oaths,
made no part of our earlier expedition.
The opposite is true in my own case;
at no point can I deny his charge.
If, when he sees me, Philoctetes
still has his bow, there is an end of me,
and you too, for my company would damn you.
For this you must sharpen your wits, to become a thief
of the arms no man has conquered.

I know, young man, it is not your natural bent
to say such things nor to contrive such mischief.   80
But the prize of victory is pleasant to win.
Bear up: another time we shall prove honest.
For one brief shameless portion of a day
give me yourself, and then for all the rest
you may be called most scrupulous of men.

Neoptolemus
    Son of Laertes, what I dislike to hear
    I hate to put in execution.
    I have a natural antipathy
    to get my ends by tricks and stratagems.
    So, too, they say, my father was. Philoctetes
    I will gladly fight and capture, bring him with us,   90
    but not by treachery. Surely a one-legged man
    cannot prevail against so many of us!
    I recognize that I was sent with you
    to follow your instructions. I am loath
    to have you call me traitor. Still, my lord,

I would prefer even to fail with honor
than win by cheating.

Odysseus
You are a good man's son.
I was young, too, once, and then I had a tongue
very inactive and a doing hand.
Now as I go forth to the test, I see
that everywhere among the race of men
it is the tongue that wins and not the deed.

Neoptolemus
What do you bid me do, but to tell lies?   100

Odysseus
By craft I bid you take him, Philoctetes.

Neoptolemus
And why by craft rather than by persuasion?

Odysseus
He will not be persuaded; force will fail.

Neoptolemus
Has he such strength to give him confidence?

Odysseus
The arrows none may avoid, that carry death.

Neoptolemus
Then even to encounter him is not safe?

Odysseus
Not if you do not take him by craft, as I told you.

Neoptolemus
Do you not find it vile yourself, this lying?

Osysseus
Not if the lying brings our rescue with it.

Neoptolemus
How can a man not blush to say such things?   110

Odysseus

When one does something for gain, one need not blush.

Neoptolemus

What gain for me that he should come to Troy?

Odysseus

His weapons alone are destined to take Troy.

Neoptolemus

Then I shall not be, as was said, its conqueror?

Odysseus

Not you apart from them nor they from you.

Neoptolemus

They must be my quarry then, if this is so.

Odysseus

You will win a double prize if you do this.

Neoptolemus

What? If I know, I will do what you say.

Odysseus

You shall be called a wise man and a good.

Neoptolemus

Well, then I will do it, casting aside all shame.   120

Odysseus

You clearly recollect all I have told you?

Neoptolemus

Yes, now that I have understood it.

Odysseus

                              Stay
and wait his coming here; I will go
that he may not spy my presence.
I will take with me to the ship this guard.
If you are too slow, I will send him back again,
disguise him as a sailor; Philoctetes
will never know him.
Whatever clever story he give you, then   130

fall in with it and use it as you need.
Now I will go to the ship and leave you in charge.
May Hermes, God of Craft, the Guide, for us
be guide indeed, and Victory and Athene,
the City Goddess, who preserves me ever.

(*Exit Odysseus.*)

Chorus

Sir, we are strangers, and this land is strange;
what shall we say and what conceal from this suspicious man?
Tell us.
For cunning that passes another's cunning
and a pre-eminent judgment lie with the prince,
in whose sovereign keeping is Zeus's holy scepter.   140
To you, young lord, all this has come,
all the power of your forefathers. Tell us now
what we must do to serve you.

Neoptolemus

Now—if you wish to see where he sleeps
on his crag at the edge—look, be not afraid.
But when the terrible wanderer returns,
be gone from the hut, but come to my beckoning.
Take your cues from me. Help when you can.

Chorus

Sir, this we have always done,   150
have kept a watchful eye over your safety.
But now
tell us what places he inhabits
and where he rests. It would not be amiss
for us to know this,
lest he attack us unawares.
Where does he live? Where does he rest?
What footpath does he follow? Is he in the house or not?

Neoptolemus

This, that you see, is his two-fronted house,
and he sleeps inside on the rock.   160

Chorus

Where is he gone, unhappy creature?

Neoptolemus

I am sure
he has gone to find food somewhere near here;
stumbling, lame, dragging along the path,
he is trying to shoot birds to prolong his miserable life.
This indeed, they say, is how he lives.
And no one comes near to cure him.

Chorus

Yes, for my part I pity him:
how unhappy, how utterly alone, always   170
he suffers the savagery of his illness
with no one to care for him,
with no friendly face near him,
but bewildered and distraught at each need as it comes.
God pity him, how has he kept a grip on life?

Woe to the contrivances of death-bound men,
woe to the unhappy generations of death-bound men
whose lives have known extremes!

Perhaps this man is as well born as any,   180
second to no son of an ancient house.
Yet now his life lacks everything,
and he makes his bed without neighbors
or with spotted shaggy beasts for neighbors.
His thoughts are set continually on pain and hunger.
He cries out in his wretchedness;
there is only a blabbering echo,
that comes from the distance speeding
from his bitter crying.   190

Neoptolemus

I am not surprised at any of this:
this is a God's doing, if I have any understanding.

These afflictions that have come upon him
are the work of Chryse, bitter of heart.
As for his present loneliness and suffering,
this, too, no doubt is part of the God's plan
that he may not bend against Troy
the divine invincible bow
until the time shall be fulfilled, at which it is decreed,
that Troy, as they say, shall fall to that bow.   200

Chorus
  Hush.

Neoptolemus
        What is it?

Chorus
              Hush! I hear a footfall,
  footfall of a man that walks painfully.
  Is it here? Is it here?
  I hear a voice, now I can hear it clearly,
  voice of a man, crawling along the path,
  hard put to it to move. It's far away,
  but I can hear it; I can hear the sound well
  the voice of a man wounded; it is quite clear now.

  No more now, my son.   210

Neoptolemus
                No more of what?

Chorus
  Your plots and plans. He is here, almost with us.
  His is no cheerful marching to the pipe
  like a shepherd with his flock.
  No, a bitter cry.
  He must have stumbled far down on the path,
  and his moaning carried all the way here.
  Or perhaps he stopped to look at the empty harbor,
  for it was a bitter cry.

Philoctetes

>Men, who are you that have put in, rowing 220
>to a shore without houses or anchorage?
>What countrymen may I call you without offense?
>What is your people? Greeks, indeed, you seem
>in fashion of your clothing, dear to me.
>May I hear your voice? Do not be afraid
>or shrink from such as I am, grown a savage.
>I have been alone and very wretched,
>without friend or comrade, suffering a great deal.
>Take pity on me; speak to me; speak,
>speak if you come as friends.
>   No—answer me. 230
>If this is all
>that we can have from one another, speech,
>this, at least, we should have.

Neoptolemus

>Sir, for your questions, since you wish to know,
>know we are Greeks.

Philoctetes

>   Friendliest of tongues!
>That I should hear it spoken once again
>by such a man in such a place! My boy,
>who are you? Who has sent you here? What brought you?
>What impulse? What friendliest of winds?
>Tell me all this, that I know who you are.

Neoptolemus

>I am of Scyrus that the sea surrounds;
>I am sailing home. My name is Neoptolemus, 240
>Achilles' son. Now you know everything.

Philoctetes

>Son of a father—that I loved so dearly—
>and of a country that I loved, you that were reared
>by that old man Lycomedes, what kind of venture
>can have brought you to port here? Where did you sail from?

Neoptolemus
At present bound from Troy.

Philoctetes
From Troy? From Troy!
You did not sail with us to Troy at first.

Neoptolemus
You, then, are one that also had a share
in all that trouble?

Philoctetes
Is it possible
you do not know me, boy, me whom you see here?

Neoptolemus
I never saw you before. How could I know you?   250

Philoctetes
You never heard my name then? Never a rumor
of all the wrongs I suffered, even to death?

Neoptolemus
I never knew a word of what you ask me.

Philoctetes
Surely I must be vile! God must have hated me
that never a word of me, of how I live here,
should have come home through all the land of Greece.
Yet they that outraged God casting me away
can hold their tongues and laugh! While my disease
always increases and grows worse. My boy,
you are Achilles' son. I that stand here   260
am one you may have heard of, as the master
of Heracles' arms. I am Philoctetes
the son of Poias. Those two generals
and Prince Odysseus of the Cephallenians
cast me ashore here to their shame, as lonely
as you can see me now, wasting with my sickness
as cruel as it is, caused by the murderous bite
of a viper mortally dangerous.

I was already bitten when we put in here
on my way from sea-encircled Chryse.   270
I tell you, boy, those men cast me away here
and ran and left me helpless. They were happy
when they saw that I had fallen asleep on the shore
in a rocky cave, after a rough passage.
They went away and left me with such rags—
and few enough of them—as one might give
an unfortunate beggar and a handful of food.
May God give them the like!
Think, boy, of that awakening when I awoke
and found them gone; think of the useless tears
and curses on myself when I saw the ships—
my ships, which I had once commanded—gone,
all gone, and not a man left on the island,   280
not one to help me or to lend a hand
when I was seized with my sickness, not a man!
In all I saw before me nothing but pain;
but of that a great abundance, boy.

Time came and went for me. In my tiny shelter
I must alone do everything for myself.
This bow of mine I used to shoot the birds
that filled my belly. I must drag my foot,
my cursed foot, to where the bolt
sped by the bow's thong had struck down a bird.   290
If I must drink, and it was winter time—
the water was frozen—I must break up firewood.
Again I crawled and miserably contrived
to do the work. Whenever I had no fire,
rubbing stone on stone I would at last produce
the spark that kept me still in life.
A roof for shelter, if only I have fire,
gives me everything but release from pain.

Boy, let me tell you of this island.   300
No sailor by his choice comes near it.

There is no anchorage, nor anywhere
that one can land, sell goods, be entertained.
Sensible men make no voyages here.
Yet now and then someone puts in. A stretch
of time as long as this allows much to happen.
When they have come here, boy, they pity me—
at least they say they do—and in their pity
they have given me scraps of food and cast-off clothes;
that other thing, when I dare mention it,   310
none of them will—bringing me home again.

It is nine years now that I have spent dying,
with hunger and pain feeding my insatiable
disease. That, boy, is what they have done to me,
the two Atridae, and that mighty Prince
Odysseus. May the Gods that live in heaven
grant that they pay, agony for my agony.

Chorus
    In this, I too resemble your other visitors.
    I pity you, son of Poias.

Neoptolemus
                                I am a witness,
    I also, of the truth of what you say.   320
    I know it is true. I have dealt with those villains,
    the two Atridae and the prince Odysseus.

Philoctetes
    Are you, as well as I, a sufferer
    and angry? Have you grounds against the Atridae?

Neoptolemus
    Give me the chance to gratify my anger
    with my hand some day!
    Then will Mycenae know and Sparta know
    that Scyrus, too, breeds soldiers.

Philoctetes

                             Well said, boy!
You come to me with a great hate against them.
Because of what?

Neoptolemus

                       I will tell you, Philoctetes—
for all that it hurts to tell it—
of how I came to Troy and what dishonor   330
they put upon me.
When fatefully Achilles came to die. . . .

Philoctetes

    O stop! tell me no more. Let me understand
this first. Is he dead, Achilles, dead?

Neoptolemus

    Yes, he is dead; no man his conqueror
but bested by a god, Phoebus the archer.

Philoctetes

    Noble was he that killed and he that died.
Boy, I am at a loss which to do first,
ask for your story or to mourn for him.

Neoptolemus

    God help you, I would think that your own sufferings
were quite enough without mourning for those of others.   340

Philoctetes

    Yes, that is true. Again, tell me your story
of how they have insulted you.

Neoptolemus

                          They came
for me, did great Odysseus and the man
that was my father's tutor, with a ship
wonderfully decked with ribbons. They had a story—
be it truth or lie—that it was God's decree
since he, my father, was dead, I and I only
should take Troy town.

This was their story. Sir, you can imagine
it did not take much time, when they had told it, 350
for me to embark with them.
Chiefly, you know, I was prompted by love of him,
the dead man. I had hope of seeing him
while still unburied. Alive I never had.
We had a favoring wind; on the second day
we touched Sigeion. As I disembarked,
all of the soldiers swarmed around me, blessed me,
swore that they saw Achilles alive again,
now gone from them forever. But he still lay
unburied. I, his mourning son, wept for him; 360
then, in a while, came to the two Atridae,
my friends, as it seemed right to do, and asked them
for my father's arms and all that he had else.
They needed brazen faces for their answer:
"Son of Achilles, all that your father had,
all else, is yours to take, but not his arms.
Another man now owns them, Laertes' son."
I burst into tears, jumped up, enraged,
cried out in my pain, "You scoundrels, did you dare
to give those arms that were mine to someone else 370
before I knew of it?" Then Odysseus
spoke—he was standing near me—"Yes, and rightly,"
he said, "they gave them, boy. For it was I
who rescued them and him, their former owner."
My anger got the better of me; I cursed him outright
with every insult that I knew, sparing none,
if he should take my arms away from me.
He is no way given to quarreling, but at this
he was stung by what I said. He answered:
"You were not where we were. You were at home,
out of the reach of duty. Since, besides,
you have so bold a tongue in your head, never 380
will you possess them to bring home to Scyrus."

There it was, abuse on both sides. But I lost
what should be mine and so sailed home. Odysseus,
that filthy son of filthy parents, robbed me.
Yet I do not blame him even so much as the princes.
All of a city is in the hand of the prince,
all of an army; unruly men become so
by the instruction of their betters.
This is the whole tale. May he that hates the Atridae
be as dear in the Gods' sight as he is in mine.   390

Chorus

Earth, Mountain Mother, in whom we find sustenance,
Mother of Zeus himself,
Dweller in great golden Pactolus,
Mother that I dread:
on that other day, too, I called on thee, Thou Blessed One,
Thou that rides on the Bull-killing Lions,
when all the insolence of the Atridae assaulted our Prince,
when they gave his arms, that wonder of the world,   400
    to the son of Laertes.

Philoctetes

You have sailed here, as it seems, with a clear tally;
your half of sorrow matches that of mine.
What you tell me rings in harmony. I recognize
the doings of the Atridae and Odysseus.
I know Odysseus would employ his tongue
on every ill tale, every rascality,
that could be brought to issue in injustice.
This is not at all my wonder, but that Ajax   410
the Elder should stand by, see and allow it.

Neoptolemus

He is no longer living, sir; never, indeed,
if he were, would they have robbed me of the arms.

Philoctetes

What! Is he, too, dead and gone?

Neoptolemus
    Yes, dead and gone. As such now think of him.

Philoctetes
    But not the son of Tydeus nor Odysseus
    whom Sisyphus once sold to Laertes,
    they will not die; for they should not be living.

Neoptolemus
    Of course, they are not dead; you may be sure
    that they are in their glory among the Greeks.   420

Philoctetes
    What of an old and honest man, my friend,
    Nestor of Pylos? Is he alive? He used
    to check their mischief by his wise advice.

Neoptolemus
    Things have gone badly for him. He has lost
    his son Antilochus, who once stood by him.

Philoctetes
    Ah!
    You have told me the two deaths that most could hurt me.
    Alas, what should I look for
    when Ajax and Antilochus are dead,
    and still Odysseus lives, that in their stead
    ought to be counted among the dead?   430

Neoptolemus
    A cunning wrestler; still, Philoctetes,
    even the cunning are sometimes tripped up.

Philoctetes
    Tell me, by the Gods, where was Patroclus,
    who was your father's dearest friend?

Neoptolemus
                          Dead, too.
    In one short sentence I can tell you this.
    War never takes a bad man but by chance,
    the good man always.

Philoctetes

You have said the truth.
So I will ask you of one quite unworthy
but dexterous and clever with his tongue.   440

Neoptolemus

Whom can you mean except Odysseus?

Philoctetes

It is not he: there was a man, Thersites,
who never was content to speak once only,
though no one was for letting him speak at all.
Do you know if he is still alive?

Neoptolemus

I did not know him,
but I have heard that he is still alive.

Philoctetes

He would be; nothing evil has yet perished.
The Gods somehow give them most excellent care.
They find their pleasure in turning back from Death
the rogues and tricksters, but the just and good
they are always sending out of the world.   450
How can I reckon the score, how can I praise,
when praising Heaven I find the Gods are bad?

Neoptolemus

For my own part, Philoctetes of Oeta,
from now on I shall take precautions.
I shall look at Troy and the Atridae both
from very far off. I shall never abide
the company of those where the worse man
has more power than the better, where the good
are always on the wane and cowards rule.
For the future, rocky Scyrus will content me
to take my pleasure at home.   460
Now I will be going to my ship. Philoctetes,
on you God's blessing and goodbye. May the Gods

recover you of your sickness, as you would have it!
Let us go, men, that when God grants us sailing
we may be ready to sail.

Philoctetes

Boy, are you going,
going now?

Neoptolemus

Yes, the weather favors.
We must look to sail almost at once.

Philoctetes

My dear—I beg you in your father's name,
and in your mother's, in the name of all
that you have loved at home, do not leave me here   470
alone, living in sufferings you have seen
and others I have told you of.
I am not your main concern; give me a passing thought.
I know that there is horrible discomfort
in having me on board. Put up with it.
To such as you and your nobility,
meanness is shameful, decency honorable.
If you leave me here, it is an ugly story.
If you take me, men will say their best of you,
if I shall live to see Oetean land.
Come! One day, hardly one whole day's space   480
that I shall trouble you. Endure this much.
Take me and put me where you will,
in the hold, in the prow or poop, anywhere
where I shall least offend those that I sail with.
By Zeus himself, God of the Suppliants,
I beg you, boy, say "Yes," say you will do it.
Here I am on my knees to you, poor cripple,
for all my lameness. Do not cast me away
so utterly alone, where no one even walks by.
Either take me and set me safe in your own home,
or take me to Chalcedon in Euboea.

From there it will be no great journey for me   490
to Oeta or to ridgy Trachis or
to quick-flowing Spercheius,
and so you show me to my loving father.
For many a day I have feared that he is dead.
With those who came to my island I sent messages,
and many of them, begging him to come
and bring me home himself. Either he's dead,
or, as I rather think, my messengers
made little of what I asked them and hurried home.
Now in you I have found both escort and messenger;   500
bring me safe home. Take pity on me.
Look how men live, always precariously
balanced between good and bad fortune.
If you are out of trouble, watch for danger.
And when you live well, then consider the most
your life, lest ruin take it unawares.

Chorus
Have pity on him, prince.
He has has told us of a most desperate course run.
God forbid such things should overtake friends of mine.
And, prince, if you hate the abdominable Atridae   510
I would set their ill treatment of him
to his gain and would carry him
in your quick, well-fitted ship
to his home and so avoid offense before the face of God.

Neoptolemus
Take care that your assent is not too ready,
and that, when you have enough of his diseased company,   520
you are no longer constant to what you have said.

Chorus
No. You will never be able in this
to reproach me with justice.

Neoptolemus

                  I should be ashamed
to be less ready than you to render a stranger service.
Well, if you will then, let us sail. Let him
get ready quickly. My ship will carry him.

May God give us a safe clearance from this land
and a safe journey where we choose to go.

Philoctetes

   God bless this day! 530
   Man, dear to my very heart,
   and you, dear friends, how shall I prove to you
   how you have bound me to your friendship!
   Let us go, boy. But let us first kiss the earth,
   reverently, in my homeless home of a cave.
   I would have you know what I have lived from,
   how tough the spirit that did not break. I think
   the sight itself would have been enough for anyone
   except myself. Necessity has taught me,
   little by little, to suffer and be patient.

Chorus

   Wait! Let us see. Two men are coming.
   One of them is of our crew, the other a foreigner. 540
   Let us hear from them and then go in.

                (*Enter the Sailor disguised as a Trader.*)

Trader

   Son of Achilles, I told my fellow traveler here—
   he with two others were guarding your ship—
   to tell me where you were. I happened on you.
   I had no intentions this way. Just by accident
   I came to anchor at this island.
   I am sailing in command of a ship outward bound
   from Ilium, with no great company, for Peparethus—
   a good country, that, for wine. When I heard
   that all those sailors were the crew of your ship, 550

I thought I should not hold my tongue and sail on
until I spoke with you—and got my reward,
a fair one, doubtless. Apparently you do not know
much of your own affairs, nor what new plans
the Greeks have for you. Indeed, not only plans,
actions in train already and not slowly.

Neoptolemus

Thank you for your consideration, sir.
I will remain obliged to your kindness
unless I prove unworthy. Please tell me
what you have spoken of. I would like to know
what are these new plans of the Greeks.   560

Trader

Old Phoenix and the two sons of Theseus are gone,
pursuing you with a squadron.

Neoptolemus

Do they intend
to bring me back with violence or persuade me?

Trader

I do not know. I tell you what I heard.

Neoptolemus

Are Phoenix and his friends in such a hurry
to do the bidding of the two Atridae?

Trader

It is being done.
There is no delay about it. That you should know.

Neoptolemus

How is it that Odysseus was not ready
to sail as his own messenger on such
an errand? It cannot be he was afraid?

Trader

When I weighed anchor, he and Tydeus' son   570
were in pursuit of still another man.

Neoptolemus

Who was this other man that Odysseus himself should seek him?

Trader

There was a man—perhaps you will tell me first
who this is; and say softly what you say.

Neoptolemus

This, sir, is the famous Philoctetes.

Trader

Do not
ask me any further questions. Get yourself out,
as quickly as you can, out of this island.

Philoctetes

What does he say, boy? Why in dark whispers
does he bargain with you about me, this sailor?

Neoptolemus

I do not know yet what he says, but he must say it,   580
openly, whatever it is, to you and me and these.

Trader

Son of Achilles, do not slander me,
speaking of me to the army as a tattler.
There's many a thing I do for them and in return
get something from them, as a poor man may.

Neoptolemus

I am the enemy of the Atridae. This
is my greatest friend because he hates the Atridae.
You have come to me as a friend, and so you must
hide from me nothing that you heard.

Trader

Well, watch what you are doing, sir.

Neoptolemus

I have.

Trader

I put the whole responsibility
squarely upon yourself.

Neoptolemus
Do so; but speak. 590

Trader
Well, then. The two I have spoken of,
the son of Tydeus and the Prince Odysseus,
are in pursuit of Philoctetes.
They have sworn, so help them God, to bring him with them
either by persuasion or by brute force.
And this all the Greeks heard clearly announced
by Prince Odysseus; for he was much surer
of success than was the other.

Neoptolemus
What can have made
the Atridae care about him after so long—
one whom they, years and years since, cast away? 600
What yearning for him came over them? Was it the Gods
who punish evil doings that now have driven them
to retribution for injustice?

Trader
I will explain all that. Perhaps you haven't heard.
There was a prophet of very good family,
a son of Priam indeed, called Helenus.
He was captured one night in an expedition
undertaken singlehanded by Odysseus,
of whom all base and shameful things are spoken,
captured by stratagem. Odysseus brought
his prisoner before the Greeks, a splendid prize.
Helenus prophesied everything to them 610
and, in particular, touching the fortress of Troy,
that they could never take it till they persuaded
Philoctetes to come with them and leave his island.
As soon as Odysseus heard the prophet say this,
he promised at once to bring the man before them,
for all to see—he thought, as a willing prisoner,
but, if not that, against his will. If he failed,

« 430 »

"any of them might have his head," he declared. My boy,
that is the whole story; that is why I urge you   620
and him and any that you care for to make haste.

Philoctetes

Ah!
Did he indeed swear that he would persuade me
to sail with him, did he so, that utter devil?
As soon shall I be persuaded, when I am dead,
to rise from Death's house, come to the light again,
as his own father did.

Trader

I do not know about that. Well, I will be going now
to my ship. May God prosper you both!

(Exit Trader.)

Philoctetes

Is it not terrible, boy, that this Odysseus
should think that there are words soft enough to win me,
to let him put me in his boat, exhibit me
in front of all the Greeks?   630
No! I would rather listen to my worst enemy,
the snake that bit me, made me into this cripple.
But he can say anything, he can dare anything.
Now I know that he will come here.
Boy, let us go, that a great sea may sever
us from Odysseus' ship.
Let us go. For look, haste in due season shown
brings rest and peace when once the work is done.

Neoptolemus

When the wind at our prow falls, we can sail, no sooner.
Now it is dead against us.   640

Philoctetes

It is always fair sailing, when you escape evil.

Neoptolemus

Yes, but the wind is against them, too.

Philoctetes
                                    For pirates
  when they can thieve and plunder, no wind is contrary.

Neoptolemus
  If you will, then, let us go. Take from your cave
  what you need most and love most.

Philoctetes
  There are some things I need, but no great choice.

Neoptolemus
  What is there that you will not find on board?

Philoctetes
  A herb I have, the chief means to soothe my wound,
  to lull the pain to sleep.   650

Neoptolemus
                        Bring it out then.
  What else is there that you would have?

Philoctetes
  Any arrow
  I may have dropped and missed. For none of them
  must I leave for another to pick up.

Neoptolemus
  Is this, in your hands, the famous bow?

Philoctetes
                                    Yes, this,
  this in my hands.

Neoptolemus
                    May I see it closer,
  touch and adore it like a god?

Philoctetes
                            You may have it
  and anything else of mine that is for your good.

Neoptolemus
  I long for it, yet only with such longing   660

that if it is lawful, I may have it, else
let it be.

Philoctetes
   Your words are holy, boy. It is lawful.
for you have given me, and you alone,
the sight of the sun shining above us here,
the sight of my Oeta, of my old father, my friends.
You have raised me up above my enemies,
when I was under their feet. You may be confident.
You may indeed touch my bow, give it again
to me that gave it you, proclaim that alone
of all the world you touched it, in return
for the good deed you did. It was for that,
for friendly help, I myself won it first.   670

Neoptolemus
I am glad to see you and take you as a friend.
For one who knows how to show and to accept kindness
will be a friend better than any possession.
Go in.

Philoctetes
   I will bring you with me. The sickness in me
seeks to have you beside me.

Chorus
In story I have heard, but my eyes have not seen
him that once would have drawn near to Zeus's bed.
I have heard how he caught him, bound him on a running wheel,
Zeus, son of Kronos, invincible.
But I know of no other,   680
by hearsay, much less by sight, of all mankind
whose destiny was more his enemy when he met it
than Philoctetes', who wronged no one, nor killed
but lived, just among the just,
and fell in trouble past his deserts.
There is wonder, indeed, in my heart
how, how in his loneliness,

listening to the waves beating on the shore,
how he kept hold at all
on a life so full of tears.   690

He was lame, and no one came near him.
He suffered, and there were no neighbors for his sorrow
with whom his cries would find answer,
with whom he could lament the bloody plague
that ate him up.
No one who would gather
fallen leaves from the ground
to quiet the raging, bleeding sore,
running, in his maggot-rotten foot.   700
Here and there he crawled
writhing always—
suffering like a child
without the nurse he loves—
to what source of ease he could find
when the heart-devouring suffering gave over.

No grain sown in holy earth was his, nor other food
of all enjoyed by us, men who live by labor,
save when with the feathered arrows shot by the quick bow   710
he got him fodder for his belly.
Alas, poor soul,
that never in ten years' length
enjoyed a drink of wine
but looked always for the standing pools
and approached them.
But now he will end fortunate. He has fallen in
with the son of good men. He will be great, after it all.   720
Our prince in his seaworthy craft will carry him
after the fulness of many months, to his father's home
in the country of the Malian nymphs,
by the banks of the Spercheius,

where the hero of the bronze shield ascended
to all the Gods, ablaze in holy fire
above the ridges of Oeta.

Neoptolemus

Come if you will, then. Why have you nothing to say?   730
Why do you stand, in silence transfixed?

Philoctetes

Oh! Oh!

Neoptolemus

What is it?

Philoctetes

            Nothing to be afraid of. Come on, boy.

Neoptolemus

Is it the pain of your inveterate sickness?

Philoctetes

No, no, indeed not. Just now I think I feel better.
O Gods!

Neoptolemus

Why do you call on the Gods with cries of distress?

Philoctetes

That they may come as healers, come with gentleness.
Oh! Oh!

Neoptolemus

What ails you? Tell me; do not keep silence.   740
You are clearly in some pain.

Philoctetes

I am lost, boy.
I will not be able to hide it from you longer.
Oh! Oh!
It goes through me, right through me!
Miserable, miserable!
I am lost, boy. I am being eaten up. Oh!

By God, if you have a sword, ready to hand, use it!
Strike the end of my foot. Strike it off, I tell you, now.
Do not spare my life. Quick, boy, quick.   750

(A long silence.)

Neoptolemus

  What is this thing that comes upon you suddenly,
  that makes you cry and moan so?

Philoctetes

Do you know, boy?

Neoptolemus

  What is it?

Philoctetes

      Do you know, boy?

Neoptolemus

What do you mean?

  I do not know.

Philoctetes

      Surely you know. Oh! Oh!

Neoptolemus

  The terrible burden of your sickness.

Philoctetes

  Terrible it is, beyond words' reach. But pity me.

Neoptolemus

  What shall I do?

Philoctetes

      Do not be afraid and leave me.
  She comes from time to time, perhaps when she has had
  her fill of wandering in other places.

Neoptolemus

  You most unhappy man,
  you that have endured all agonies, lived through them,   760
  shall I take hold of you? Shall I touch you?

Philoctetes

    Not that, above everything. But take this bow,
as you asked to do just now, until the pain,
the pain of my sickness, that is now upon me, grows less.
Keep the bow, guard it safely. Sleep comes upon me
when the attack is waning. The pain will not end till then.
But you must let me sleep quietly.
If they should come in the time when I sleep,
by the Gods I beg you do not give up my bow
willingly or unwillingly to anyone.
And let no one trick you out of it, lest you prove
a murderer—your own and mine that kneeled to you.

Neoptolemus

    I shall take care; be easy about that. It shall not pass
except to your hands and to mine. Give it to me now,
and may good luck go with it!

Philoctetes

                  Here,
take it, boy. Bow in prayer to the Gods' envy
that the bow may not be to you a sorrow
nor as it was to me and its former master.

Neoptolemus

    You Gods, grant us both this and grant us
a journey speedy with a prosperous wind
to where God sends us and our voyage holds.

Philoctetes

    An empty prayer, I am afraid, boy:
the blood is trickling, dripping murderously
from its deep spring. I look for something new.
It is coming now, coming. Ah!
You have the bow. Do not go away from me.
    Ah!
O man of Cephallenia, would it were you,
Would it were your breast that the pains transfix.
    Ah!

770

780

790

Agamemnon and Menelaus, my two generals,
would it were your two bodies that had fed
this sickness for as long as mine has. Ah!

Death, death, how is it that I can call on you,
always, day in, day out, and you cannot come to me?
Boy, my good boy, take up this body of mine
and burn it on what they call the Lemnian fire.   800
I had the resolution once to do this for another,
the son of Zeus, and so obtained the arms
that you now hold. What do you say?
What do you say? Nothing? Where are you, boy?

Neoptolemus
   I have been in pain for you; I have been
   in sorrow for your pain.

Philoctetes
   No, boy, keep up your heart. She is quick in coming
   and quick to go. Only I entreat you, do not
   leave me alone.

Neoptolemus
   Do not be afraid. We shall stay.   810

Philoctetes
   You will?

Neoptolemus
   You may be sure of it.

Philoctetes
   Your oath,
   I do not think it fit to put you to your oath.

Neoptolemus
   I *may* not go without you, Philoctetes.

Philoctetes
   Give me your hand upon it.

Neoptolemus
    Here I give it you,
    to remain.

Philoctetes
    Now—take me away from here—

Neoptolemus
                          What do you mean?

Philoctetes
                                    Up, up.

Neoptolemus
    What madness is upon you? Why do you look
    on the sky above us?

Philoctetes
              Let me go, let me go.

Neoptolemus
    Where?

Philoctetes
        Oh, let me go.

Neoptolemus
             Not I.

Philoctetes
    You will kill me if you touch me.

Neoptolemus
    Now I shall let you go, now you are calmer.

Philoctetes
    Earth, take my body, dying as I am.
    The pain no longer lets me stand.   820

Neoptolemus
    In a little while, I think,
    sleep will come on this man. His head is nodding.
    The sweat is soaking all his body over,
    and a black flux of blood and matter has broken
    out of his foot. Let us leave him quiet, friends,
    until he falls asleep.

Chorus

Sleep that knows not pain nor suffering
kindly upon us, Lord,
kindly, kindly come.
Spread your enveloping radiance,   830
as now, over his eyes.
Come, come, Lord Healer.

Boy, look to your standing,
look to your going, look to your plans
for the future. Do you see? He sleeps.
What is it we are waiting to do?
Ripeness that holds decision over all things
wins many a victory suddenly.

Neoptolemus

Yes, it is true he hears nothing, but I see we have hunted in vain,
vainly have captured our quarry the bow, if we sail without him.   840
His is the crown of victory, him the God said we must bring.
Shame shall be ours if we boast and our lies still leave victory
   unwon.

Chorus

Boy, to all of this the God shall look.
Answer me gently;
low, low, whisper,
whisper, boy.
The sleep of a sick man has keen eyes.
It is a sleep unsleeping.

But to the limits of what you can,
look to this, look to this secretly,   850
how you may do it.
You know of whom I speak.
If your mind holds the same purpose touching this man,
the wise can see trouble and no way to cure it.
It is a fair wind, boy, a fair wind:
the man is eyeless and helpless,

outstretched under night's blanket—
asleep in the sun is good—
neither of foot nor of hand nor of anything is he master,   860
but is even as one that lies in Death's house.
Look to it, look if what you say
is seasonable. As far as my mind,
boy, can grasp it, best is the trouble taken
that causes the least fear.

Neoptolemus

Quiet, I tell you! Are you mad? He is stirring,
his eyes are stirring; he is raising his head.

Philoctetes

Blessed the light that comes after my sleep,
blessed the watching of friends.
I never would have hoped this,
that you would have the pity of heart to support   870
my afflictions, that you should stand by me and help.
The Atridae, those brave generals, were not so,
they could not so easily put up with me.
You have a noble nature, Neoptolemus,
and noble were your parents. You have made light
of all of this—the offense of my cries and the smell.
And now, since it would seem I can forget
my sickness for a while and rest, raise me yourself,
raise me up, boy, and set me on my feet,
that when my weariness releases me,
we can go to the ship and sail without delay.   880

Neoptolemus

I am glad to see you unexpectedly,
eyes open, free of pain, still with the breath of life.
With suffering like yours, all the signs pointed
to your being dead. Now, lift yourself up.
If you would rather, these men will lift you. They
will spare no trouble, since you and I are agreed.

Philoctetes
> Thanks, boy. Lift me yourself, as you thought of it.
> Do not trouble them, let them not be disquieted   890
> before they need by the foul smell of me; living
> on board with me will try their patience enough.

Neoptolemus
> Very well, then; stand on your feet; take hold yourself.

Philoctetes
> Do not be afraid; old habit will help me up.

Neoptolemus
> Now is the moment. What shall I do from now on?

Philoctetes
> What is it, boy? Where are your words straying?

Neoptolemus
> I do not know what to say. I am at a loss.

Philoctetes
> Why are you at a loss? Do not say so, boy.

Neoptolemus
> It is indeed my case.

Philoctetes
> Is it disgust at my sickness? Is it this   900
> that makes you shrink from taking me?

Neoptolemus
> All is disgust when one leaves his own nature
> and does things that misfit it.

Philoctetes
> It is not unlike your father, either in word
> or in act, to help a good man.

Neoptolemus
> I shall be shown to be dishonorable:
> I am afraid of that.

Philoctetes
Not in your present actions. Your words make me hesitate.

Neoptolemus
Zeus, what must I do? Twice be proved base,
hiding what I should not, saying what is most foul?

Philoctetes
Unless I am wrong, here is a man who will   910
betray me, leave me—so it seems—and sail away.

Neoptolemus
Not I; I will not leave you. To your bitterness,
I shall send you on a journey—and I dread this.

Philoctetes
What are you saying, boy? I do not understand.

Neoptolemus
I will not hide anything. You must sail to Troy
to the Achaeans, join the army of the Atridae.

Philoctetes
What! What can you mean?

Neoptolemus
                              Do not cry yet
until you learn.

Philoctetes
Learn what? What would you do with me?

Neoptolemus
First save you from this torture, then with you
go and lay waste the land of Troy.   920

Philoctetes
                              You would?
This is, in truth, what you intend?

Neoptolemus
                              Necessity,
a great necessity compels it. Do not be angry.

Philoctetes

 Then I am lost. I am betrayed. Why, stranger,
 have you done this to me? Give me back my bow.

Neoptolemus

 That I cannot. Justice and interest
 make me obedient to those in authority.

Philoctetes

 You fire, you every horror, most hateful engine
 of ruthless mischief, what have you done to me,
 what treachery! Have you no shame to see me
 that kneeled to you, entreated you, hard of heart?   930

 You robbed me of my livelihood, taking my bow.
 Give it back, I beg you, give it back, I pray, my boy!
 By your father's Gods, do not take my livelihood.
 He does not say a word,
 but turns away his eyes. He will not give it up.

 Caverns and headlands, dens of wild creatures,
 you jutting broken crags, to you I raise my cry—
 there is no one else that I can speak to—
 and you have always been there, have always heard me,
 Let me tell you what he has done to me, this boy,   940
 Achilles' son. He swore to bring me home;
 he brings me to Troy. He gave me his right hand,
 then took and keeps my sacred bow,
 the bow of Heracles, the son of Zeus,
 and means to show it to the Argives,
 as though in me he had conquered a strong man,
 as though he led me captive to his power.
 He does not know he is killing one that is dead,
 a kind of vaporous shadow, a mere wraith.
 Had I had my strength, he had not conquered me,
 for, even as I am, it was craft that did it.
 I have been deceived and am lost.
 What can I do?

Give it back. Be your true self again. Will you not?   950
No word. Then I am nothing.

Two doors cut in the rock, to you again,
again I come, enter again, unarmed,
no means to feed myself! Here in this passage
I shall shrivel to death alone. I shall kill no more,
neither winged bird nor wild thing of the hills
with this my bow. I shall myself in death
be a feast for those that fed me. Those that I hunted
shall be my hunters now.
Life for the life I took, I shall repay
at the hands of this man that seemed to know no harm.   960

My curse upon your life!—but not yet still
until I know if you will change again;
if you will not, may an evil death be yours!

Chorus
    What shall we do? Shall we sail? Shall we do as he asks?
    Prince, it is you must decide.

Neoptolemus
    A kind of compassion,
    a terrible compassion, has come upon me
    for him. I have felt for him all the time.

Philoctetes
    Pity me, boy, by the Gods; do not bring on yourself
    men's blame for your crafty victory over me.

Neoptolemus
    What shall I do? I would I had never left
    Scyrus, so hateful is what I face now.   970

Philoctetes
    You are not bad yourself; by bad men's teaching
    you came to practice your foul lesson. Leave it to others
    such as it suits, and sail away. Give me my arms.

Neoptolemus
   What shall we do, men?

                                   (*Odysseus appears.*)

Odysseus
   Scoundrel, what are you doing? Give me those arms.

Philoctetes
   Who is this? Is that Odysseus' voice?

Odysseus
                                   It is.
   Odysseus certainly; you can see him here.

Philoctetes
   Then I have been sold indeed; I am lost. It was he
   who took me prisoner, robbed me of my arms.

Odysseus
   Yes, I, I and no other. I admit that.   980

Philoctetes
   Boy, give me back my bow, give it back to me.

Odysseus
   That he will never
   be able to do now, even if he wishes it.
   And you must come with the bow, or these will
   bring you.

Philoctetes
   Your wickedness and impudence are without limit.
   Will these men bring me, then, against my will?

Odysseus
   Yes, if you do not come with a good grace.

Philoctetes
   O land of Lemnos and all mastering brightness,
   Hephaestus-fashioned, must I indeed bear this,
   that he, Odysseus, drags me from you with violence?

Odysseus
   It is Zeus, I would have you know, Zeus this land's ruler,
   who has determined. I am only his servant.   990

Philoctetes
Hateful creature,
what things you can invent! You plead the Gods
to screen your actions and make the Gods out liars.

Odysseus
They speak the truth. The road must be traveled.

Philoctetes
I say No.

Odysseus
I say Yes. You must listen.

Philoctetes
Are we slaves and not free? Is it as such
our fathers have begotten us?

Odysseus
No, but as equals
of the best, with whom it is destined you must take Troy,
dig her down stone by stone.

Philoctetes
Never, I would rather suffer anything than this.
There is still my steep and rugged precipice here.   1000

Odysseus
What do you mean to do?

Philoctetes
Throw myself down,
shatter my head upon the rock below.

Odysseus
Hold him. Take this solution out of his power.

Philoctetes
Hands of mine, quarry of Odysseus' hunting,
now suffer in your lack of the loved bowstring!

You who have never had a healthy thought
nor noble, you Odysseus, how you have hunted me,
how you have stolen upon me with this boy

as your shield, because I did not know him, one
that is no mate for you but worthy of me,
who knows nothing but to do what he was bidden,   1010
and now, you see, is suffering bitterly
for his own faults and what he brought on me.
Your shabby, slit-eyed soul taught him step by step
to be clever in mischief against his nature and will.
Now it is my turn, now to my sorrow you have me
bound hand and foot, intend to take me away,
away from this shore on which you cast me once
without friends or comrades or city, a dead man among the living.

My curse on you! I have often cursed you before,
but the Gods give me nothing that is sweet to me.   1020
You have joy to be alive, and I have sorrow
because my very life is linked to this pain,
laughed at by you and your two generals,
the sons of Atreus whom you serve in this.
And yet, when you sailed with them, it was by constraint
and trickery, while I came of my own free will
with seven ships, to my undoing, I
whom they dishonored and cast away—
you say it was they that did it and they you.

But now why are you taking me? For what?
I am nothing now. To you all I have long been dead.   1030
God-hated wretch, how is it that now I am not
lame and foul-smelling? How can you burn your sacrifice
to God if I sail with you? Pour your libations?
This was your excuse for casting me away.

May death in ugly form come on you! It will so come,
for you have wronged me, if the Gods care for justice.
And I know that they do care for it, for at present
you never would have sailed here for my sake
and my happiness, had not the goad of God,

a need of me, compelled you.
Land of my fathers, Gods that look on men's deeds,   1040
take vengeance on these men, in your own good time,
upon them all, if you have pity on me!
Wretchedly as I live, if I saw them
dead, I could dream that I was free of my sickness.

Chorus

He is a hard man, Odysseus, this stranger,
and hard his words: no yielding to suffering in them.

Odysseus

If I had the time, I have much I could say to him.
As it is, there is only one thing. As the occasion
demands, such a one am I.
When there is a competition of men just and good,   1050
you will find none more scrupulous than myself.
What I seek in everything is to win
except in your regard: I willingly yield to you now.

Let him go, men. Do not lay a finger on him.
Let him stay here. We have these arms of yours
and do not need you, Philoctetes.
Teucer is with us who has the skill and I,
who, I think, am no meaner master of them
and have as straight an aim. Why do we need you?
Farewell: pace Lemnos. Let us go. Perhaps   1060
your prize will bring me the honor you should have had.

Philoctetes

What shall I do? Will you appear
before the Argives in the glory of my arms?

Odysseus

Say nothing further to me. I am going.

Philoctetes

Your voice has no word for me, son of Achilles?
Will you go away in silence?

Odysseus

Come, Neoptolemus.
Do not look at him. Your generosity
may spoil our future.

Philoctetes

You, too, men, will you go   1070
and leave me alone? Do you, too, have no pity?

Chorus

This young man is our captain. What he says to you
we say as well.

Neoptolemus (to the Chorus)

Odysseus will tell me
that I am full of pity for him. Still
remain, if he will have it so, as long
as it takes the sailors to ready the tackle
and until we have made our prayer to the Gods.
Perhaps, in the meantime, he will have better thoughts
about us. Let us go, Odysseus.
You, when we call you, be quick to come.   1080
(*Exeunt Odysseus and Neoptolemus.*)

Philoctetes

Hollow in the rock, hollow cave, sun-warmed, ice cold,
I was not destined, after all, ever to leave you.
Still with me, you shall be witness to my dying.
Passageway, crowded with my cries of pain,
what shall be, now again, my daily life with you?
What hope shall I find of food to keep my wretched life alive?   1090
Above me, in the clouds, down the shrill winds
the birds; no strength in me to stop them.

Chorus

It was you who doomed yourself,
man of hard fortune. From no other,
from nothing stronger, came your mischance.
When you could have chosen wisdom,

with better opportunity before you,
you chose the worse.   1100

Philoctetes
Sorrow, sorrow is mine. Suffering has broken me,
who must live henceforth alone from all the world,
must live here and die here;
no longer bringing home food nor winning
it with strong hands. Unmarked, the crafty words   1110
of a treacherous heart stole on me. Would I might see him,
contriver of this trap,
for as long as I am, condemned to pain.

Chorus
It was the will of the Gods
that has subdued you, no craft
to which my hand was lent.   1120
Turn your hate, your ill-omened curses, elsewhere.
This indeed lies near my heart,
that you should not reject my friendship.

Philoctetes
By the shore of the gray sea he sits and laughs at me.
He brandishes in his hand the weapon which kept me alive,
which no one else had handled. Bow that I loved,
forged from the hands that loved you, if you could feel,
you would see me with pity, successor to Heracles,   1130
that used you and shall handle you no more.
You have found a new master, a man of craft, and shall be bent
   by him.
You shall see crooked deceits and the face of my hateful foe,
and a thousand ill things such as he contrived against me.

Chorus
A man should give careful heed to say what is just;   1140
and when he has said it, restrain his tongue from rancor and taunt.
Odysseus was one man, appointed by many,
by their command he has done this, a service to his friends.

« 451 »

Philoctetes

Birds my victims, tribes of bright-eyed wild creatures,
tenants of these hills, you need not flee from me or my house.
No more the strength of my hands, of my bow, is mine.   1150
Come! It is a good time
to glut yourselves freely on my discolored flesh.
For shortly I shall die here. How shall I find means of life?
Who can live on air without any of all that life-giving earth sup-
plies?   1160

Chorus

In the name of the gods, if there is anything that you hold in respect,
draw near to a friend that approaches you in all sincerity.
Know what you are doing, know it well.
It lies with you to avoid your doom.
It is a destiny pitiable to feed
with your body. It cannot learn how
to endure the thousand burdens with which it is coupled.

Philoctetes

Again, again you have touched my old hurt,   1170
for all that you are the best of those that came here.
Why did you afflict me? What have you done to me?

Chorus

What do you mean by this?

Philoctetes

Yes, you have hoped to bring me
to the hateful land of Troy.

Chorus

I judge that to be best.

Philoctetes

Then leave me now at once.

Chorus

Glad news, glad news.
I am right willing to obey you.
Let us go now to our places in the ship.   1180

Philoctetes

    No, by the God that listens to curses, do not go,
    Ï beseech you.

Chorus

               Be calm!

Philoctetes

                   Friends, stay!
    I beg you to stay.

Chorus

                  Why do you call on us?

Philoctetes

    It is the God, the God. I am destroyed.
    My foot, what shall I do with this foot of mine
    in the life I shall live hereafter?
    Friends, come to me again.   1190

Chorus

    What to do that is different
    from the tenor of your former bidding?

Philoctetes

    It is no occasion for anger
    when a man crazy with storms of sorrow
    speaks against his better judgment.

Chorus

    Unhappy man, come with us, as we say.

Philoctetes

    Never, never! That is my fixed purpose.
    Not though the Lord of the Lightning, bearing his fiery bolts,
    come against me, burning me
    with flame and glare.
    Let Ilium go down and all that under its walls   1200
    had the heart to cast me away, crippled!
    Friends, grant me one prayer only.

Chorus

                  What is it you would seek?

Philoctetes
>A sword, if you have got one,
>or an ax or some weapon—give it me!

Chorus
>What would you do with it?

Philoctetes
>   Head and foot,
>head and foot, all of me, I would cut with my own hand.
>My mind is set on death, on death, I tell you.

Chorus
>Why this?   1210

Philoctetes
>   I would go seek my father.

Chorus
>Where?

Philoctetes
>   In the house of death.
>He is no longer in the light.
>City of my fathers, would I could see you.
>I who left your holy streams,
>to go help the Greeks, my enemies,
>and now am nothing any more.

Chorus
>I should have been by now on my way to the ship,
>did I not see Odysseus coming here   1220
>and with him Neoptolemus.

>   (*Enter Odysseus and Neoptolemus in front of the cave, talking.*
>   *Philoctetes withdraws into the cave.*)

Odysseus (*to Neoptolemus*)
>You have turned back, there is hurry in your step.
>Will you not tell me why?

Neoptolemus
>I go to undo the wrong that I have done.

Odysseus
A strange thing to say! What wrong was that?

Neoptolemus
I did wrong when I obeyed you and the Greeks.

Odysseus
What did we make you do that was unworthy?

Neoptolemus
I practiced craft and treachery with success.

Odysseus
On whom? Would you do some rash thing now?

Neoptolemus
Nothing rash. I am going to give something back. 1230

Odysseus
What? I am afraid to hear what you will say.

Neoptolemus
Back to the man I took it from, this bow.

Odysseus
You cannot mean you are going to give it back.

Neoptolemus
Just that. To my shame, unjustly, I obtained it.

Odysseus
Can you mean this in earnest?

Neoptolemus
                    Yes, unless
it is not in earnest to tell you the truth.

Odysseus
What do you mean, Neoptolemus, what are you saying?

Neoptolemus
Must I tell you the same story twice or thrice?

Odysseus
I should prefer not to have heard it once.

Neoptolemus
You can rest easy. You have now heard everything.   1240

Odysseus
Then there is someone who will prevent its execution.

Neoptolemus
Who will that be?

Odysseus
The whole assembly
of the Greeks and among them I myself.

Neoptolemus
You are a clever man, Odysseus, but
this is not a clever saying.

Odysseus
                              In your own case
neither the words nor the acts are clever.

Neoptolemus
                                        Still
if they are just, they are better than clever.

Odysseus
How can it be just to give to him again
what you won by my plans?

Neoptolemus
It was a sin,
a shameful sin, which I shall try to retrieve.

Odysseus
Have you no fear of the Greeks if you do this?   1250

Neoptolemus
I have no fear of anything you can do,
when I act with justice; nor shall I yield to force.

Odysseus
Then we shall fight
not with the Trojans but with you.

Neoptolemus
    Let that be as it will.

Odysseus
                    Do you see my hand,
    reaching for the sword?

Neoptolemus
                    You shall see me do as much
    and that at once.

Odysseus
                    I will let you alone;
    I shall go and tell this to the assembled Greeks,
    and they will punish you.

Neoptolemus
                    That is very prudent.
    If you are always as prudent as this,
    perhaps you will keep out of trouble.   1260

                                        (*Exit Odysseus.*)

    I call on you, Philoctetes, son of Poias,
    come from your cave.

                    (*Philoctetes appears at the mouth of the cave.*)

Philoctetes
                    What cry is this at the door?
    Why do you call me forth, friends? What would you have?
    Ah! This is a bad thing. Can there be some fresh mischief
    you come to do, to top what you have done?

Neoptolemus
    Be easy. I would only have you listen.

Philoctetes
    I am afraid of that.
    I heard you before, and they were good words, too.
    But they destroyed me when I listened.

Neoptolemus
    Is there no place, then, for repentance?   1270

Philoctetes

You were just such a one in words when you stole my bow,
inspiring confidence, but sly and treacherous.

Neoptolemus

I am not such now. But I would hear from you
whether you are entirely determined
to remain here, or will you go with us?

Philoctetes

Oh, stop! You need not say another word.
All that you say will be wasted.

Neoptolemus

You are determined?

Philoctetes

More than words can declare.

Neoptolemus

I wish that I could have persuaded you.
If I cannot speak to some purpose, I have done.

Philoctetes

You will say it all   1280
to no purpose, for you will never win my heart
to friendship with you, who have stolen my life
by treachery, and then came and preached to me,
bad son of a noble father. Cursed be you all,
first the two sons of Atreus, then Odysseus,
and then yourself!

Neoptolemus

Do not curse me any more.
Take your bow. Here I give it to you.

Philoctetes

What can you mean? Is this another trick?

Neoptolemus

No. That I swear by the holy majesty
of Zeus on high!

Philoctetes
> These are good words,   1290
> if only they are honest.

Neoptolemus
> The fact is plain.
> Stretch out your hand; take your own bow again.

> *(Odysseus appears.)*

Odysseus
> I forbid it, as the Gods are my witnesses,
> in the name of the Atridae and the Greeks.

Philoctetes
> Whose voice is that, boy? Is it Odysseus?

Odysseus
> Himself and near at hand.
> And I shall bring you to the plains of Troy
> in your despite, whether Achilles' son
> will have it so or not.

Philoctetes
> You will rue your word
> if this arrow flies straight.

Neoptolemus
> No, Philoctetes, no!   1300
> Do not shoot.

Philoctetes
> Let me go, let go my hand, dear boy.

Neoptolemus
> I will not.

> *(Exit Odysseus.)*

Philoctetes
> Why did you prevent me killing my enemy,
> with my bow, a man that hates me?

Neoptolemus
> This is not to our glory, neither yours nor mine.

Philoctetes
>   Well, know this much, that the princes of the army,
>   the lying heralds of the Greeks, are cowards
>   when they meet the spear, however keen in words.

Neoptolemus
>   Let that be. You have your bow. There is no further cause
>   for anger or reproach against me.

Philoctetes
>   None.
>   You have shown your nature and true breeding,   1310
>   son of Achilles and not Sisyphus.
>   Your father, when he still was with the living,
>   was the most famous of them, as now he is of the dead.

Neoptolemus
>   I am happy to hear you speak well of my father
>   and of myself. Now listen to my request.
>   The fortunes that the Gods give to us men
>   we must bear under necessity.
>   But men that cling wilfully to their sufferings
>   as you do, no one may forgive nor pity.   1320
>   Your anger has made a savage of you. You will not
>   accept advice, although the friend advises
>   in pure goodheartedness. You loathe him, think
>   he is your enemy and hates you.
>   Yet I will speak. May Zeus, the God of Oaths,
>   be my witness! Mark it, Philoctetes, write it in your mind.
>   You are sick and the pain of the sickness is of God's sending
>   because you approached the Guardian of Chryse,
>   the serpent that with secret watch protects
>   her roofless shrine to keep it from violation.
>   You will never know relief while the selfsame sun   1330
>   rises before you here, sets there again,
>   until you come of your own will to Troy,
>   and meet among us the Asclepiadae,

who will relieve your sickness; then with the bow
and by my side, you will become Troy's conqueror.

I will tell you how I know that this is so.
There was a man of Troy who was taken prisoner,
Helenus, a good prophet. He told us clearly
how it should be and said, besides, that all Troy   1340
must fall this summer. He said, "If I prove wrong
you may kill me."
Now since you know this, yield and be gracious.
It is a glorious heightening of gain.
First, to come into hands that can heal you,
and then be judged pre-eminent among the Greeks,
winning the highest renown among them, taking
Troy that has cost infinity of tears.

Philoctetes
Hateful life, why should I still be alive and seeing?
Why not be gone to the dark?
What shall I do? How can I distrust   1350
his words who in friendship has counseled me?
Shall I then yield? If I do so, how come
before the eyes of men so miserable?
Who will say word of greeting to me?
Eyes of mine, that have seen all, can you endure
to see me living with my murderers,
the sons of Atreus? With cursed Odysseus?
It is not the sting of wrongs past
but what I must look for in wrongs to come.
Men whose wit has been mother of villainy once   1360
have learned from it to be evil in all things.
I must indeed wonder at yourself in this.
You should not yourself be going to Troy
but rather hold me back. They have done you wrong
and robbed you of your father's arms. Will you go and help them
fight and compel me to the like?
No, boy, no; take me home as you promised.

Remain in Scyrus yourself; let these bad men
die in their own bad fashion. We shall both thank you,   1370
I and your father. You will not then, by helping
the wicked, seem to be like them.

Neoptolemus
What you say
is reasonable; yet I wish that you would trust
the Gods, my word, and, with me as friend, fare forth.

Philoctetes
What, to the plains of Troy, to the cursed sons
of Atreus with this suffering foot of mine?

Neoptolemus
To those that shall give you redress,
that shall save you and your rotting foot from its disease.

Philoctetes
Giver of dread advice, what have you said!   1380

Neoptolemus
What I see fulfilled will be best for you and me.

Philoctetes
And saying it, do you not blush before God?

Neoptolemus
Why should one feel ashamed to do good to another?

Philoctetes
Is the good for the Atridae or for me?

Neoptolemus
I am your friend, and the word I speak is friendly.

Philoctetes
How, then, do you wish to betray me to my enemies?

Neoptolemus
Sir, learn not to be defiant in misfortune.

Philoctetes
You will ruin me, I know it by your words.

Neoptolemus
> Not I. You do not understand, I think.

Philoctetes
> Do I not know the Atridae cast me away?   1390

Neoptolemus
> They cast you away; will, now again, restore you.

Philoctetes
> Never, if of my will I must see Troy.

Neoptolemus
> What shall we do, since I cannot convince you
> of anything I say? It is easiest for me
> to leave my argument, and you to live,
> as you are living, with no hope of cure.

Philoctetes
> Let me suffer what I must suffer.
> But what you promised to me and touched my hand,
> to bring me home, fulfil it for me, boy.
> Do not delay, do not speak again of Troy   1400
> I have had enough of sorrow and lamentation.

Neoptolemus
> If you will then, let us go.

Philoctetes
> Noble is the word you spoke.

Neoptolemus
> Brace yourself, stand firm on your feet.

Philoctetes
> To the limit of my strength.

Neoptolemus
> How shall I avoid the blame of the Greeks?

Philoctetes
> Give it no thought.

Neoptolemus
> What if they come and harry my country?

Philoctetes
> I shall be there.

Neoptolemus
> What help will you be able to give me?

Philoctetes
> With the bow of Heracles.

Neoptolemus
> Will you?

Philoctetes
> I shall drive them from it.

Neoptolemus
> If you will do what you say,
> come now; kiss this ground farewell, and come with me.

> (*Heracles appears standing on the rocks above the cave of Philoctetes.*)

Heracles
> Not yet, not until you have heard
> my words, son of Poias.
> I am the voice of Heracles in your ears;   1410
> I am the shape of Heracles before you.
> It is to serve you I come and leave my home among the dead.
> I come
> to tell you of the plans of Zeus for you,
> to turn you back from the road you go upon.
> Hearken to my words.

> Let me reveal to you my own story first,
> let me show the tasks and sufferings that were mine,
> and, at the last, the winning of deathless merit.   1420
> All this you can see in me now.
> All this must be your suffering too,
> the winning of a life to an end in glory,
> out of this suffering. Go with this man to Troy.

First, you shall find there the cure of your cruel sickness,
and then be adjudged best warrior among the Greeks.
Paris, the cause of all this evil, you shall kill
with the bow that was mine. Troy you shall take.
You shall win the prize of valor from the army
and shall send the spoils to your home,
to your father Poias, and the land of your fathers, Oeta.   1430
From the spoils of the campaign you must dedicate
some, on my pyre, in memory of my bow.

Son of Achilles, I have the same words for you.
You shall not have the strength to capture Troy
without this man, nor he without you,
but, like twin lions hunting together,
he shall guard you, you him. I shall send Asclepius
to Ilium to heal his sickness. Twice
must Ilium fall to my bow. But this remember,   1440
when you shall come to sack that town, keep holy in the sight of
    God.
All else our father Zeus thinks of less moment.
Holiness does not die with the men that die.
Whether they die or live, it cannot perish.

Philoctetes
Voice that stirs my yearning when I hear,
form lost for so long,
I shall not disobey.

Neoptolemus
Nor I.

Heracles
Do not tarry then.
Season and the tide are hastening you on your way.   1450

Philoctetes
Lemnos, I call upon you:
Farewell, cave that shared my watches,
nymphs of the meadow and the stream,

the deep male growl of the sea-lashed headland
where often, in my niche within the rock,
my head was wet with fine spray,
where many a time in answer to my crying
in the storm of my sorrow the Hermes mountain sent its echo!   1460
Now springs and Lycian well, I am leaving you,
leaving you.
I had never hoped for this.
Farewell Lemnos, sea-encircled,
blame me not but send me on my way
with a fair voyage to where a great destiny
carries me, and the judgment of friends and the all-conquering
Spirit who has brought this to pass.

Chorus

Let us go all
when we have prayed to the nymphs of the sea   1470
to bring us safe to our homes.   1471